Supervision of Psychotherapists
The Discovery-oriented Approach

SUPERVISION OF PSYCHOTHERAPISTS

THE DISCOVERY-ORIENTED APPROACH

Alvin R. Mahrer PhD

University of Ottawa, Canada

WHURR PUBLISHERS
LONDON AND PHILADELPHIA

© 2005 Whurr Publishers Ltd
First published 2005
by Whurr Publishers Ltd
19b Compton Terrace
London N1 2UN England and
325 Chestnut Street, Philadelphia PA 19106 USA

British Library Cataloguing in Publication Data

A catalogue record for this book
is available from the British Library.

ISBN 1 86156 484 8

Typeset by Adrian McLaughlin, a@microguides.net
Printed and bound in the UK by Athenæum Press Limited, Gateshead, Tyne & Wear

Contents

Preface

Whether you are learning psychotherapy or counseling or case work or whatever it is suitable to call it, whether you are just starting out or have had a fair number of years of experience, being with a fine supervisor can offer some benefits. First you can learn what the supervisor has to teach you about the field, more from the body of knowledge underlying the field, and the supervisor's approach to psychotherapy. Second you can also have a colleague or supervisor to talk with about issues that are important to you.

Being a supervisor for a short or a long time can also offer some genuine benefits. First, you can teach what there is to be taught about the field, increase the supervisees' understanding of the body of knowledge underlying the field, and show supervisees how to do the approach that you know and practice. Second you can also help supervisees talk about the issues that are important for them to talk about. Of course, there can be other benefits to fine supervision, but supervision can be good, helpful, worthwhile, important, and valuable.

Now, let us quietly tip-toe away from commonplace supervision, and take a peek at the 'discovery-oriented approach'. Instead of listening to supervisors and supervisees, listen to discovery-oriented students/colleagues/trainees/practitioners talking about the discovery-oriented approach to learning psychotherapy.

> 'I discovered some great ideas I never knew I had, what makes people tick, the structure of personality. Everything. Like opening up a part of my brain I never knew was there.'
>
> 'We were like explorers, together, going deeper and deeper into my own notions and ideas, not surface ones, no. The ones deeper inside. Inside exploration. That's what it was.'
>
> 'I had a chance to think seriously about things I sort of was curious about, but I never really thought about seriously. You know what I mean?'

'Up to then, I was a dedicated cognitive therapist, but during those discovery-oriented sessions I found the ideas I've been writing about since I graduated. Otherwise they would have been undiscovered deeper ideas in just another cognitive therapist.'

'It was the only time I could look down inside and discover deep ideas that could make such huge differences in how I thought about and did therapy. Those sessions were better than five years of doctoral training and three years of therapy. Honest!'

'I supervise like that, now, and trainees love it. It's like a breath of fresh air, and it works. Besides, it's fun!'

'I found a way of thinking about therapy and doing therapy . . . like it came from inside me, but it really fit me, mine, you know what I mean? I didn't invent some new therapy, but it was like finding the therapy that was hidden deep inside me all the time.'

'I remember probing inside, and discovering, yeah, really discovering little notions I had about how far change can happen, how much change there can be, and I remember spending the next week in the library, just studying, like for the first time in my life! That was the most exciting week in my whole doctoral program!'

'Well of course, it was not really supervision cause you don't show the supervisee how to do therapy, and you don't monitor and take case responsibility. So you need regular supervision I suppose. But those discovery-oriented sessions sure were the only time I actually thought about psychotherapy, and found ideas I never though I had! Funny, cause that's when I learned how to do psychotherapy, real psychotherapy!'

'Discovery-oriented' supervision is not really supervision. It seems to be different from almost everything that supervision is. It doesn't try to do what supervision is good at doing. It is a whole new dimension to supervision. It is a whole new departure from what most supervision is.

Discovery-oriented supervision is the best way I know to explore deep down inside the other person's ideas about psychotherapy. These are what discovery-oriented supervision is for, whether the person is or will be a supervisor or a discovery-oriented teacher. Maybe it should be called discovery-oriented teaching.

I hope that you use this volume to become acquainted with discovery-oriented supervision, or teaching, to try it out yourself, and to make it better.

I want to share with the reader my appreciation and gratitude to three people for the important role they played in enabling this volume to come to life: one is Carl Rogers. Thank you for one paragraph, published in 1957. That paragraph said, in a nutshell, what this volume tries to say. The second is a small group of interns and postdoctoral trainees who solved my lingering problem of supervisory mediocrity by nudging me toward discovery-oriented training. The third is Colin Whurr, a special fellow who granted an old revolutionary the means of tilting at windmills.

Alvin R. Mahrer, PhD

A friendly preview to help you see if this volume is for you

This volume has something to say about a generally new way of doing supervision of trainees who are learning and doing psychotherapy. It looks for supervisors whose way of thinking fits reasonably well with this relatively new way of doing supervision. The purpose of this preview is to tell you enough for you to decide if you are sufficiently interested to read more of what this book has to say.

This volume is mainly for supervisors of psychotherapy trainees

Picture trainees who are just beginning to do psychotherapy. They are still in the training program. They may be just beginning to do work on their internships, residencies, field training. Or they may be well along on their training, completing the program, specializing in some particular approach, in an advanced phase. They may even be seasoned practitioners who are working with a supervisor in order to keep on improving or to learn some new way of doing psychotherapy.

This volume is mainly for the supervisors, the ones who are doing the training, the teaching. Even further, this volume is not for most supervisors, but mainly for the supervisors who have a spark of genuine interest in this particular way of doing supervision.

Although this volume is mainly for supervisors, there are two other groups with whom this volume would like to talk. One of these groups includes the trainees. If this 'discovery-oriented' approach to supervision is going to work, it requires trainees who are interested, and it requires trainees who are drawn toward this 'discovery-oriented' approach when it comes time for them to do supervision. Another group consists of the teachers who teach the courses in the training program. The 'discovery-oriented' approach can apply both to on-the-job supervision and to didactic classroom teaching and education of psychotherapists.

Picture trainees having their own 'deeper frameworks' for psychotherapy

By 'deeper framework' I mean that each trainee can have an inner deeper pool of ideas about things that relate to psychotherapy. These can include: ideas about what psychotherapy can and cannot achieve; how and why a person feels bad, has bad feelings; how much and how far a person can change; what pieces and parts make up what is called 'personality;' how a person got to be the way he or she is, the origins of 'personality;' what a person is like deep inside, at the bottom; what determines the way the person acts and behaves, relates and interacts, the kind of personal world that he or she has; how and why change can occur, how and why deep-seated change can occur at the very basis of what the person is; what accounts for a person feeling good, happy; how and why a person can feel much better; whether or not to picture what a person can become, can be; whether to picture an optimal state and what that state is like; how quickly and how deep and how far a person can change; and whether change can occur gradually or in quantum leaps.

Can you picture that most trainees have inner deeper ideas on these kinds of issues and topics, and that these ideas are largely rather diffuse, unclarified, undifferentiated, undeveloped? Picture a rather loose pool of these kinds of ideas deep inside most trainees.

Picture that the ideas in the inner deeper framework may be rather similar to the much more conscious and aware ideas that the person has on the surface. It may be that, if the trainee holds to a Jungian approach or a cognitive–behavioral approach, his or her inner deeper framework may be cordial. On the other hand, allow for the alternative possibility that for most trainees, once they discover their inner deeper framework, it can be substantially different from their on-the-surface ideas. As a matter of fact, the inner deeper framework can be remarkably different from what they believe on the surface. Their inner deeper framework can be a genuine discovery, a genuine surprise, a genuine departure.

The deeper ideas may have relatively high or surprisingly low 'goodness of fit' with the more surface ideas. In any case, their discovery is a genuine discovery in that the trainee is entitled to say: 'I didn't know I believed that . . . If that idea has been deep inside all along, I never knew it was there . . . So that is my deeper idea! What do you know? . . . That idea is a real surprise to me, and it has been there inside me all along!' In other words, the actual nature and content of the deeper framework are almost always a genuine discovery for the trainee, even though the deeper idea may be familiar to some part of the larger field of psychotherapy. The idea may be new to the trainee, but not to the field of psychotherapy.

Picture interested supervisors helping interested trainees to discover their own inner deeper frameworks for psychotherapy

Most supervisors have a mind-set in which they are here to teach what they are here to teach. This is what supervision mainly is. This is what their job is. They know integrative therapy or client-centered therapy or constructivist therapy or psychodynamic therapy, and they are here to supervise trainees in learning and doing the therapy they are here to supervise.

Now picture one out of every 20 or 30 supervisors as having a glow of genuine interest in helping an interested trainee to discover and develop the framework that lies deeper inside the trainee. This supervisor may do this full-time, or part-time, with the balance of the time dedicated to the supervisor supervising the therapy that the supervisor knows. This supervisor is special because he or she believes in the value of helping interested trainees discover and develop their inner deeper frameworks. This is the way the supervisor thinks, and this is the way the supervisor supervises.

Picture some trainees with a glow of enthusiasm for discovering their own inner deeper frameworks for psychotherapy

Most trainees, even beginning trainees, usually have some approach that they have adopted. They like their approach. They identify with their selected approach. They may be dedicated proponents or not especially so, but they can say that they are solution-focused thera-pists, or they are psychodynamic, gestalt, integrative, or cognitive–behavioral ones.

For these trainees, the idea of looking inside, of searching for some inner deeper framework, is rather strange and alien, not quite sensible. Of course they can learn more about their chosen approach, but, no thanks, they are not interested in some notion of an inner deeper framework. It has little or no meaning, and even less appeal.

Can you picture the occasional trainee who does have a spark of enthusiasm for probing down into his or her own inner pool of ideas about psychotherapy? This trainee may have some chosen approach. It may even fit rather well, but there is a glow of passionate readiness to go deeper inside. This trainee may even know what it is like to ruminate about the deeper issues in psychotherapy, to puzzle over the deeper questions, to think about how a person gets to be the way the person is, what makes for pain and suffering. This trainee may have some pet ideas and notions about psychotherapy, ideas and notions that are aside from and separate from whatever approach the trainee has on the surface. Here is the right trainee for the discovery-oriented approach to supervision.

Picture some special payoffs from trainees discovering their own inner deeper frameworks for psychotherapy

There is a kind of joyful curiosity and passionate interest in exploring down into one's own notions and ideas about psychotherapy, in devel-oping these notions and ideas into one's own deeper framework for psychotherapy. But there are also some rather practical payoffs. Here are a few:

1. The trainee can be able to have a framework for psychotherapy, an approach to psychotherapy, that truly fits. It is the right approach. It may be a modification of the trainee's chosen cognitive approach, or it may be a particular integrative approach. On the other hand, it may be a sweeping change so that the avowed cognitive therapist finds that it is the client-centered approach that fits the trainee's own inner deeper framework.

2. When the trainee carries out a therapeutic approach that arises out of and truly fits the trainee's inner deeper framework, then the actual doing of psychotherapy can take on an added feature. There can be an added joy,

pleasure, buoyancy, excitement in doing psychotherapy. The shift is not typically one from boring dullness to exciting enthusiasm. Yet there can be a heightened pleasure in the sheer doing of psychotherapy. It is a pleasure, rather than a good job. It can be fun, rather than a good way of earning a living. Years and years later, when many practitioners have moved on to administration or to other pursuits or to a burned-out retirement, doing psychotherapy is still a source of solid enjoyment and pleasure.

3. A surprisingly large proportion of these trainees seem to move on to becoming exceptional therapists, master therapists. During their training, these trainees seemed to become quite competent therapists, well above what I would have expected, well above what most other trainees seemed to achieve. Long after their training, when I was able to talk to them at some length, and listen to their audiotapes, I was impressed that these were exceptional psychotherapists, exceedingly competent psychotherapists, even master practitioners.

Nor did they seem to congregate around any particular kind of therapy. One did experiential psychotherapy, and the rest represented all sorts of therapeutic approaches. In fact, I was impressed with how broad a range of approaches they represented. What seemed to characterize so many of these former trainees was their sheer expertise. They were truly outstanding therapists, and recognized as such by their colleagues and peers in their local communities, not so much because of their publications or workshops or professional offices, but rather because of their being such unusually fine practitioners.

Partly because sheer competence seemed like such an important topic, and partly because this topic could be so touchy, I was appreciative of these former trainees' impressions about what seemed to help them become so good. They mentioned at least three factors. One was that the passion they had for discovering their own deeper frameworks also included a passion for becoming master therapists. Exploring into their own deeper framework seemed to fuel their becoming exceptional therapists, and their yearnings to become master therapists in turn fueled their curiosity about their own deeper frameworks. Second, they talked about the sense of solidness and sheer trust they had in doing therapy on the basis of their own deeper framework. This was more important than whatever brand of therapy they followed. If they did cognitive therapy, it was cognitive therapy as rooted in their own deeper framework. Third, and in a lighter vein, almost all of these former trainees recited a kind of truism: if you do a therapy that fits with your own deeper framework, you can become a master practitioner.

These are the main points the volume tries to offer. Are you interested enough to read on?

How is this volume organized?

Chapter 1 describes how I was introduced to the idea of supervision as helping trainees to discover and carry forward their deeper frameworks about psychotherapy, and my searching throughout the supervision literature to learn about this interesting way of supervising so I could appreciate its history, content, and practical guidelines in order to do it reasonably well.

Chapter 2 aims to highlight the special features and advantages of the discovery-oriented approach to supervision. These are special in that they are substantially different from the features and advantages of the more commonplace approaches to supervision. The underlying message is: 'If these features and advantages are appealing to you, then go ahead and try the discovery-oriented approach.'

Chapter 3 offers suggestions for how the discovery-oriented approach can be a friendly added ingredient in psychotherapy training programs, including both internship, field, and residency programs, and the more didactic, academic, course-work programs of psychotherapy training. The spirit is to add a friendly new ingredient throughout the course of psychotherapy training, rather than to substantially replace current training programs with a wholesale, new, discovery-oriented training program.

Not all teachers and supervisors, and not all students, trainees, and supervisees, are particularly suited to the discovery-oriented approach. Chapter 4 suggests some helpful qualities of those who can be discovery-oriented supervisors, and Chapter 5 suggests some helpful qualities of those who seem fitting and appropriate to be discovery-oriented students, trainees, and supervisees.

Chapter 6 gets down to business by describing some of the more practical–logistical guidelines for the discovery-oriented training of psychotherapists.

What does the discovery-oriented supervisor actually do? What are some discovery-oriented methods? Part II offers five methods that the supervisor can follow. They are given in Chapters 7–11. Each chapter describes a method well enough for a supervisor to carry it out, and includes illustrative examples to show the supervisor what to do and how to do it.

The volume ends with some overall conclusions about the discovery-oriented approach, and some invitations to interested supervisors and teachers and also to the field of psychotherapy itself.

Throughout this final section, the underlying question, for supervisors, teachers, students, trainees, and supervisees, is: 'Are you interested in the discovery-oriented approach to the training and supervision of psychotherapists, in learning and doing this approach, in making it better and better?'

This preview likewise ends with a hope that you are interested enough to keep on reading, to know more about this approach, and perhaps even to consider being a part of this approach to psychotherapy training, teaching and education, supervision, and on-the-job discovery of the deeper frameworks of the psychotherapy student, trainee, and supervisee.

Part I

Introduction to the discovery-oriented approach

Chapter 1

An introductory background to the discovery-oriented approach to supervision

If you look over the literature on supervision, you will probably find little or nothing called a discovery-oriented approach. Here is an introductory background on what this is and how it seems to have come about.

Supervision was so hard for me when I began doing supervision

When I graduated with a doctorate, my first and second jobs were as director of training in a department of psychology in a large training hospital, and then in another large training hospital – a total of 13 years.

There were plenty of trainees, interns, and residents. My job included a large component of supervision of both trainees and other supervisors who supervised trainees. However, there were at least two reasons why supervision was so hard for me.

I did not know how to do psychotherapy well

It was hard for me to be a supervisor because I knew I was not very good at what I was supposed to be supervising. I may have been at about the same level as most of my colleagues, but I certainly felt like I was not very good at being a psychotherapist, and it seemed both sad and silly that I was supposed to supervise others in what I was sure I was not especially good at.

When I was in my doctoral program, I believe I had some fine teachers. On my internship, I believe I had some fine supervisors.

However, from the time I started doing supervision, I knew I was not doing very well at doing psychotherapy. One of the problems was that the only psychotherapy about which I had actually heard and studied was from tapes of my supervisees. I had never even thought about recording or studying and learning from what the old fellow did whose couch I had made my home during the 5 years of my doctoral training. I had never heard or studied tapes of actual therapists doing actual therapy with actual patients.

During the 13 years I worked in hospitals, I managed to start a precious collection of audiotapes of actual sessions of actual psychotherapy. These tapes were gifts by the good grace of so many practitioners, some of whom were quite well known. By studying these precious audiotapes, I found some enormously wonderful sessions from which I could learn how to start becoming a fine practitioner, but these audiotapes were evidence that I had a long way to go to become a fine therapist, or even proficient and competent enough to be a supervisor.

When I started doing supervision, and for about a decade or so, the main sense I had was that I was not ready to do supervision because I did not know how to do psychotherapy well enough to supervise trainees. I was much more ready to be a learner than a supervisor.

I had little or no idea of my own deeper framework for psychotherapy

When I first started doing psychotherapy, I knew a lot about psychotherapy theories and research and even practice. I could wax scholarly and eloquent about my own chosen approach to psychotherapy. I could explain it well, and I could defend it against other theories and approaches to it.

I knew what I believed on the surface. I identified with the social learning approach to which I attached myself in my doctoral program, but I gave myself the right to be friendly to a little bit of a psychoanalytic approach and a personal construct approach, perhaps because some of my friends in the doctoral program joined those teams. I was a card-carrying, social learning therapist.

I also knew that I had little or no idea what I really believed. I could recite the social learning catechism with regard to almost everything about psychotherapy because I was a fine student. But I was ignorant about my own inner deeper notions and ideas about psychotherapy, what human beings were like, how we were constructed, why we had such awful feelings, how change occurred, and most of the secrets of psychotherapy. No one had ever asked me. I had never asked myself.

When I started doing supervision, it was hard because I was better suited to be a student, rather than a supervisor, with little or no idea of my own deeper framework to psychotherapy.

Psychotherapy was even harder when I discovered my own deeper framework and became a fairly proficient practitioner

From the time I started doing supervision, it took about 30–40 years for me to discover and to seriously explore my own inner deeper notions and ideas about psychotherapy, and develop this pool of nascent notions and ideas into a somewhat respectable conceptual system (Mahrer, 1989), a rationale, and a way of doing it (Mahrer, 1996/2004). The first finally emerged as a full-blown, comprehensive 'experiential psychology', and the last emerged as something I called 'experiential psychotherapy'.

During those 30–40 years, I had little or no idea what my way of thinking and my psychotherapy might look like when they developed and took shape. They may have been similar to some other established and popular psychology and psychotherapy, or they may have been somewhat different. As it happened, they both seemed to be relatively unique, I believe. What was somewhat embarrassing was that neither my experiential psychology nor my experiential psychotherapy was seriously similar to the theory or the psychotherapy that I had been touting, claiming, and fervently espousing during my doctoral program and in the first few decades of doing supervision!

During those 30–40 years I also developed into a fairly proficient practitioner of what I called experiential psychotherapy. However, after all those years, supervision was even harder for me.

The main reason seemed to be that what the experiential therapist did, the on-the-surface rationale, and something about the underlying belief system apparently instantly galvanized virtually every trainee into a rabid disbeliever, a resistant critic, a rebellious opponent. They instantly saw this psychotherapy and its belief system as weird, deviant, and violating just about all the beliefs that the trainees did not even know they believed in. This seemed to be true for all kinds of trainees, from sweet and kindly souls to hard and tough thinkers, from trainees with or without any approach that they called their own, from beginning trainees to old postdoctoral practitioners.

Almost all the trainees had instant strong reactions to the manifest or underlying belief system of this psychotherapy as exciting, stimulating, freeing, captivating, appealing, innovative, provocative, distinctive, unique, ominous, threatening, dangerous, and frighteningly challenging and destructive to their own manifest and probably deeper system of beliefs about human beings and psychotherapy.

From the first supervision session on, almost all trainees could not and would not even consider experiential psychotherapy, even though many of them wanted to have sessions with an experiential psychotherapist! Experiential supervision was a colossal and consistent failure with almost all except perhaps one from every group of 20–30 trainees.

Supervision was hard for me when I started doing it. It became much harder to do supervision when, after many years, I finally discovered my own deeper framework and became a fairly good practitioner of experiential psychotherapy. I had a serious problem.

The solution: discover and develop the trainee's own deeper framework for psychotherapy!

Two things seemed to help solve the problem. One was that some therapists all over the world seemed to find my publications on experiential psychology and experiential psychotherapy exciting, sensible, and something that they could either adopt or modify to suit themselves. That helped because I found myself relieved of so much personal pressure to try to get my own supervisees to accept and do experiential psychotherapy. The burden I did not realize I had was almost gone.

The second thing that happened was that I must have somehow started listening to a few special trainees. They were actually able to get me to see that they were ready and eager to discover their own inner deeper framework by saying things along these lines:

'Look, you figured out the way of making sense of therapy that made sense for you, so why can't we?'

'Instead of trying to get us to do therapy your way, could you help us to figure out what we think about psychotherapy?'

'We know what our supervisors want us to do in therapy, but sometimes we want to have a way of putting it all together, or at least together for us. Would you help us?'

'I like cognitive-behavioral therapy, and I guess that's the therapy for me. But sometimes I'm not sure. Can you help me figure out if that's the therapy for me?'

'We've never really had a chance to dig into our own thoughts about psychotherapy. I think I know what I think, but I'm not sure. Can you help us see more of what we really think?'

'What you say, the way you think about therapy, that challenges us. We can argue with you, but we don't really know what we think. Or we're not sure, anyhow. Can you help us find out what we really think? Then we can really argue with you!'

'The longer I do therapy, the more confused I get. I do all right, but I have some big questions. Could you help me to talk about these questions? I guess I want to learn about my own ways of thinking about these questions.'

These people seemed like good people. They were not malcontents. They were good trainees. Some had been doing therapy for a fair number of years. They did not seem to be here to gossip about other supervisors or to complain about the program. They did not seem like they were lost, without some ground or base, destined to be eternal searchers for some system that fits.

What they said was the doorway to the solution of my finding supervision so very difficult. It seemed so simple. The solution had been the one I followed when I spent so many years trying to discover my own deeper framework for psychotherapy. To those trainees, thank you!

The solution was for me to do what I could to enable ready and eager trainees to discover their own inner deeper framework to psychotherapy.

The discovery-oriented solution could and should have been familiar to me and to the field of psychotherapy

The idea behind the discovery-oriented approach seems rather simple and rather common. One way to know something is to look deeper inside it. See what it is made of. Probe deeper inside. Simple enough.

It seems sensible that psychotherapy research would be fueled, at least in part, by the idea that one way to know something is to look deeper inside it. See what it contains. Explore down inside. Understand what you are studying by probing down inside it. Take a closer look down inside. Explore what comprises it. Be curious about the deeper insides.

This is the simple idea behind my interest in psychotherapy research, my way of doing it, and my way of using the findings of my psychotherapy research. I even called this a 'discovery-oriented' approach to psychotherapy research (Mahrer, 1985, 1988, 1996/ 2004, 2004b; Mahrer and Boulet, 1999).

It also seemed sensible that the field of psychotherapy would salute the idea that looking deeper inside a patient can be helpful, important, perhaps even crucial, in understanding the patient and in doing therapy with the patient. It seemed sensible that particular therapies might even want to look deeper inside the patient to 'discover' the person's deeper thoughts and ideas, ways of making sense of things, personal outlook, fantasies, worries, ruminations.

In my own work, I followed this common theme by dedicating the first of four steps in each experiential session to probing inside to discover what lay deeper, and I called what was found a 'deeper potential for experiencing' (Mahrer, 1996/2004, 2002, 2004c). My experiential psychotherapy was solidly lined up with other therapies that saluted the importance of looking deeper inside. My therapy and many other therapies were 'discovery oriented' in this same sense of looking deeper inside for things that are thought of as important and useful.

Psychotherapy research and psychotherapy practice seemed quite familiar with the discovery-oriented idea. Look deeper inside. That is a key. You can find some wonderful and useful things. It could and should have been a tiny step from psychotherapy research and practice over to psychotherapy education, training, teaching, and supervision. What was, for me, a solution to a problem of supervision could and perhaps should have been relatively standard in psychotherapy supervision, and education, training, and teaching. Do these things by doing what is so familiar in research and practice, namely look deeper inside the student, the trainee, the supervisee. Discover the supervisee's own deeper thoughts and ideas. This could and should have been the easy and common thing for the supervisor to do. Or so it could and should have seemed to me.

The discovery-oriented way of thinking of psychotherapy research and practice could and should have been common enough in psychotherapy education, teaching, training, and supervision. It seemed sensible that the actual working methods would differ when you are being discovery oriented in doing research or practice or supervision. That seemed clear. However, the underlying 'discovery-oriented' idea would seem to be common in all three. Or so it seemed to me (Mahrer, 1995, 1998).

I replaced the role of being a supervisor with becoming a discovery-oriented teacher

It seemed rather clear to me that the usual role of supervisor was not especially helpful for me to do what I wanted to do with trainees. In fact, the usual role of supervisor made it quite difficult and clashed with what I wanted to do. What I needed was a qualitatively new role, one suited to my aims and goals. It turned out to be a new role of discovery-oriented teacher (Mahrer and Boulet, 1997).

I was not sure what this new role might be, but it seemed much better to help me in what I was trying to accomplish in my work with trainees. Gradually I learned what this new role could be, and I developed a way of understanding its features because I was developing into a reasonably helpful discovery-oriented teacher with my trainees.

I also saw what becoming a discovery-oriented teacher could be like in the classroom. For me, at least, it meant highlighting what I believed were the basic and fundamental issues and questions in the field of psychotherapy, issues and questions such as: What are human beings like? Why do people have good feelings and bad feelings? How does a person come to be the person that he or she seems to become? What can a person become? What do you do in initial sessions? How do you listen and what do you listen for? What can you do to help bring about in-session change? What accounts for dreams? And many more.

In the classroom, I found myself doing my best to have the students appreciate what these basic and fundamental issues and questions were, and to learn some of the traditionally fine positions on the basic and fundamental issues, and some of the traditionally fine answers to these basic and fundamental questions (Mahrer, 2000, 2003, 2004a). I also did what I could to enable students to discover their own positions on these issues, and their own answers to these questions. I was learning, and it was fun.

What did the literature on supervision say about this way of not doing supervision?

I had read little or nothing on how to do supervision, and here I was engaged in doing a kind of supervision that seemed exciting but a bit weird. I therefore asked the trainees to please go to the library to find books and articles on anything even remotely related to this way of doing supervision or, as the trainees preferred, this way of not doing supervision. I wanted to know if others found this way of not doing supervision as exciting as I did, and I wanted to benefit from others' experience of how to do it better and better.

The trainees were surprised that the literature on supervision was a rather recent popular item, complete with its own journals and classic landmarks.

Supervisors must show supervisees how to do psychotherapy the right way

The trainees who scoured the literature started me off with works by Goodyear and Bradley (1983), Stoltenberg and Delworth (1987), and the classic landmark in supervision (Hess, 1980a). After a fair amount of reading, I believed I could perhaps attend a conference on supervision, but I would probably not find a few renegades who were excited about this way of not doing supervision. Put it this way: if I wrote about this way of working with trainees, the introduction might be short, because I found few respectable colleagues with whom to share the blame.

What I did find, as I read more and more, was a picture of the way many supervisors seemed to think about themselves and their supervisees. It seemed that trainees were thought of as children, here to learn, and the supervisors were like parents who were here to foster growth and development, and to impart their knowledge. The supervisors were to guide the trainees through the stages of increasing knowledge and competencies, culminating in a final stage of independence and autonomy as a professional psychotherapist (Hogan, 1964; Hess, 1980b, 1986, 1987; Hill, Charles, and Reed, 1981; Stoltenberg, 1981; Loganbill, Hardy, and Delworth, 1982; Blocher, 1983; Goodyear and Bradley, 1983; Heppner and Roehlke, 1984; Worthington, 1984).

In line with this common picture, teachers and supervisors were the first to teach what is basic and fundamental, the rudimentary knowledge, the primary skills. Once the trainees have gained the solid base, they can proceed to the more advanced and specialized knowledge and skills.

I found it hard to accept this picture of trainees being like children proceeding through stages of growth and development. I found myself drawing further and further away from this picture, and I found myself becoming increasingly critical of supervisors with such a picture. How patronizing they seemed to be. How like missionaries dedicated to bringing the word to inferior cultures. It was hard to see supervisors as good and helpful people, rather than fitting my prejudiced view of them. It was not easy to tell myself that I knew so little about supervision, so be quiet and appreciate that most supervisors were good people doing their best to train supervisees. For example, most supervisors appreciated that trainees generally differ from one another, and their differences are to be respected and appreciated and taken into account. Supervisors rarely if ever talked about trying to produce practitioners on an assembly line, with each being a clone of the other, with any practitioner being replaceable by another. There was plenty of appreciation of trainees being different from each other, and good supervision appreciating these differences.

However, almost uniformly, these differences were surface. They referred to idiosyncratic qualities and characteristics that were surface. These on-the-surface differences rarely if ever involved the trainee's inner deeper notions and ideas, or pursuing the pool of undeveloped notions and ideas lying deeper inside him or her. For example, the common picture, in the supervisory literature, similar to the common picture in the literature on child development, is that trainees, similar to children, often have their own individual personalities and their own individual styles of relating to the training program, their teachers, and supervisors, and all of this is to be taken into account in supervision (e.g. Hogan, 1964; Andrews, Norcross, and Halgin, 1992). This recognition of individual style can carry over into the trainee's actual in-session work, into the trainee's own distinctive way of putting the approach into operation (Yontef, 1997). Yet trainees have nevertheless to learn the approach and do it properly in actual operation. Trainees differ in their style of learning about doing surgery or flying a plane or preparing a meal or playing the piano. Yet they are to be able to do it properly and well, even with understandable variation in their personal style.

Beyond differences in style, the supervision literature recognizes that the supervisor could and should acknowledge the trainee's own personal interests, preferences, choices, and inclinations in doing psychotherapy, and in doing this particular brand of psychotherapy. Trainees must be seen as differing in many ways, and these ways include differences in 'preferences, values, needs, the degree and type of dedication to the task of helping patients, his or her perspective on relations' (Yontef, 1997, p. 152). There is ample recognition of individual differences, but trainees must nevertheless learn what they are here to learn.

If a trainee arrives for supervision with a leaning towards or preference for some way of thinking, the general picture is that the trainee's way of thinking came largely from some other teachers or some other supervisors. Accordingly, scattered throughout the supervisory literature are warnings that the trainee's preferred way of thinking, therapeutic approach, should be taken into account in assigning the trainee to the fitting supervisor (e.g. Patterson, 1997). One theme is that there can be trouble if a person-centered trainee is assigned to a cognitive supervisor, or a Jungian trainee to a behavioral supervisor. A quite different theme is that, for the sake of balance and fairness, the person-centered trainee ought to be assigned to the cognitive supervisor, and the Jungian trainee to the behavioral supervisor.

In any case, the literature is relatively clear that the supervisor has a way of thinking and teaches the trainee that way of thinking:

> A teacher must pass on a way of thinking as well as a set of skills. Teachers of therapists have special requirements. Therapists must know how to treat their clients; teachers must know not only how to treat clients but also how to think about that action in ways that can be transmitted to others.
>
> Haley (1996, p. 199)

There are at least two possibilities here:

1. Trainees come to supervision with essentially no way of thinking. The supervisor has a way of thinking, and teaches that way to the trainee.

2. Trainees come to supervision with a way of thinking, but it is to be set aside and replaced by the supervisor's way of thinking.

In either case, the trainee's own way of thinking is generally presumed to be either non-existent or irrelevant, and this general attitude is in sharp contrast to an attitude that most trainees have ways of thinking, these ways of thinking can have deeper roots, and it is the supervisor's job to work with the trainees in finding, discovering, exploring, and developing the trainees' own ways of thinking.

Some exceedingly soft hints

There were a few scattered and exceedingly soft hints without fingers pointing in the right direction. For example, there were suggestions that supervisors might be able to stimulate and encourage trainees' capacity for wonder, curiosity, and awe in what can and does occur in psychotherapy (Watkins, 1996; compare Cooper and Witenberg, 1984), and for supervisors to encourage trainees to go ahead and do some experimenting on their own, with different approaches, perhaps even going beyond what a particular approach talks about (Watkins, 1990). However, none of these suggestions flagged the idea of trainees' own inner deeper frameworks, of finding them, developing them, applying them. But these were nevertheless some exceedingly soft hints.

In much the same vein, in one of the pioneering classics in psychotherapy supervision, Ekstein and Wallerstein (1972) saw training for psychotherapy as likewise having the possibility of emphasizing trainees' capacity for wonder and curiosity, experimenting and trying new things, exploring new ideas, and coming up with new methods. Ekstein and Wallerstein (1972, pp. 4–5) wondered 'if we should train researchers, explorers, curious people who are out to develop new methods and theories and will help us make the advances so essential in this new, still largely unexplored field'. Ekstein and Wallerstein, Cooper and Witenberg, and Watkins at least raised the possibility of valuing trainees' curiosity, having new ideas, exploring the unknown. But these were more tantalizing soft hints, with occasional cameo appearances rather than leading to discussion of supervision as a way of helping trainees to explore, be curious about, think about their own inner pool of notions and ideas about psychotherapy.

Sometimes I came across hints that I thought were hints because I had little puffs of excitement that the supervisors were going to use these hints to discover the trainees' own ways of thinking, their own deeper ideas. But I was disappointedly wrong in each case. From the supervisors' viewpoints, these were not hints at all. They were problems that needed solution so that the trainees could learn the approaches they were here to learn, so that the trainees could learn to do psychotherapy the right and proper way. For example, suppose that the trainee comes to supervision with a preference for an approach that is different from the approach that the supervisor is to teach. The supervisor's approach is cognitive–behavioral, and the trainee's approach is Jungian or Adlerian or Eriksonian. Or suppose that the supervisor's crisis intervention approach differs from the trainees' approach, with the trainees being police officers with police officers' built-in, police-approved, police-instilled way of dealing with psychological crises in interpersonal relationships.

I was excited that perhaps the differences could be used to explore and develop the trainee's own deeper ideas, but I was wrong. What I mistook for a soft hint was consistently treated as a problem to be solved so that the trainee could learn what the trainee was supposed to learn. For instance, in getting the police officers to learn the supervisor's crisis intervention approach, one way to solve the problem is to start with the police officers' own police-approved way of dealing with crisis intervention, and to gradually hang the supervisor's approach on to the hooks offered by the approach that the police officers brought to supervision in the first place (Burkhardt, 1980). This may be a clever solution to the problem, but it is not really the soft hint I had mistakenly thought it might be.

As another example, Alonzo (1985) cites a situation where a trainee has come to have serious doubts about the approach the trainee is learning. Again I was excited that the serious doubts could be a direct doorway into the trainee's own underlying notions and ideas, but again I mistakenly saw the soft hint I was wanting to see, and my mistake was corrected when the trainee's serious doubts were indications of an impasse in supervision, a problem that the supervisor is to fix, solve, do something about.

It can be easy to see soft hints where they do not exist, to mistakenly misread what the author is not really saying. In describing his role as a supervisor, Corey says (Haynes, Corey, and Moulton, 2003, p. 13): 'I see my role as a supervisor as being a guide in a process of self-discovery.' I misread this as Corey's being a guide in the trainee's discovery of his or her own inner deeper pool of ideas about psychotherapy. I was seriously mistaken. As Corey went on to explain, his role is to guide the trainee's own path toward discovering the right way to do psychotherapy, instead of the supervisor telling the trainee directly. It is as if Corey had said: 'Rather than my telling you the right way to do psychotherapy, I can help you discover it for yourself.'

The soft hints I had thought I found were either mistaken misinterpretations or they were exceedingly soft hints indeed. But I persisted searching because the idea seemed so simple, such a matter of psychotherapeutic common sense.

Another kind of soft hint came from acknowledgments of the value and importance of exploring the supervisor's own deeper beliefs and ideas about psychotherapy. This was an exciting soft hint because it seemed so easy, natural, and a short step to doing the same for trainees. If supervisors can have deeper beliefs and ideas about psychotherapy, and if it can be important to explore them, how about granting the same rights to trainees, and exploring their deeper beliefs and ideas about psychotherapy?

In reading Jay Haley's (1996) book on supervision, I was impressed with his uncommonly interesting and creative ideas about supervision, and I kept having two reactions:

1. How appealing it would be to talk with him so I might be able to learn more about his interesting and creative ideas about supervision.

2. Here is one supervisor who is likely to value the importance of exploring trainees' own beliefs and ideas about psychotherapy.

I still would like to talk with Haley about his interesting and creative ideas about supervision, and also about my disappointment that nowhere in his book did he feature exploration of trainees' own beliefs and ideas about psychotherapy.

Haley was, for me, an example of a supervisor with interesting and creative ideas. So were many other supervisors. This led to a question that kept coming to mind: if I am so interested in their ideas, would it not be sensible that at least some supervisors would also be interested in the ideas of students, trainees, supervisees? Could it really be that supervisees have interesting ideas only when they graduate and become supervisors? It is rather easy for me to picture Haley as a supervisee, and a supervisor being honestly interested in the trainee's notions and ideas about psychotherapy.

If supervisors are supposed to have deeper notions and ideas about psychotherapy, and are to pay attention to their deeper notions and ideas in choosing an approach, why should the same courtesy not be extended to supervisees? Something seemed strange.

What seemed strange was that the literature included acknowledgments that many supervisors' approaches were rooted in deeper beliefs, ideas and notions, principles, and deeper frameworks. It was granted that a supervisor's 'therapeutic orientation is deeply rooted in personal beliefs and existing behavior patterns and would be difficult, if not impossible to change significantly. Supervisors are advised to use the supervisory approach and techniques that are in agreement with their theoretical orientation to therapy' (Hart, 1982, p. 32).

It would seem that a tiny step would extend a similar picture to trainees, that trainees would also be seen as having their own deeper beliefs, ideas and notions, principles, and deeper frameworks. However, it seemed that the supervisory literature essentially lacked this tiny step. In a way, this failure seemed somewhat odd and surprising because, for many graduates, about 6 months later many of these graduates would themselves be supervisors.

It seems odd, disappointing, and yet exciting that discussions about the training of supervisors include the precious idea of beginning supervisors looking into their own personal beliefs. As a further example of the various theories and approaches to supervision, it can help to take into account the beginning supervisor's own beliefs about human nature and how change occurs. 'Select a theory that comes closest to your beliefs about human nature and the change process' (Haynes, Corey, and Moulton, 2003, p. 129). Many beginning supervisors are entitled to say: 'I would like to, but I don't know how to do that. My psychotherapy training did not pay even a little attention to trying to help me find out my own deeper ideas, personal beliefs about human nature or why people feel bad or how patients change.'

What seems so odd, disappointing, and yet frustrating is that supervisors can talk about the value of supervisors looking into, exploring, developing, and using their own personal beliefs, ideas about human nature, what people are like and how change occurs. It would seem to be just a tiny, easy, sensible, almost natural step to do much the same thing in the training of psychotherapists. Except that the literature on supervision maintains a long-standing track record of not exploring the deeper ideas, the deeper frameworks, of psychotherapy trainees. What a pity.

Another glow of a hint consisted of the supervisor asking questions that enabled the trainee to think about therapeutic issues, especially in regard to treatment of the particular client. For example, if the trainee faces a dilemma between encouraging a client's sense of independence and autonomy, and her responsibility to her children, the supervisor can ask: 'Do you have to choose between the two sides of the dilemma, or can they co-exist?' (Nielson, 2002, p. 147). Although questions such as these can enable trainees to think about therapeutic issues, and that could be an exciting hint, in fact this method was used to guide the trainee in the direction of arriving at the 'right' answer. Nevertheless, here is yet another rare soft hint.

In his book on supervision, Haley (1996) explicitly features some fascinating therapeutic issues. Here is a brief sample: Should everything be shared with the client? Does the past cause the present? Does personal therapy make for a better therapist? Does the therapist's religion matter? Do symptoms have useful social functions? Who should have therapy? Could and should therapy be done in the client's home? What theories should be taught? A whimper of disappointment might be heard when it becomes clear that Haley raises these questions in order to provide his own answers, rather than using these good questions as entries into the trainees' own beliefs and ideas about psychotherapy. Another soft hint bites the dust.

In reading text after text, it became easy to misinterpret sentences as hinting toward the value of exploring and developing the trainees' own deeper ideas, e.g. 'Supervisory sessions may at times serve to help validate or evaluate a theoretical perspective by examining it in the context of the trainee's ongoing cases' (Greenberg, 1980, p. 88). I misinterpreted this as reading: 'Supervisory sessions may at times serve to help validate or evaluate or develop the trainee's own theoretical perspective by examining it in the context of the trainee's ongoing cases.' It took a few re-readings for me to realize that what was validated or evaluated was the theoretical perspective that the trainee was here to learn. Nevertheless, a little creative misinterpretation was almost in the direction of a soft hint.

What seemed missing, in the supervision literature that I was studying, was a body of writings that pictured trainees as having a valuable pool of their own, inner, deeper notions and ideas, a kind of soup that could be discovered and could become the trainees' own deeper frameworks for psychotherapy. The apparent absence of these writings left me surprised, somewhat worried, and also excited. I was surprised because the idea seemed so simple and fitting for supervision. I was worried because I might be ignorant of the parts of the literature that delved into this topic at length, and because I started having doubts about the worth of trying to discover trainees' own deeper frameworks. I was excited because the next book or chapter or article might well be just what I was searching for.

Three gems and the mother lode

I finally came across what I had been searching for. These were not whole books or chapters or articles, but they were enough to encourage me that I might be following the tracks of other clinical supervisors. My reaction to the first was that these supervisors saw what I saw, and likewise valued the trainees' own deeper personal notions and ideas about psychotherapy. Gilbert and Evans (2000) mentioned special moments in supervision, 'accompanied by an emotional and cognitive re-examination of previously held assumptions and beliefs. These assumptions may be related to the theoretical basis of the supervisee's work or to more personal assumptions about the nature of life and reality that inform the supervisee's vision of the world' (p. 54). Hooray! We found the same kinds of special moments that were like windows into the deeper notions and ideas of the supervisees.

I was eager to read on. How would the supervisors use these special moments? What can I learn? But that was that. A brief mention and nothing more. How disappointing. But at least here was something. Surely there would be more in the rich literature on supervision.

The trainees I worked with found a second gem, but again it was a brief mention, a kind of incidental but interesting aside in the course of talking about how supervisees can go about choosing a fitting approach. Shertzer and Stone (1968) suggest that for a trainee to select a fitting orientation or approach, it can be helpful for him or her to try to understand his or her own personal view of what human beings are like and how change occurs. Here is a second mention of the idea that trainees can be seen as having their own deeper frameworks for psychotherapy, and that knowing about their deeper framework can be important.

A third gem came from a description of a regularly occurring seminar for beginning therapists in training. One part of the seminar was to show trainees the extent to which their own personal notions and ideas about some deeper and basic issues can influence what occurs in their actual in-session work. The message was for trainees to dig into and explore their own personal answers to these deeper and basic issues, and this is what stamped this as an exciting gem:

> In introducing beginning therapists to the impact of their own values upon their psychotherapy transactions, we explore personal answers to several fundamental questions. The first is, 'What is the nature of man?' . . . The second fundamental question is, 'What is the meaning of

life?' . . . Each therapist must ponder these issues and have a personal answer to the question.

Lewis (1978, p. 20)

Once again, here was a brief mention that neither was elaborated nor played much of a role in the overall training program.

Nevertheless, here were at least three interesting recognitions of trainees' own personal notions and ideas, of the possibility of exploring trainees' own deeper frameworks. In addition to teaching trainees what they are here to learn, perhaps it can be important to delve into trainees' own personal thoughts, notions and ideas, positions on basic issues, answers to basic questions. Here were three gems, even though each was a spare and isolated few sentences or lonely paragraph.

Then the trainees gave me the mother-lode gift. Like the others, it was only a spare paragraph, but what a paragraph! It was a concentrated summary of the main ideas I was stumbling around, a clarification of what I was beginning to see. It was not written by one of the grand deans of psychotherapy supervision. Nor was it written by an obscure supervisor whose brilliant pioneering ideas about supervision were later discovered by the field of supervision. It was written by Carl Rogers, and it was written some time ago (Rogers, 1957, p. 87):

> I believe that the goal of training in the therapeutic process is that the student should develop his own orientation to psychotherapy out of his own experience. In my estimation every effective therapist has built his own orientation within himself and out of his own experience with his clients or patients. It is quite true this orientation as finally developed may be such that it closely resembles that of others, or closely resembles the orientation to which he was exposed.

Rogers did not elaborate on this paragraph in the balance of the chapter. Nor did the paragraph explicitly spell out the idea of searching for the trainee's inner deeper framework. Nevertheless, a case can be made that here is the basis for working with the trainee to discover and to develop the trainee's own notions and ideas about psychotherapy. I had found what I was looking for.

This single paragraph provided the jewel of an idea and the rationale I was searching for. We searched through Rogers' subsequent writings. Nothing. That was hard to believe. What about the writings of other client-centered psychotherapists, especially those who wrote about supervision? Again, nothing. This was surprising, and it was a disappointment.

What was even more surprising was that a leading client-centered voice explicitly asserted the converse of what Rogers had suggested. In writing about supervision, Patterson (1997) was quite clear that (1) the supervisor was here to teach client-centered therapy, rather than to help the trainee explore his or her own inner thoughts and ideas, and (2) the trainee was here to learn client-centered therapy. Indeed, the supervisee's commitment was virtually a requirement for client-centered supervision to be successful. There could be an interesting conversation between the 1957 Rogers and the 1997 Patterson!

When it became rather clear that the supervisory literature did not seem to especially take notice of what I regarded as Rogers' exciting paragraph, and that client-centered supervisors themselves seemed oblivious to it, I kept re-reading it. Maybe I misread this paragraph as I had misread so many other false hints. Maybe I was crediting the paragraph with meanings and implications it never had in mind. Maybe that paragraph appeared only in the copy of the book from the university library.

Then I came across that same paragraph, quoted in full in an article on training and supervision by some client-centered leaders (Truax, Carkhuff, and Douds, 1964). At least the paragraph was real. However, my naive and brittle hopes were again dashed when the authors used that precious paragraph to reinforce the importance of using the trainee's own experience as a therapist in learning what they and Patterson presumed was to be client-centered therapy. Similar to Patterson, client-centered trainees were here to learn client-centered therapy.

I was not finished with combing the literature on supervision, but that one paragraph by Rogers was beginning to look more and more lonely, thin, and frail. And my laudable search to learn more and more about this way of doing supervision became increasingly less exciting and increasingly more questionable, hesitant, lonely, and worrisome. Maybe I was on the wrong track. Maybe I was just plainly wrong.

A few colleagues, some dedicated students, and I continued what seemed to us to be an exhaustive search for direct or indirect mentioning of this way of doing supervision, We combed through the supervision literature from the sparse writings in the early 1900s to the current stream of journals and books on supervision. We found essentially nothing.

One of the reasons we were so surprised was that the idea Rogers had enunciated in 1957 seemed so simple and so sensible as a kind of friendly adjunct or complement to the good ideas in the supervision literature. Another related reason was that the field of psychotherapy placed such importance on probing into what the client thinks, the client's own belief system, the client's deeper thoughts and ideas, and it seemed so sensible that supervisors would extend the same interest in the trainee's own thoughts, belief system, ideas, deeper framework. But we were apparently wrong, and this still seems so surprising.

Can a respectable volume have so few references?

I was indebted to Gilbert and Evans (2000), Shertzer and Stone (1968), Lewis (1978), and especially to Rogers (1957) for having provided the basis for this way of doing supervision, but now I was facing a dilemma: How could a book on supervision have so few references? At least three voices answered:

1. One voice told me to ask the experts. I dutifully asked many of the experts on supervision if there were other publications about exploring the trainee's own 'deeper framework' for psychotherapy. Although the experts offered no further publications, I kept hearing the voice almost insisting that there must be other publications somewhere.

2. The second voice was more of a whisper. It advised me to find a fair number of references, and for me to sprinkle them throughout the volume so that the chapters would at least have a respectable appearance. Find references that can be stretched into looking relevant, and cite them here and there. I tried to let these nasty whispers pass by.

3. The third voice was more elevated and also more critical. If there is no body of literature on this way of doing supervision, that is the way things are. If there were only a few others who mentioned the idea, cite them and leave the matter be. Do not pad the volume with references that really do not belong, references hired mainly for the sake of appearance.

My decision was to flag the few publications that seemed relevant, to decline adding references in a game of trying to look respectable, to admit that there may be additional publications that do fit but I could not find, and to invite readers to please let me know about publications that ought to have been cited.

The discovery-oriented approach is for beginning trainees and seasoned practitioners

Discovering and developing one's own deeper framework, figuring out what it is and helping it to become a workable approach are for beginning students in their academic classes in psychology, psychiatry, counseling, social work, or any of the psychotherapy-related professions. They are for students in any appropriate program, with or without masters or doctoral degrees.

The discovery-oriented approach is also useful for those who are engaged in on-the-job training, whether it is called practicum, field experience, internship, residency, postdoctoral training, or whatever.

It is also appropriate and fitting for seasoned practitioners with 5 or 15 or more years of doing psychotherapy. These people may be especially ready to explore their own deeper frameworks, perhaps to deepen and solidify what they already know and do, perhaps in a readiness to discover a moderately different deeper framework, or perhaps with no agenda at all, except to discover whatever they may discover by seeking down into their own inner deeper framework, whatever it turns out to be.

One way of picturing the deeper framework is that it consists of a relatively fixed set of notions and ideas. Find them, incorporate them, and move on to one's career. I hold to a different picture with at least three parts:

1. As you discover one part of your deeper framework, as you develop and use that part, other parts of your deeper framework can take shape, come to the fore, carry forward.

2. As you have further experience as a psychotherapist, other parts of your deeper framework can evolve, develop, take form and shape, be ready for you to discover.

3. As you have further experience as a psychotherapist, new parts can be born in the deeper framework, new notions and ideas can take shape, come about.

In other words, the discovery of your own deeper framework can be marvelously helpful and useful in the beginning of your training, and throughout your career.

This discovery-oriented approach is for interested supervisors and teachers

From my reading of some of the literature, the discovery of the student's or trainee's own deeper framework for psychotherapy did not seem to be prominently featured in many training programs. Actually, it seemed to be rarely mentioned. Accordingly, this book is for those teachers and supervisors who may have some interest in this added wrinkle.

I picture this as a modest added ingredient in some courses of an academic program and in the supervision of trainees, rather than as a serious contender for the main feature of the program. Even if a fair proportion of teachers and supervisors are friendly to including this ingredient, I still picture it as a minor but quite helpful ingredient in the beginning or the middle or toward the end of the teaching and supervision programs.

Chapter 2

Some advantages of discovering and developing the trainee's deeper framework for psychotherapy

Some of the advantages are relatively immediate and some are more long term. The advantages are for each individual trainee, and for the field of psychotherapy in general. Almost without exception, the advantages are quite real and practical rather than vague and amorphous.

Joyful excitement in discovering each trainee's own deeper ideas about psychotherapy

The belief is that each trainee has a pool of deeper ideas about psychotherapy. They are ideas about what human beings are like, how a person came to be the person that he or she is, how and why people feel good or bad, how change can come about, what a person can become. They are ideas that are the basis of what psychotherapy is. The belief is that deep inside each trainee is a pool of these kinds of ideas, notions, thoughts.

The belief is that these ideas are truly deeper inside each trainee. Some trainees may have a dim sense of the presence of such ideas, but few trainees can say what they are. In other words, these ideas are deeper. They were probably there before the trainee even became a trainee, but the belief is that they are there now. They are present and they can be found.

The deeper pool of ideas may be rather vague, poorly formed, unclear. They may well be disorganized, undeveloped, without much shape or form, somewhat undifferentiated, cloudy. But the belief is that these ideas are there, deep inside each trainee.

For some trainees, there are times when it is exciting to probe down inside, to explore and to discover their own inner deeper notions and ideas. 'So this is what I believe! . . . Yes, this is what I think . . . That seems fitting. I never quite put it into words like this, but yes, this is what I think about that . . .' There can be a titillating curiosity and excitement at going down inside to discover the thoughts and ideas, the positions and beliefs that are yours, that are yours from deeper inside. Now you know. This is exciting, for some trainees at some times.

It can also be exciting to develop these deeper ideas, to let them grow, to see more of what they are like, to see how they fit with other ideas. 'It is like what happened in infancy and childhood can be changed. It doesn't have to be worked around. The effects can be altered. So what might that mean? I wonder . . . .' Once the trainee finds these deeper ideas, they can be further refined and developed. It is far more than just discovering some dead ideas. They can be developed, and this can be exciting.

The trainee can become more open to exploration, inquiry, discovery

Most trainees learn what the program provides for them to learn. It is as if the program says 'We are here to teach you how to be professional psychotherapists', and the trainees reply, 'And we are here to learn.'

When the trainees have learned a substantial amount of what the program teaches, trainees are often able to incorporate and apply that knowledge so that trainees have a way of understanding, making sense of what happens in their sessions. Trainees are able to label, categorize, and understand the change in the way the client relates to the therapist, the recrudescence of the initial symptoms, the resistance to carrying out the homework assignment. Most trainees learn how to make sense of their subject matter, to understand and explain most of what happens in the normal course of unfolding events in the session, to monitor and guide the in-session process of psychotherapy.

Something more seems to happen with trainees who seem geared toward discovering their own deeper ideas about psychotherapy. These trainees seem to be or to become quite interested in exploration, inquiry, discovery. They are more able to be curious about psychotherapy, to be inquisitive, more inclined to probe, ask questions, go deeper into issues and in-session events, to have a passion for studying and knowing and understanding and getting deeper into things. These trainees are inclined to welcome a state of not knowing, of being quizzical, unsure, seeking more clarity. They tend to become involved with deeper questions and issues about psychotherapy. They puzzle about and address questions such as: Just what is an intake session for? Why do clients seek out psychotherapists? How do I arrive at what I think this person ought to be like? How could this session have been quite different and much better? What would make me know that I am totally off base in the way I see this client?

Once trainees get an exciting taste of exploring down into their own ideas and notions, they are inclined to find in-session events and to probe more deeply into them. They tend to find those that are significant and impressive, or bothersome and troublesome, or puzzling and inexplicable, and they are inclined to study them, to pore deeply into them. 'Her headache suddenly went away! How come? I am curious about what caused that!' 'Right then I froze! For almost no reason! But I was panicky for a few seconds. How come? I want to study that more.'

These trainees find themselves drawn toward probing deeper inside the people they work with, curious about this person's thoughts, fascinated by that person's feeling. There is a heightened pull to explore deeper inside the person, the person's inner nature, qualities, possibilities.

It seems sensible that these trainees might have had a readiness to explore, inquire, discover, even before they participated in this kind of training. However, what seems quite clear is that discovering their own deeper frameworks tends to heighten these trainees' general tendencies to probe deeper, to inquire down into, to scrutinize, to be curious, to discover what may be hidden, to know more. For many trainees, and perhaps even for the field as a whole, this can be a solid advantage of discovery-oriented work with trainees.

The trainee's therapeutic approach is custom fitted, 'solidly suited', the right one for the trainee

In most training programs, there are plenty of overt and covert pressures for the trainees to choose some therapeutic approach. Frequently, the pressures begin even before the trainees are accepted into the training program. If they say the right things in their applications and their interviews, they might be accepted into the training programs. If they say the wrong things, the chances are low that they will be accepted. And the overt and covert pressures are there right from the start.

The most common scenario is that the trainee arrives for training with some preferences for this or that approach or kind of approach, and selects one from those generally offered by the training program. The program may offer two or three flavors, and the trainee picks one. The program offers cognitive–behavioral, some psychodynamic, and a little integrative, and the trainees make their choices.

Some trainees arrive with a selection: 'I am a behaviorist.' Most trainees find some club to join during the training program. By the time of graduation, most of them are wearing the uniform of their chosen approach.

It is relatively common that many training programs offer a menu or selection of a number of approaches, usually with one department favored but with the others as tolerable options. In every group of trainees there are often a few who decline to become card-carrying proponents of one of the available options, and who instead are inclined to take the apparently sensible position that each has something to offer. These are the trainees who prefer taking a little of this and a little of that. They can say that several approaches probably have a corner on the truth so it makes good sense to be able to draw from a number of viable approaches. They adopt what is often called an integrative or eclectic stance, but without adopting any particular integrative or eclectic approach.

Of course, there are occasional trainees who are devout believers in an approach that is nowhere to be found in the training program. Until the trainee can be educated or shown how to think in the right way or ushered out of the program, she insists on following through with her passion for implosive therapy or Eriksonian hypnotherapy or logotherapy.

Under ordinary circumstances, the trainee selects an approach for all sorts of reasons, and the chosen approach usually bears a surface goodness of fit with her surface outlook. She selects an approach, and the approach fits, on the surface at least.

This may not be a problem at all. The trainee selected and followed an approach that fits her on the surface, and that is good enough. The approach that she adopted is usually the approach she follows throughout her career. They meet early in training and they stay with one another forever. Sometimes the trainee moves on to some related or even unrelated approach, but that occurs almost naturally, without jolting aches and pains, without problems to speak of.

What is missing in these common scenarios is the wonderful opportunity to find and to have the therapeutic approach that is one's soul-mate, that is truly custom fitted, that is solidly suited, that is the genuinely right one for this trainee. Picture a therapeutic approach that has special goodness of fit with the trainee's own deeper pool of notions and ideas, which comes out of and represents his own deeper framework of what human beings are and can be, what psychotherapy is, which in turn comes from his own deeper insides. This is an advantage that can be gained by discovering and developing his own deeper framework for psychotherapy.

Sometimes the deeper framework may fittingly undergird the trainee's own chosen approach. Usually, however, the deeper framework is different from whatever approach he had or chose on the basis of more surface considerations.

There is a wonderful sense of finding the approach that comes out of and is the expression of the trainee's own deeper notions and ideas. There usually is a newly felt sense of: 'This is me! This is truly my approach! It fits! It is truly the right approach for me!' Here is the simple, precious, powerful, sensitive advantage of finding the approach that is custom fitted, solidly suited, and the right one for the trainee.

The deeper framework can be right for both inside and outside the office

For virtually every trainee, there is a framework, a conceptual system, a set of principles that guides the way he is in the office, in actual psychotherapeutic work, and a framework or set of principles that guides the way he is outside the office, in daily life, in simply living and being. Sometimes these two frameworks are rather similar or at least complementary. Sometimes these two frameworks differ, perhaps clash, conflict, or grate with each other.

In his life with his family and friends, the trainee exemplifies self-reliance, autonomy, independence; in his work with clients there is little of this to be found. In another trainee's work with clients, she relies on careful and attentive listening, but this is not especially present in her own relationships with her 8-year-old daughter. In his daily life, the third trainee relies on his characteristic sense of humor and lighthearted silliness; in his in-session work, he is mainly in the role of the rather neutral observer. In her work with clients, she prizes the clients' own resources for growth and development; in her relationships with her husband and friends, she tolerates and understands their frailties and incapacities. In his relationships with neighbors and acquaintances, he is the model of accommodation and helpfulness; with clients, he plays out the role of the grand sanctuary from external threats and stresses, pressures and plights. For better or for worse, there often is a lack of goodness of fit between the principles that underlie and guide the person's in-session work and those that underlie and guide the person's out-of-office daily living.

There is almost always a bonus when the trainee discovers his or her own inner deeper framework. The bonus is that the inner deeper framework seems to underlie and undergird the way he or she is both inside and outside the office. It is as if there can be a new framework that guides both in-session work and daily living. The two worlds can fit each another. Sometimes the greater changes occur in in-session work, sometimes in daily living and being in the world. Yet the bottom line seems to be that the discovered deeper framework brings into good relationship the way the trainee is in and outside the office. For most trainees, this is a bonus.

The trainee can be free of the common problems of having an approach that seems superficially right but is fundamentally wrong

Most trainees and most practitioners are afflicted with some exceedingly common problems from adopting an approach that seems right, but is only superficially right, and has little goodness of fit with the trainees' own deeper pool of notions and ideas. What usually makes the problems even worse is that they do not know that the adopted approach is fundamentally wrong for them. Here are some of these common problems.

Much lower general level of competence than it could or should be

This sprawling, across-the-board, gross accusation applies both to most individual practitioners and to the field as a whole. Spelled out even further, the accusation is that the general level of competence, capability, and excellence is much lower than it could be or should be if practitioners were to function on the basis of their own deeper frameworks for psychotherapy. If I were to build a case in support of my accusation, I would include at least these considerations:

- I was surprised and impressed when trainees and seasoned practitioners were able to discover their own deeper frameworks, and then make what seemed like giant leaps forward in terms of simple competency and capability. They seemed to jump a few levels of competency. They seemed to become so much better as practitioners.

- For over four decades, I searched for, begged and pleaded for, tapes of sessions that were outstanding, unusual, magnificent, extraordinary. I nagged practitioners who were well known, and I looked for those who had little or no national reputation but who were highly respected and sought by colleagues in their communities. These tapes of unusual sessions raised the bar of competence to a special level. I heard directly what practitioners can be capable of achieving.

- As a result of this exceedingly long-term fascination with collecting audiotapes of sessions, I was able to come across actual data inclining me to believe that perhaps many practitioners remain, throughout most of their careers, essentially at the general level of competence they were when they were initially accredited, registered, licensed, or certificated. My impression is that these practitioners became increasingly comfortable, seasoned, and experienced remaining at their initial level of professional expertise.

- My tape library includes some tapes of trainees who, a year or so later, were doing supervision as part of their jobs, and it also includes some tapes of supervisors who, a year or so earlier, were completing their training programs. Listening to these tapes helped steer me toward being impressed that, if this is the level of competence of at least some supervisors, I have some worries about the level of competence in many supervisees, as well as the level of competence of the field in general.

I concede that my case is quite weak. Nevertheless, I do believe that the ordinary or generally accepted level of competency is much lower than it could or should be, and that the number and proportion of highly competent master practitioners is far lower than it could or should be. I go from there to wondering if more supervisees and more practitioners might be able to discover, develop, and function on the basis of their own deeper frameworks.

Underlying nagging sense that one's chosen approach is not quite one's ideal soul-mate

This is a somewhat common problem, but it is far from universal. Not many practitioners proclaim that their chosen approach is all right, reasonably acceptable, but not the ideal approach, and that they are still waiting for and looking for the ideal approach that is just right for them. Often this is more of an underlying nagging sense with an indistinct and cloudy form and shape. There may be a sense of making do with their chosen approach, of this approach being acceptable, of their being faithful to this approach, of this approach having served them well. There may be a sense of covert glancing at other approaches, as if perhaps to meet the perfect soul-mate, a glow of readiness to accept the ideal approach if it should ever come along and present itself.

More commonly, this underlying nagging sense is sealed under a dedicated devotion to one's chosen approach, a devotion that can elevate one's chosen approach to its idealization. Of course I am an Ericksonian; it is the best approach for me. I am a solid proponent of this integrative therapy; I am a dedicated follower. I have always been a Jungian; it is the best approach by far. Cognitive therapy is the only therapy; it is ideal, the supreme approach.

This underlying nagging sense can have a strong effect on your attitude toward other approaches which become rivals, inferior, lesser. Your approach is of course superior. You may tolerate other approaches, but they are not possibilities for you. You spend your career not mingling with the enemy, not knowing much about them. Some of their practitioners might be your friends, but you have little or no real respect for the approaches that your friends espouse, have chosen, do.

This problem, in most of its forms and guises, can easily come from having chosen an approach that may seem superficially right but is fundamentally the wrong one for the trainee. The trainee can usually be free of this problem by discovering and developing his or her own inner deeper framework, and thereby finding an approach that is fundamentally right for him or her.

- If she had any approach at all, it was feminist oriented, but she did not parade this publicly until she explored deep inside and found a thoroughgoing feminist underlying framework. Feminist therapy now felt right.

- For nearly 13 years, he was a practicing Jungian analyst, until he discovered a much more ingrained deeper existential framework that fit, fit truly well.

- This trainee had been an avowed cognitive-behavioral therapist until a deeper exploration revealed an ingrained social constructionist foundation of beliefs. When he accepted this deeper framework, the persistent nagging sense of 'not quite right' faded away.
- She remained a devout integrative therapist throughout her traineeship, but a deeper exploration brought her to her own 'self-psychology' foundational framework, which became her personal approach to therapy.

There may be undergirdings or underminings of the approach the trainee had chosen, but finding the right and proper deeper framework usually relieves him or her or the practitioner of the nagging sense that the chosen approach does not quite fit, is not really and truly his or her soul-mate.

Many trainees tend to adopt an approach that fits their lifelong, superficial 'folk psychology'

Over the course of their lives, long before they became trainees, most trainees have gradually honed and developed, put into place and counted on, their own personal notions of what people are basically like, what makes people be the way they are, why people do what they do, what good people are like, how people change, how and why some people do or do not have these particular qualities and characteristics, how to be with friends or people who are scary, how to get others to do what you want them to do, how and why people have bad feelings, what good or bad parents are like, how people should be. In other words, in order to be and behave in their worlds, most trainees have developed their own working, superficial 'folk psychology', and most have it long before they enter the training program.

Once in the training program, something interesting happens when the trainee comes face to face with a fleshed-out therapeutic approach. There is a connection or lack of connection between the therapeutic approach and the trainee's own 'folk psychology'. There is a goodness of fit or a sense of being alien between the therapeutic approach and the trainee's own 'folk psychology'. The therapeutic approach is familiar or strange. There is a bond or distance. The therapeutic approach speaks to the trainee or it blabbers mostly noise. The therapeutic approach makes sense or nonsense. For example, almost without explicitly knowing, Jane has almost always had a sense of having a common bond with most others, something shared with others, an underlying humanness. Hearing about and reading about Jung gave Jane a sense of true knowing and understanding of what he was saying. The notion of a collective unconscious was all too familiar in some way. Archetypes made sense. Jung's analytic psychology was the formal explication of what Jane somehow had always believed and known. She found her therapeutic approach.

Her fellow trainee, James, had no such connecting bond with Jung. James had almost always had an inner sense that family and culture had imposed ways of thinking, ways of believing, that made most people the way they were, for better or for worse. For James, what made ingrained sense, without his saying outright that it made ingrained sense, was that things could be better if a person had the right outlook, the right perspective, the right way of thinking. When James was introduced to cognitive psychology, he found his therapeutic approach. It spoke to him directly and personally. It represented an established approach that exemplified what James had somehow known and believed throughout his life.

Of course, trainees can rarely say: 'I have found a therapeutic approach that exemplified and fits my lifelong "folk psychology".' Instead, when there is a goodness of fit, many trainees typically voice academically acceptable reasons for choosing a therapeutic approach: 'It is empirically supported. It is a validated approach . . . It is manualized . . . It meets the criteria of an adequate theory . . . Its theory and practice are grounded in controlled empirical research.'

The problem can be that the trainee can be drawn toward a therapeutic approach that seems appealing, but it lacks that special click, that sense of goodness of fit that can come from exemplifying the trainee's lifelong 'folk psychology'.

Trainees typically adopt an approach that is able to provide the important personal feelings that go with being a therapist

Trainees can be adept at explaining why they pick the approach they do. It appeals to them 'conceptually'. It makes the best sense. It is best supported by research. They admire the heroes of that approach. They respect the supervisors who have that approach. Trainees are rarely caught without sound justifying reasons for whatever approach they follow.

From the experiential way of making sense of things, trainees tend to find an approach for the same reasons that they help create most other situations in their lives. They seek those particular friends, that particular person to live with, that particular place to work, largely because that situation enables them to have the precious personal feelings and experiencing that it is important for the trainee to have. Trainees also tend to adopt the approach that can provide them with the precious personal feelings and experiencing that it is important for them to have. This is the reason, from the experiential perspective, for whether or not the trainee knows this, and most trainees will not know this.

Here is a sample of the kinds of precious feelings and experiencing that are important for many trainees to have in the role of therapist. Whatever approach can offer the precious personal feelings and experiencing for this particular trainee is likely to be the approach he or she will adopt, and then will voice all sorts of other reasons for having adopted the approach.

It is the rarest and most extraordinary of trainees who would even admit that the highlight of the session is having this or that special feeling, that the real reason for being a therapist is to be able to have such a precious personal feeling, that the most important thing that happened in this session is that he or she had this particularly wonderful personal feeling, that the most appealing thing about this approach is that he or she can enjoy such wonderful feelings.

Instead, with such predictable regularity as to approach a law with essentially no exceptions, trainees will find other things as the highlights of the session. They talk about the therapeutic relationship, their interventions, the fluctuations in the client's condition, and dozens of other topics that are professionally acceptable. The wonderfully precious and highly personal feelings they had in the session are inevitably sidetracked, marginalized, trivialized, secondary, unmentioned, unimportant. Indeed, again with rare exception, most trainees keep them hidden and unknown, even to themselves.

Trainees have all sorts of reasons why they chose the approach they follow. There may be an exception, but they do not say that they chose this approach because it gives them a good chance to have precious personal feelings such as the following, that the greatest and most wonderful thing that happened in the session is when they had this precious feeling:

> 'I have such special knowledge of what you are really like, your inner world, the deeper mysterious world of your insides.'

> 'I am so mentally healthy, so well-adjusted, in such fine shape, without pathology and problems.'

'I am the one who can tell what is wrong with you. I know what the real problem is. I see into your psychopathology. I see the serious flaws in your personality. I can tell what the mental illness is in you.'

'I am perfection, the ideal person, the optimal being. I am the Godlike one, the exemplar of ideal mental health.'

'I give you precious understanding, sympathy, empathy. I share what you feel. I truly know how you feel. I know how it really is for you.'

'I am the grand healer, the reliever of pain. I take away your hurt, your anguish, your suffering. It is gone. I did this for you.'

'What I say is so important. You listen raptly to what I say. I give you the grand explanation. I provide you with understanding. My words are to be respected.'

'I am so wise, so sage. I pour out the wisdom of the ages. I know what is true. I know how people really are. I know how the world works. I know the truth about human beings, about life, about pain and suffering, about healing and human development.'

'You fully depend on me. You entrust yourself to me. You put yourself in my safe hands. I am the one you turn to for the important decisions, the management of your life.'

'I give you special intimacy and closeness. You feel these things with me. No one else can or ever has offered you such wonderful intimacy and closeness and oneness with another human being.'

'I am in charge of the man, my client. I am the superior one. I make him grovel. I am authoritative over him. I have power over him. Look what I can make him do.'

'I am so seductive, so sexual. I am sought after, lusted after. I can feel the erotic sensations in my body.'

'I am omniscient, the all-powerful one. I am God on earth. I have the knowledge and the power.'

'I am the grand savior from psychic catastrophe, the one who rescues the patient from psychic disaster, from the swirling underground mental illness.'

'I can reach the unreachable, the utterly withdrawn, the lost soul who is yearning to take my hand.'

'I am the respected professional, the one who is looked up to. I am the doctor.'

These are only a small sample of the many kinds of precious personal feelings that trainees and professional psychotherapists have in their sessions, the veritable peaks and highlights of their sessions.

Yet trainees rarely say these words out loud. They rarely think these things inside themselves. They rarely even know that these are the precious highlights of the session. They rarely know that these precious personal feelings are the main reasons that underlie and account for why they chose whatever approach they chose and for why they are here with this client, doing the things they actually do with this client in this session.

From the experiential perspective, these moments of such precious personal feeling and experiencing are the highlights of the session for most therapists carrying out most approaches. Therapists engage in psychotherapy, do what they do in the sessions, and hold to justifying rationales and therapies, mainly as support for having their precious in-session feelings and experiencing. These feelings and experiencing fuel what is called psychotherapy, drive what is called psychotherapy. Strip away the jargon, the talk about psychopathology, the mental health talk, the platitudes and propositions of psychotherapy, and what is left are the precious personal feelings and experiencing that the therapist has in the session.

By discovering the trainee's inner deeper framework, what tends to be resolved is the delicious problem of adopting whatever approach can provide the not-talked-about precious personal feelings and experiencing. This exceedingly common problem is inclined to wash away when the trainee is custom fitted with an approach that fits well with his or her own deeper framework.

Doing psychotherapy tends to become more mechanical and perfunctory and less joyful and exciting

For most psychotherapists, their approach may well seem superficially fitting and right, but it is not rooted in or the live expression of their deeper frameworks. This usually means that doing psychotherapy easily becomes rather mechanical and perfunctory. It is their work. It is their job. It is relatively routine. It is what they do. It may border on being somewhat monotonous, especially when they are experienced at the job.

For most psychotherapists, doing psychotherapy is not unpleasant. It may of course be important to them, a source of pride. They enjoy their work. They like being psychotherapists. Yet doing psychotherapy is more mechanical and perfunctory than it is joyful and exciting.

There is less of a sense of passion and excitement, of bubbly enthusiasm.

Furthermore, most trainees and most psychotherapists are not especially aware of this pervading sense of what they are doing as essentially mechanical and perfunctory, as lacking a solid sense of joy, buoyancy, passion, excitement.

This is the somewhat subtle but common problem when psychotherapists follow an approach that seems superficially right, but is fundamentally wrong because it is not an approach coming from their own inner deeper framework.

When the deeper framework becomes the trainee's own approach, this background sense of mechanicalness washes away. It is replaced with a quiet bubbliness, a tingling excitement that occurs before, during, and after the actual session. There is a solid and stable interest in the doing of psychotherapy. The trainee can think about the session, is drawn toward going over compelling parts because there are compelling parts and because he or she is interested in them.

Eventually many psychotherapists seem to give up doing psychotherapy

During training, many trainees are dedicated psychotherapists. When they meet each other, after 15–25 years or so, it is relatively common that a rather large proportion are no longer doing psychotherapy. They have become administrators. They are consultants. They do research on other topics. They are engaged in other interests.

The change may be referred to as 'burn-out', or perhaps 'career development', yet they are often no longer active practitioners. They may well be satisfied and happy in their new pursuits, yet they are no longer active practitioners.

This is a relatively common consequence when their approach seems superficially right, but is fundamentally wrong, when their approach has little or no basis in their own inner deeper frameworks.

In happy contrast, there is a kind of bubbly zest in the practitioner whose therapeutic approach comes from the deeper framework. The practitioner may be 83 years old, but waiting for and having a session with the other person, and talking it over with an 80-year-old colleague, he or she can be as vibrant and alive as the 8-year-old hockey player heading for the arena.

The trainee can become a master practitioner

This advantage is for trainees, and also for psychotherapists who have experience as practitioners. The advantage is that they seem to become much better practitioners. The ceiling on competence is raised much higher. Once they discover and develop their own inner deeper framework, their level of competence seems to soar.

Occasionally, a trainee has that spark of wanting to be a great practitioner, a truly master practitioner. Great supervisors can help. But a necessary added ingredient is discovering and developing that trainee's own inner deeper framework. This is the gift a supervisor can give to that rare trainee.

The rule seems to be as follows: when the trainee discovers and develops his or her own deeper framework for psychotherapy, his or her level of competence will be inclined to rise significantly.

What is the convincing evidence? It is a little humorous to look for a body of research studies on this. I have a hard time picturing researchers interested in this topic, an even harder time picturing the researchers finding subjects to study, and a still harder time picturing a large enough sample to satisfy many researchers.

What has convinced me are the trainees and practitioners who were able to dig down and discover their own inner deeper frameworks, and to watch how their levels of competency kept going up and up. This seemed to happen almost right away, and then these rare practitioners seemed to reach the level of master practitioners years later.

What has also convinced me is serious talk with master practitioners, the truly gifted and fine practitioners of our field, often people whose audiotapes I have had the privilege of studying. Almost without exception, these rare people have done the exciting and difficult job of probing inside to find their own inner deeper frameworks, usually being the prime creators of their own approaches.

Finding the occasional trainee whose deeper framework is friendly to my experiential psychotherapy

When I start with a trainee, I am virtually unable to know if he or she can do my experiential psychotherapy. If a number of trainees seem enthusiastic about this approach, what generally happens is that most of them do not have the inner frameworks that fit well with this approach. There is a grating poorness of fit. They do not think 'experientially'.

However, when I concentrate on helping the trainees to discover their own inner deeper frameworks, I occasionally come across one whose deeper framework seems to be friendly to the experiential way of thinking. Here is the rare trainee who is likely to be a good candidate for my experiential psychotherapy. I say 'rare' because it seems to be approximately one in every 40 or 50 trainees whose inner deeper framework is friendly to that of experiential psychotherapy.

In other words, helping trainees discover and develop their own inner deeper frameworks seems to be a relatively painless, effective, but somewhat lengthy screening device for finding the occasional fitting candidate for my experiential psychotherapy.

These are some of the advantages, the aims and goals, the payoffs, of helping trainees discover and develop their own inner deeper notions and ideas about psychotherapy, their own inner deeper frameworks for psychotherapy. I believe these advantages are important for supervisors, especially important for trainees, and exceedingly important for the advancement of the field of psychotherapy, and have some important implications for our training programs.

Chapter 3

How can a training program include the discovery-oriented approach?

Picture masters programs, doctoral programs, or postdoctoral programs in most of the psychotherapy-related fields such as psychology, psychiatry, and others that have university-based training programs in psychotherapy or counseling. Picture training programs that train psychotherapists in specialties such as school counseling, psychoanalytic psychotherapy, family psychotherapy, or Jungian analysis. Picture both the classroom or academic part of the training program and the internship, residency, field-work part of the training program.

It seems that few if any training programs include a substantial element that focuses on the discovery and development of the trainees' own inner deeper framework for psychotherapy. The question is: 'How could training programs include a substantial component of the discovery-oriented approach to teaching and training?'

Picture that some of these training programs simply add this component to what they already include in their training programs. The picture is not that these training programs twist themselves out of shape and emphasize the discovery-oriented approach. Indeed, my impression is that, for the good of both the trainees and the field of psychotherapy, it is most sensible for the discovery-oriented approach to be included as a friendly added component. That is enough.

At least some of the faculty hold a 'multiple mind-set' perspective, rather than the common 'single-truth mind-set'

In a training program, there is some room for the discovery-oriented approach when at least some of the faculty have a way of seeing the world that includes a foundational belief in different ways of seeing the world, different basic outlooks, different personal worlds, different ways of building and organizing one's personal world, different mind-sets.

According to this perspective, this mind-set, some of these multiple mind-sets may be better or more useful than others, depending on the intended aim or purpose or goal.

The foundational belief is that there can be different sets of foundational beliefs

There is room for the discovery-oriented approach when at least some of the faculty can hold a foundational belief that there can be different sets of foundational beliefs in the broad field of psychotherapy. This is a relatively uncommon foundational belief.

In the much more common mind-set, it is virtually taken for granted that there is one set of what may be called basic dictums, fundamental principles, anchoring cornerstones, foundational beliefs. Although these are rarely if ever spelled out in a concrete, authoritative way (Mahrer, 2000, 2003), here is an amateur, provisional, unauthorized sample of some of these foundational beliefs at the base of the traditional 'single-truth mind-set' of the field of psychotherapy (Mahrer, 2003, 2004a):

- There is a cumulative body of psychotherapeutic knowledge; research is a primary gatekeeper for what is admitted into or withdrawn from the cumulative body of knowledge.

- The cumulative body of knowledge is relevant and applicable across virtually all psychotherapeutic theories and approaches.

- Conceptual systems of psychotherapy are to include common foundations comprising fundamental truths, postulates, and axioms.

- Theories of psychotherapy are judged, examined, and tested by deriving hypotheses that are subjected to scientific verification, confirmation, disconfirmation, refutation, and falsification.

- The outcomes of psychotherapy can be rigorously assessed as successful, effective, beneficial, or not, essentially apart from philosophical value systems.

- Biological, neurological, physiological, and chemical events and variables are basic to psychological events and variables.

- The brain is a basic determinant of human behavior.

- Human beings are essentially information-processing biological organisms.
- There are biopsychological stages of human growth and development.
- The person and the external world are integral independent entities that interact and affect one another.
- Responses followed by satisfying consequences tend to be strengthened; responses followed by unsatisfying consequences tend to be weakened.
- Causal determinants of human behavior generally lie in antecedent events.
- There are mental illnesses, diseases, and disorders.
- Clients seek psychotherapy for, and psychotherapy is, treatment of psychological/psychiatric problems, distress, mental disorders, personal difficulties, problems in living.
- The practitioner initially assesses and diagnoses the problem or mental disorder, and then selects and applies the appropriate treatment.
- The therapist-client relationship is a prerequisite to successful psychotherapy.
- Insight and understanding are a prerequisite to successful psychotherapy.
- There are common factors across successful and effective psychotherapies, and it is beneficial for research to identify them and for psychotherapies to incorporate them.
- There are differential treatments of choice for differential psychological problems and mental disorders.
- Clients with low ego strength and inadequate defenses may be harmed by excessive stress in psychotherapy.
- Psychotherapeutic training is to include training in the common core of basic psychotherapy skills and methods.

Most of the faculty in most programs know that trainees will learn the common established way of listening to clients, establishing the proper therapist–client relationship, carrying out an initial assessment and evaluation, diagnosis and problem identification, and selection of the appropriate treatment program and methods.

Most of the faculty in most programs share a common 'single-truth mind-set', with its common set of foundational beliefs and its common core of basic skills for doing psychotherapy. Once this common foundation is established, trainees can then be exposed to different approaches to psychotherapy and their different treatment methods and techniques.

The discovery-oriented approach has little or no place in such training programs dominated by a faculty with the 'single-truth mind-set'. The discovery-oriented approach can have a fair chance when at least some of the faculty hold a 'multiple mind-set' perspective in which there truly can be different mind-sets and different sets of foundational beliefs, in which the 'single-truth mind-set' is only one of basically different mind-sets.

'I can help you discover your own deeper framework' is a better credo than 'I tell you the truth; you are here to learn the truth'

Most of the faculty in most training programs come out of a mold in which they have the knowledge. They know the truth. They know the theory and the methods of psychodynamic therapy or cognitive–behavioral therapy. They are here to provide the knowledge. Trainees are here to learn. Trainees are to be schooled, taught, given the knowledge. Trainees are like vessels into which the faculty pours the knowledge. When trainees can show that they have the right amount of the right knowledge, they are probably ready to complete the training program.

The discovery-oriented faculty has a different mind-set with a different credo. According to this credo, they value an added ingredient. The faculty offers the trainees an opportunity to explore inside, to discover the pools of notions and ideas that are the foundation of their own inner deeper frameworks. If the trainees are ready and eager, this faculty can be of help. The members can work with the trainees to help dig down inside and to explore, discover, and develop each trainee's own inner deeper framework.

A new dimension in training programs: what are the foundational issues and questions, and what are our positions and answers?

A training program can include the discovery-oriented approach, and help the trainee explore and discover his or her own inner pool of notions and ideas, by saying: 'Here are many of the foundational issues and questions in the field of psychotherapy. Here are the traditional positions and answers by our traditional approaches. What are your own positions on these foundational issues, and what are your own answers to these foundational questions?'

Picture this new dimension in any kind of training program, whether it ends with a certificate or a diploma, a masters or a doctoral program, a training program in Jungian analysis or cognitive therapy, a graduate or postgraduate training program, a training program that is specialized or generalized.

This is a new dimension because it is essentially lacking, to any substantial degree, in virtually all training programs in psychotherapy.

What is missing in virtually all training programs is a dimension of acknowledging and studying foundational questions and answers

Training programs include courses on topics such as cognitive therapy, the therapist–client relationship, psychotherapy research, psychopathology, basic techniques in psychotherapy, diagnostic evaluation, stress management. Almost without exception, these courses consist of material and topics with virtually no focus on the underlying foundational issues and questions. Students finish the course and have little or no idea that there are underlying foundational issues and questions, what they are, and that virtually all of the course material and topics represent some kind of generally accepted position on the hidden foundational issues and some kind of generally accepted answer to the hidden foundational questions. Students finish the course without even knowing that there are foundational issues and questions, much less what they are. Students are typically ignorant of the floor underneath the course material and topics that they were given to learn.

Students are typically given a position or answer without knowing the deeper issue, the basic question, or alternative positions and answers

Students are typically given a single position or answer to underlying issues and questions that they are rarely shown. They are taught the cognitive or the psychodynamic or the mainstream positions and answers without knowing that these are positions on deeper issues and answers to deeper questions. Students learn the catechism without even knowing that there is a deeper world of issues and questions, and without knowing that there can be other positions on underlying issues that they do not know about, and that there can be other answers to underlying questions that they do not know about.

Almost without exception, their teachers are in a similar mind-set of not knowing. The teachers teach the material without knowing that what they teach are positions on hidden issues and answers to hidden questions.

The training of psychotherapists rarely opens the door to the underlying issues and questions largely because the teachers are rarely aware that such an underlying world even exists. Teachers generally teach the facts, the content, the knowledge, and rarely even know about the existence of the underlying issues and questions for which their facts, content, and knowledge are positions or answers.

How to judge whether a course and a program are good or poor in this dimension

Look at a given course in a training program. Look at the training program as a whole. There are ways to judge whether the course and the program are good and adequate or poor and inadequate with regard to the dimension of including foundational issues and questions. Here are four ways to judge:

1. Do the course and the training program dedicate at least 10–20 percent of their time to focusing on these underlying foundational issues and questions? Most courses and training programs fail here.

2. Do the course and the training program cover a fair number of the relevant foundational issues and questions? Most courses and training programs fail here.

3. Do the course and the training program highlight that their content and knowledge constitute positions and answers to foundational issues and questions? Most courses and training programs fail here.

4. Do the course and the training program value and provide space for the students to find, discover, and formulate their own positions and answers to the foundational issues and questions? Most courses and training programs fail here.

Indeed, most courses and training programs are exceedingly poor on this dimension.

How to use a list of foundational issues and questions

Here are five ways to use such a list:

1. Organize what you teach in the course as one or more positions on these particular issues or as one or more answers to these particular questions. Be open and clear in specifying the underlying foundational issues or questions for this course.

   Feel free, as the teacher, to say that you agree with this particular position or answer, or that here is your own, perhaps somewhat different, position or answer.

   There is a list of 75 'foundational beliefs' that may be generally accepted in the field of psychotherapy (Mahrer, 2003). Tick off the foundational beliefs that apply to or are relevant to this course.

2. Invite students to follow the procedure (Mahrer, 2003) to arrive at their own personal acceptance, modification, or replacement of each of the foundational beliefs relevant to this course.

3. For each of the following foundational issues and questions, students should answer these questions: 'On each foundational issue or question, what is the position or answer that is generally accepted by the field of psychotherapy as correct, right, traditional, authority backed?' 'What are some plausible alternative positions or answers to these generally accepted positions or answers?'

4. Invite students to study each foundational issue or question and to arrive at their own position or answer. Students may think of this assignment as a matter of choosing or selecting their own from the positions or answers that are presented in the course. However, make it clear that the emphasis is to be on the student's own position or answer, one that feels right for the student, that comes from the student. The student's position or answer may be a slight modification on one that is established in the field, or it may be a substantial modification, or an original position or answer. Yet the continuing emphasis is that it is to be a position or answer that comes from the student, fits the student, and feels just right for the student (Mahrer, 1987; Mahrer and Boulet, 1989).

   The assignment consists of the student writing down his or her own position or answer on each of the foundational issues or questions. These views need not be defended and justified. They need not be of publishable quality. They do not need corroborating or justifying with references and citations. The assignment is merely to give the student a chance to spell out what he or she thinks, believes, in response to each foundational issue or question. The assignment is one of providing informal notes, loose ideas, a stream of thoughts, rather than a formal, well-organized paper.

5. Provide students with an opportunity to study perhaps 10-15 pages of almost any published text to learn how to identify the underlying foundational issues or questions to which the text provides positions or answers. Examine each paragraph to see whether this paragraph provides a position on some underlying issue or provides an answer to some underlying question. If so, what is the underlying foundational issue or question?

An amateur attempt to start formulating a list

The list below is not intended to be formal or authoritative. It is merely a beginning, a provisional and amateur attempt to formulate some of the foundational questions in the field of psychotherapy (Mahrer, 2004a). Some of the questions may fall outside the field. Some are more basic and some deeper than others. They are in no particular order. They are not intended to be comprehensive or exhaustive. They represent varying levels of abstraction and generality. They are not intended to be in some final form.

A sample of some foundational questions in the field of psychotherapy

These questions are to do with *conceptualization* in the field of psychotherapy:

- Can constructs in one conceptual system relate to and have effects on constructs in a different conceptual system?
- What are the relationships between, on the one hand, biological, neurological, physiological, chemical events and variables and, on the other, psychological events and variables?
- Are there psychological laws of human nature? If so, what are they?
- How can a conceptual system be improved, advanced?
- Can conceptual systems be combined or integrated into a new conceptual system?
- On what basis may a conceptual system be judged as adequate or inadequate?
- What are the criteria of a science of psychotherapy?
- What are the criteria for judging psychotherapeutic data as hard, objective, real?

- What are the criteria for judging an explanation as worthy, adequate, satisfactory'?

Here is a small sample of some foundational questions dealing with *psychotherapy research*:

- On what basis is something included or excluded from the cumulative body of psychotherapeutic knowledge?
- How can research examine and advance a psychotherapeutic conceptual system?
- Is there a single 'scientific method' or are there multiple 'scientific methods'?
- How can research show that a hypothesis is wrong, falsified, refuted?
- What are systematic methods of arriving at a research hypothesis?
- How can research be done to discover more of what can be known about psychotherapy?

Here is a small sample of some foundational questions dealing with *personality*:

- What are the basic foundations of 'personality'?
- What accounts for feelings that are pleasant or unpleasant, pleasurable or painful?
- How and why does a person dream?
- How and why does a person seem to behave in ways that are accompanied by feelings that are unpleasant, hurtful, painful?
- What are the components of what is referred to as 'personality'?
- What accounts for change in what is referred to as 'personality'?
- What are the limits on how broad and deep 'personality change' can be?

The following questions are a sample of foundational questions to do with *psychotherapy*:

- What are the purposes, aims, and goals of psychotherapy'?
- How are the purposes, aims, or goals arrived at for this person in this session?
- On what bases can these purposes, aims, or goals be judged as (1) more appropriate and fitting for this person in this session or (2) superior to other plausible purposes, aims, or goals?

- On what bases is a given session judged as worthwhile, successful, effective?

- What factors and agents limit, restrict, and constrain the extent and nature of potential change?

- What accounts for some in-session changes being judged as welcomed and desirable?

- What are the defining characteristics of what is and is not judged as 'psychotherapy'?

- How can a new psychotherapy be created, originated, brought about?

- What concrete methods help bring about what concrete in-session changes?

- How can personal change be brought about that can be regarded as deep-seated, radical, transformational?

- How can a person become the person that he or she is capable of becoming?

- How can dreams be used to achieve psychotherapeutic change'?

Training programs can add a new dimension that is aimed at helping students to discover and develop their own deeper framework. One way is to start with a list of foundational beliefs, and to use the guidelines to help students discover and develop their own foundational beliefs (Mahrer, 2003). A second way is to start with the above list of foundational questions, ask students to write down the more or less standard, accepted, traditional answers, and then to give students an opportunity to write down their own, personal answers to each of the foundational questions.

Explicit features of the training program: the discovery and development of the students' own deeper framework for psychotherapy

Either formally or informally, the training program says to its students: 'We value and respect that you may have your own deeper notions and ideas about psychotherapy, some of which you may be aware of, most of which are probably deeper, loosely formed pools of notions and ideas. Part of what this training program offers, for any of you who are truly interested, is an opportunity to dig down into your own deeper framework, to explore and discover what these inner deeper notions and ideas are, to help you develop them into whatever they may become, into your own framework for psychotherapy, whatever it seems to be, whether it is similar to some generally accepted approach or whether it bears your own distinctive deeper notions and ideas.'

The training program may put this into more formal words, and include this formal feature as one of the formal features of the program. Or the training program may incorporate the spirit of these words into the more informal character of the program.

In any case, most students can know full well whether or not the program includes this distinctive feature. It shows. It shows in the bits and pieces that hold together the training program, and it shows in the teachers and the clinical supervisors.

Inclusion of some teachers who genuinely value helping students discover their own deeper framework for psychotherapy in the training program

I picture only a sprinkling of such teachers, rather than most of the faculty. The students who are ready and eager to discover their own deeper frameworks can do so with a sprinkling of such teachers. If most teachers in the program have this value, it is easy to see discovering one's own deeper framework as taking on the appearance of a requirement that might pull disinterested students into the need to conform when really they do not think that way.

I can picture this dimension as characterizing these teachers' courses, as being a special added feature of their courses. I can also picture a special course on this topic, a course explicitly focused on enabling students to discover and develop their own frameworks.

It would be wonderful if interested teachers included this discovery-oriented dimension in their courses. However, it is not the purpose of the rest of this book to show teachers how to do this. Rather, the purpose is to talk with clinical supervisors and supervisees.

Inclusion of some clinical supervisors who genuinely value helping students discover their own deeper framework for psychotherapy in the training program

Again, I picture only a sprinkling of the clinical supervisors. Not every clinical supervisor has a mind-set that includes this value. Having a sprinkling of available clinical supervisors may be enough.

Once again, both the supervisors and the students almost certainly know which of the clinical supervisors value doing supervision in this way and for this purpose. As is seen in the remainder of this book, dedicating supervision to helping the trainees discover and develop their own deeper frameworks usually means that this is the main feature of the supervision.

The remainder of this book is dedicated to showing these supervisors how to do supervision in this way.

Chapter 4

Some qualities of a good discovery-oriented teacher

In the field of psychotherapy, the common meaning of 'teacher' refers to the one who teaches an academic course, and the common meaning of 'clinical supervisor' refers to the one who 'supervises' the trainee in on-the-job training and psychotherapy. In this volume, the role of the person who helps the on-the-job trainee discover his or her own deeper framework is more of a 'teacher' than a 'supervisor'. It seems awkward to keep referring to this person as 'the supervisor who does discovery-oriented teaching', but the description fits. Nevertheless, I use the word 'teacher' and the phrase 'discovery-oriented teacher' to mean the person who helps the on-the-job trainee discover his or her own deeper framework for psychotherapy.

The more I read about the training of psychotherapists, the more impressed I became with the big gap, the altogether different mindsets, between the common picture of what a good teacher and supervisor is like, and the qualities of a good discovery-oriented teacher. I also became increasingly impressed with how little has been written on the qualities of a teacher who might value the discovery-oriented approach to training.

I genuinely hope that at least some teachers and supervisors are ready and eager to become discovery-oriented teachers, to add a dash or a substantial dimension of the discovery-oriented approach to their teaching and training of psychotherapists.

The purpose of this chapter is to describe some of the qualities of a good discovery-oriented teacher. I wish I could say that these qualities came from careful study of a number of discovery-oriented teachers, but I cannot. I have known or read the writings of teachers who seem to have many or most of these qualities, but these people seem rare and precious, and it seems somewhat unfair to claim them to be discovery-oriented teachers as described in this volume. Instead, these qualities came from my own impressions, and these are feeble justifications.

As you read each quality, you may keep some questions in mind:

- Do you qualify as a good discovery-oriented teacher?
- To what extent would you like to have these qualities?
- If you are a teacher or a trainee, to what extent would you value a teacher with these qualities, and see some value in having a few teachers with these qualities in your training program?
- If you are a trainee, to what extent would you want to have a teacher with these kinds of qualities?

A case for being difficult to be a good discovery-oriented teacher

As you read this chapter, please consider a case that few supervisors have the qualities, the knowledge, the competencies of a good discovery-oriented teacher. It can take a fair amount of training and experience to acquire this knowledge, to gain these particular competencies, to develop these particular qualities.

Consider a kind of test. On graduation, the challenge is that very few graduates would have the qualities, requisite knowledge, and competencies of a reasonably good discovery-oriented teacher. As you read this chapter, see if you are inclined to agree or to disagree.

In contrast, it is often the case that recent graduates have 'supervision' as part of their first job. They are often hired to do a job that includes some supervision. What is more, a fair proportion of these recent graduates can do a reasonable job as supervisor. The clever observation or truth is that it takes around 3–6 months to go from trainee to supervisor, to go from the student's side of the desk to the other side as supervisor. Indeed, many recent graduates quickly and easily get the hang of being one of the supervisors. All of this is evidence on behalf of a case that the qualities, knowledge, and competencies of most trainees are sufficient for the graduate to be a supervisor and, the case holds, generally insufficient and inadequate for the recent graduate to be a reasonably good discovery-oriented teacher. As you read this chapter, see if you are inclined to agree or to disagree.

The teacher believes in different ways of making sense of things, some of which may be more useful than others, rather than being the one and only eternal truth

The discovery-oriented teacher believes that there can be different ways of describing things, each of which may be accurate or correct, and neither of which is ultimately correct, eternally correct, or more correct than the others. That thing may be described as white, ceramic, and a cup.

None of these descriptions is the only true description, closer to the real truth. However, these descriptions may well differ in usefulness (Mahrer, 2004a). If I am thirsty and want to drink, describing that thing as a cup is more useful than describing it as white or ceramic, even though that thing may well be white and ceramic.

Each approach, each conceptualization, each way of making sense of things, may have its own foundational beliefs, its own basic propositions, cornerstones on which the approach rests. The discovery-oriented teacher believes in the sensibility and worth of different kinds of foundational beliefs, rather than in foundational dictums, axioms, theorems, assumptions that are elevated to the status of eternal truths that every approach must salute.

Here are a few foundational beliefs, with the first aiming to put into words what the field apotheosizes as eternal truths, and the second being a companion foundational belief from the experiential way of making sense of things:

- There is a cumulative body of knowledge; research is a primary gatekeeper for what is admitted into or withdrawn from the cumulative body of knowledge.

  Each distinctive conceptual approach has its own relatively distinctive body of knowledge; research plays a minor role in what is admitted into or withdrawn from each conceptual approach's body of knowledge.

- Prediction and explanation of empirically validated facts are important criteria for judging the worth of theories of psychotherapy.

  Conceptual systems of psychotherapy are to be judged largely on the basis of their demonstrated usefulness in helping to achieve the aims for which they were generated and used.

- Research is to confirm, verify, disconfirm, refute, and falsify the tested hypothesis.

   Psychotherapy research is predominantly to discover further and increasingly better answers to the important questions in the field of psychotherapy.

- Psychotherapeutic theories, orientations, and approaches acquire, maintain, or lose acceptability largely on the basis of careful evaluation of their conceptual soundness and clinical efficacy.

   Psychotherapeutic theories, orientations, and approaches acquire, maintain, or lose acceptability largely on the basis of the constituency with beliefs that have reasonably high goodness of fit with the beliefs of the psychotherapeutic theory, orientation, and approach.

- Biological, neurological, physiological, and chemical events and variables are basic to psychological events and variables.

   In the philosophy of science accepted by the experiential perspective, the events that are of interest to the experiential perspective are described and understood in terms of the experiential system of constructs, rather than in terms of supposedly more basic events and variables in such bodies of constructs as biology, neurology, physiology, and chemistry.

- The brain is a basic determinant of human behavior. Different construct systems may well provide their own different descriptions and explanations of events.

   In the experiential system, human behavior is understood as a function of, and is determined by, potentials for experiencing and their relationships.

- Human beings have inborn, intrinsic, biological and psychological needs, drives, instincts, and motivations; these include needs and drives for survival, sex-aggression, object-seeking, contact comfort.

   Each person is understood in terms of deeper and basic potentials for experiencing that are relatively unique to this person, rather than universal, that are experiential, rather than biological or biopsychological, and not characterized by properties of need, drive, or force.

- Pain is aversive; behavior tends to reduce, avoid, or eliminate pain.

   Behavior is an effective way of enabling experiencing, whether the experiencing is accompanied with feelings that are good and pleasant, or with feelings that are bad and painful.

These are only 8 of 75 foundational beliefs taken from the field of psychotherapy (Mahrer, 2003, 2004a), with each followed by a different foundational belief from the experiential perspective (Mahrer, 1989).

The teacher believes that there can be different ways of making sense of things, different basic principles, rather than one single view or set of beliefs that are to be worshiped as eternally true. The teacher accepts that one's own foundational beliefs may be more useful than others, but not necessarily truer than others.

The discovery-oriented teacher declines the role of authoritative purveyor-enforcer of the right way to think about and do psychotherapy

The typical role of supervisor usually includes at least two parts. These parts may be conspicuous and manifest, or they may be somewhat hidden and cloaked. In either case, both parts of the message typically get through to many trainees.

These two parts help to define the role of supervisor. They can be described in a friendly or a somewhat unfriendly way, a way that many supervisors may well accept or a way most supervisors would object to as wrong or offensive or both.

One part of the ordinary role of supervisor is 'purveyor of truth'. The message that the supervisor sends is along these lines: 'I am here to represent and to show you the right way, the correct way, the accepted way, to think about and to do psychotherapy, or at least this way of thinking about and doing psychotherapy. I know the truth, and I will make sure that you learn the truth.' The supervisor can convey this message in a way that is or is not so friendly, direct or somewhat indirect, and includes large or small doses of respect, value, caring, and understanding of the trainee. In almost any case, the role of supervisor almost always includes a defining part of the supervisor as the purveyor of truth.

In addition, the role of supervisor includes a component of the supervisor as enforcer. In effect, the message to the trainee is something along these lines: 'I am here to make sure that you have the right way of thinking about and doing psychotherapy. I assess and evaluate you. I judge you. You are to conform. You are to think the right way, and you are to do psychotherapy the right way. If you do, I am satisfied and pleased. If you do not, then you can be in trouble.'

Most supervisors are able to convey this message in ways that are friendly, reassuring, humane, but this is a second defining part of the supervisor's role.

What can be a curious paradox is the degree to which these two messages are also present when the supervisor and trainee are in the role of psychotherapist. Perhaps their role of psychotherapist also includes smaller or larger chunks of the psychotherapist as the purveyor and enforcer of truth. Could it be that some supervisors and some supervisees convey to their clients messages along the following lines? 'I am here to show you what is true, what is the correct and better way to think and to be. I know the truth about mental health, and I am here to pass this truth along to you. I know the way for you to think and to be. Furthermore, I am here to judge you, to evaluate you. If you think and act the way I want you to think and act, that is good. If, however, you resist, if you do not think and act the way I want you to think and act, then you can be in big trouble.'

If some supervisors find good reasons to object to their role as including that of the purveyor and the enforcer of truth, these supervisors can find even better reasons for objecting to their role of psychotherapist as including that of the purveyor and enforcer of truth. I tend to consider these two parts as defining parts of the role of most supervisors. I also tend to consider the presence of these two parts of the role of many psychotherapists as curiously interesting paradoxes.

In rather sharp contrast, the discovery-oriented teacher firmly, and with all due disrespect, declines the role of supervisor, with its dual defining parts of the supervisor as the purveyor and enforcer of the right way to think about and do psychotherapy. The discovery-oriented teacher declines this role not because of some lofty value system or because the teacher prefers being some sort of nice person. Instead, the teacher declines this role because it is not useful, an abysmal failure, at helping to achieve the intended goals of the discovery-oriented approach. Neither a mind-set of the single eternal truth nor the role of supervisor as purveyor–enforcer of a single-truth way of thinking and doing psychotherapy is useful in enabling the teacher to work with the trainee in discovering and developing his or her own deeper framework for psychotherapy. This is the practical reason for the teacher declining the traditional role of supervisor.

The teacher believes in the idea of deeper frameworks, and the value of discovering and developing each trainee's deeper framework

The teacher believes in the idea that each trainee may be described as having a deeper pool of notions about psychotherapy, a pool of notions that may be nebulous, hazy, partly formed, poorly organized, generally unclarified. These notions may be essentially unknown to the trainee, and might even be surprising if the trainee were to find out what they are.

The teacher does not picture the deeper framework as a chest that needs only to be unlocked, and there are well-formed jewels, carefully written basic principles, organized sets of propositions, well-thought-out foundational beliefs. Instead, the teacher's picture is that the deeper framework is made up of ill-formed and partly formed notions and ideas that call for some careful drawing out, evolution, organization, given some form and shape.

The teacher knows the value of discovering and developing the trainee's deeper framework. If the trainee has similar values, the teacher can work together with the trainee in discovering and developing the trainee's deeper framework.

The teacher also knows that the work is piecemeal, slow, gradual. Discovering and developing one part can help other parts to come forward, to be ready for study, to be examined and evolved. Yet the whole enterprise is important and valued by the teacher.

The teacher appreciates that the trainee's deeper framework is likely to differ from his or her own framework

Most supervisors are keenly alert to the trainee's wrong way of thinking and doing psychotherapy. Most supervisors know that the trainee needs education and proper guidance in learning what the supervisor has to offer as the right way to think about and do psychotherapy. Most supervisors are either minimally tolerant or acutely intolerant of the trainee's different way of thinking about and doing psychotherapy. Most trainees know that getting along with this supervisor, progressing through the training program, and learning what this supervisor has to offer mean adopting the role of learning whatever this supervisor has to offer.

In contrast, the good discovery-oriented teacher has a mind-set in which the trainee's deeper framework is likely to be quite different from the teacher's own adopted framework. The trainee will probably have a different way of thinking about and doing psychotherapy, different positions on foundational issues, and different answers to foundational questions.

The good teacher values the discovery and development of the trainee's own framework. The good teacher can know and expect that the trainee will probably be surprised, perhaps even somewhat distrusting, that the former can welcome and appreciate genuine differences between the latter's own deeper framework and the framework that the teacher actually holds. The good teacher can genuinely value and appreciate discovering the trainee's deeper framework even though the emerging framework is not at all the teacher's framework.

The test of this quality does not particularly come on lighter, more superficial, principles and issues such as the components of a good therapist–client relationship. The trainee may well come to value therapist openness and self-disclosure much more than the teacher. Rather, the test usually comes on much deeper and fundamental principles and issues, e.g. a trainee's deeper framework may differ from the teacher on the matter of what is required for profound and in-depth personal change. The teacher holds to a cognitive perspective on that matter, whereas the trainee's deeper framework includes a certain death of one's self by plunging into a state of complete madness and utter chaos, or a full dedication to follow the teachings of God. On the deeper issue of the actual origins of personality, the teacher holds to a cognitive position, whereas the trainee's deeper framework is much closer to a social learning position, or one that rests on ideas about the gradual evolution of a collective unconscious. Although the teacher and the trainee may have somewhat different views on the more superficial matters, the differences can be serious, striking, and therefore challenging, with regard to the deeper and more fundamental matters.

The teacher is able to appreciate, accept, and welcome that there may well be significant differences between the trainee's emerging deeper framework and his or her own framework, and that these differences can and do occur with regard to genuinely basic issues such as the structure of personality, and what the higher and more ennobling goals of psychotherapy can be. The teacher is able to pass the test of appreciating the trainee's deeper framework when his or her deeper framework (1) differs from that of the teacher, (2) openly opposes that of the teacher, and especially (3) may well be more creative, powerful, profound, and sophisticated than that of the teacher.

It can be easy for some teachers to say: 'You have mastered virtually everything I have to teach. You are now ready for teachers who have more to teach you.' This can be pictured with many teachers of rare and special and gifted trainees in ballet, music, mathematics, physics, chess, and boxing. This kind of acknowledgment can be rare, in the teaching and training of psychotherapists. However, what can be even more rare is when the teacher's work with psychotherapy trainees brings them to deeper frameworks that ask for appreciation and welcoming, rather than rejection and replacement with his or her own framework.

The teacher reserves the right to be disappointed in what may emerge as the trainee's deeper framework

Almost always, the teacher is proud and pleased with helping the trainee to discover the deeper framework. On the other hand, there are at least two conditions in which the teacher is entitled to reserve the right to be disappointed in discovering what emerges.

One condition is when the trainee's deeper framework includes pieces and parts that the teacher is simply unable to accept. Now that the pieces and parts are dusted off, refined, clarified, and brought to the surface, the teacher sees them as far beyond merely different from what the teacher believes. Instead, the teacher sees them as dangerous, utterly wrong, far too threatening to him or her, e.g. 'I am not able to welcome and accept a deeper framework that holds itself as the single truth, the ultimate truth, the only way of making sense of things. Such a position is simply much too threatening to me. I am unable to do my job as a discovery-oriented teacher. I am far beyond disappointment. I am disappointedly unable to work with such a deeper framework.'

A second condition is when the emerged deeper framework proves, once again, that the trainee's deeper framework is not at all the framework that the teacher holds: 'In a quiet way, I am disappointed when neither the trainee's surface framework nor his or her deeper framework has much in common with my own experiential way of thinking and doing psychotherapy. But the feelings are usually much stronger when he or she likes my approach on the surface, is here to learn my approach, and espouses my approach, and yet the emerged deeper framework is not at all that of my framework.'

These two conditions are worthy tests of the teacher's good quality of truly believing in the idea of a deeper framework, and in the value of discovering and developing that of the trainee.

The teacher has a fair knowledge of the foundational issues and questions

The discovery-oriented teacher knows that there are foundational issues and questions, and has a fair knowledge of what they are. Most other teachers do not. Most other teachers have a position on foundational issues and an answer to foundational questions, but have little or no knowledge of the underlying issues or questions (Mahrer, 2003, 2004a).

Some of the foundational issues and questions seem to have little or no relevance for the trainee as practitioner. These foundational questions include, for example, those dealing more directly with research. Here are a few: (1) How and why are some research methods better than others? (2) Do research questions lead to and determine research methods, or do standard and established research methods lead to, limit, and restrict the research questions?

On the other hand, some foundational questions seem to have rather direct relevance for the working practitioner. Here are a few examples:

- What stamps a goal or direction of change as a good one, as better than some other goal or direction of change for this particular person at this particular time?
- What accounts for a person seeking out a meeting with a psychotherapist?
- How can a therapist know what the other person is thinking, feeling, experiencing?
- How does a therapist arrive at the meaning of what the client is saying?
- How and why does a person have bad feelings, do things that are accompanied with or provide bad feelings?
- How can a person be free of painful bad feelings, problems, situations, conditions, states?

Some foundational questions seem to have more indirect relevance for the working practitioner. Here are a few examples:

- What are the purposes, aims, goals of psychotherapy?
- How can one branch, approach, school of psychotherapy be distinguished from others?

- Are the methods and techniques of psychotherapy owned by given psychotherapies, or are they parts of a 'public marketplace' of methods and techniques?

- What accounts for personality change?

- What is regarded as optimal, fully developed, fully functioning, ideal, what a person can become?

- What are the pieces and bits, the components and parts, of what is referred to as 'personality'?

The good teacher has a fair knowledge of most of the foundational issues and questions, and can study the audiotape with the trainee, listen to what the trainee's deeper notions are, and say: 'I think I can begin to see that you are coming face to face with a foundational issue or question, and maybe that you seem to have your own position or answer.'

The teacher has a fair knowledge of the different positions and answers to foundational issues and questions

The teacher may be a logotherapist or a behavioral therapist, but she is also a little bit of a scholar who knows some of the different positions on foundational issues, and some of the different answers to foundational questions. When the trainee is face to face with a foundational question of what accounts for bad and painful feelings, or what role dreams can play in psychotherapy, the teacher knows a bit about some of the different answers to these questions. She may not be a dedicated scholar, but she can do a fair job of speaking on behalf of some of the different answers to these foundational questions.

The teacher's knowledge is probably thin, perhaps rather narrow. She probably has little experience and much less proficiency in carrying out the different answers to the questions. However, she usually appreciates that proponents of each position or answer can make strong cases on behalf of their respective positions and answers.

Perhaps what might be most important is that she knows enough to be able to steer the trainee toward helpful resources. She can suggest that the trainee see Dr Rodriguez to get more about that particular position or answer. She can suggest that the trainee look through this book because it provides a fine review of many of the various ways of accounting for bad and painful feelings, or for how to use dreams in psychotherapy. Even further, the teacher can suggest that the trainee look up some of the writings of these particular people to learn more about the particular position or answer that seems to be emerging from exploration of the trainee's own deeper framework.

The teacher can draw from a fair knowledge of therapies and methods

Most supervisors know their own approach rather well. So do most teachers. But, in addition, teachers also have appreciation and knowledge of other therapies and of a relatively broad range of therapeutic methods. Their knowledge goes beyond their own approach.

The good teacher would probably not be a competent practitioner of these other therapies, and would probably be an embarrassed failure at carrying out other therapies and other methods, but at least he or she knows that they exist. The good teacher may not be able to give courses on these other therapies and other methods, but he or she would at least know that there are such courses, and might even have a passing familiarity with a bit of the actual content.

The teacher is rarely a scholar in these other therapies and methods, but can draw from a fair enough knowledge to help in lifting out and developing the trainee's own deeper framework. The teacher can recognize and steer the trainee toward learning more about logotherapy or Jungian analysis or Adlerian analysis or solution-focused therapy. The teacher can help the trainee become more familiar with the role of expectancy, attachment theory, social role-playing, and methods such as the two-chair method, hypnosis, or homework assignments. And if the teacher does not know enough, he or she can suggest the right other person with whom the trainee can talk.

The teacher knows how to discover the trainee's deeper framework

The good teacher has some special qualities and characteristics. But there is more. The good teacher has also learned a number of relatively explicit skills, developed some specific competencies designed to help in discovering the trainee's own deeper framework.

One set of skills helps the teacher to work with the trainee to discover his or her position on foundational issues and his or her answers to foundational questions. The teacher knows how to do this, and has the requisite skills and competencies.

The second set of skills is what this book is mainly about. These are the explicit skills that start with the taped sessions, and enable the teacher and the trainee to uncover, discover, and then carry forward and develop, the trainee's own deeper framework.

These are learnable skills. The good teacher has acquired these skills and is reasonably competent in using them.

The teacher is able to appreciate, adopt, and work within the trainee's own deeper framework

Of course the teacher has his own approach, his own way of thinking about and doing psychotherapy. But in addition, the teacher has that special quality of being able to appreciate the trainee's own framework, and to take the giant next step of being able to let go of his own framework, and to adopt, get inside of, work within, the trainee's own way of seeing things, the trainee's own deeper framework.

Indeed, the teacher is able to do this at least as well as the trainee, and usually better than her. One of the main reasons for this is that the trainee is typically fuzzy about the deeper framework, is separated and distanced from the deeper framework, and has a lot of interfering clutter blocking the deeper framework, whereas the teacher is generally free of these encumbrances.

It is refreshing when the teacher and the trainee both give voice to the emerging and developing deeper framework. They can be a real team, with each pushing the other forward.

The teacher can play the role of the inquisitive apprentice who seeks to understand the trainee's framework

In the ordinary role, the supervisor is the one with the knowledge, and the trainee is there to learn. In the discovery-oriented approach, the teacher has the ability to reverse the roles, i.e. the teacher can play the role of the trainee's student, his apprentice who wants to learn his way of thinking about and doing psychotherapy. The trainee is in the role of the teacher, the one who explains, the one who shows the student or apprentice how to think about and do his approach to psychotherapy.

The teacher may even define the role explicitly: 'Suppose that I am your student, your trainee, your apprentice, and I am here to learn your way of thinking about and doing psychotherapy. Is this all right? Can we do this?' In this role, the teacher is the one who asks questions, who keeps inquiring and clarifying so that the teacher can become increasingly clear about how to think about and do psychotherapy the trainee's way.

The teacher declines the role of the one with power over the trainee and the trainee's 'personality'

Most supervisors carry out a role in which they have personal, administrative, and professional power over the supervisee. This role is easy to justify, collectively accepted as part of the job of supervisor, and typically dignified as the supervisor's professional responsibility. Sometimes the power is explicit, sometimes implicit, but almost always there. Sometimes the power is benign, sometimes it can have a tough edge.

The supervisor is the one to write a formal report on the supervisee, to judge and evaluate him, to help continue or retard his progress through the program. The supervisor can have a hand in passing or failing the supervisee, in assigning the grade.

As a result, supervisors and trainees can play out various roles with each other, for better or worse. The supervisor can be the one who does things on behalf of the trainee, defends him, and the trainee can fulfill the role of the one who needs and appreciates the favor. The supervisor can fulfill the role of the one who nurtures and cares for the trainee, and the trainee is in the role of the one who seeks and develops through the good nurturing. The supervisor is in the role of the one who punishes and rewards the trainee, and the trainee is in the role of the person whose way of being and behaving is guided by the punishments and rewards. The supervisor can be in the role of the one who selects out the trainee as special, as the favored one, and the trainee is the one who is chosen and selected above others. The supervisor can fulfill the role of the one who is pleased or displeased, and the trainee can carry out the role of one who pleases or displeases.

Many supervisors accept or give themselves the right and the responsibility to judge, evaluate, deal with, do things to, and treat the supervisee's 'personality'. It is common and easy to justify this as a part of the supervisor's responsibility (Mahrer and Boulet, 1997).

Supervisors can point out the supervisee's personal problems, difficulties, unresolved issues, interfering conflicts, underlying psychopathologies, unrealized virtues and talents, personal qualities and characteristics. Supervisors can be concerned with light and superficial things about the trainee, or with inner, deeper issues and problems of the very person whom the trainee is.

The supervisor can fulfill the role of the one who makes judgments about the trainee's personality, either the friendly and interested judge who can be pleased with the right kinds of changes in him or her, or the critical judge who labels him or her as having serious personality problems and flaws. The supervisor can fulfill the role of the one who helps the trainee with personality problems by using the special relationship that the supervisor develops and plays out with him or her. The supervisor can fulfill the role of the one who actually does things to treat the trainee's personality problems as his or her unofficial, informal, personal psychotherapist.

When most supervisors work on the personal issues and problems of the supervisee, their being with one another may be for better or worse, may give pleasure or be painful for either or both. The highlight of their being with one another may well be the treasured gift that the trainee receives from the supervision. Or it may be that the supervisor's messing with the trainee's personality is a kind of personal abuse that the trainee carries away from the course of the supervision.

In any case, it is exceedingly common that most supervisors place themselves in a role of having the power to deal with and do something about the 'personality' of their supervisees. This power may be for better or worse.

The discovery-oriented teacher respectfully declines this role (Mahrer and Boulet, 1997). The teacher respectfully declines assuming this role for himself, and respectfully declines the trainee's offer for him to accept the role of having power over the trainee and the trainee's 'personality'. The teacher respectfully declines this role mainly because playing this common role interferes with the role of teacher, and interferes with achieving what he is here to help the trainee achieve.

In effect, the teacher says to the trainee: 'I value and respect that you may have your own deeper notions and ideas about psychotherapy, some of which you may be aware of, most of which are probably deeper, loosely formed pools of notions and ideas. I am here to offer you, if you are truly interested, an opportunity to dig down into your own deeper framework, to explore and discover what these inner deeper notions and ideas are, to help you develop them into whatever they may become, into your own framework for psychotherapy. I am here to work with you in gaining the advantages of discovering and developing your own framework for psychotherapy.'

This is the role the teacher accepts for himself, rather than the role of supervisor with personal, administrative, and professional power over the supervisee and the supervisee's 'personality'.

The teacher invites, elicits, honors, and relies on the trainee's own personal honesty

Almost every time that the teacher says something, the teacher is virtually asking: 'What do you really think? What is your honest reaction? What is your honest belief? What notion or idea do you honestly have here? Of these possibilities, which honestly appeals to you more? What are your honest feelings about this notion, this idea, this possibility?'

From the very beginning, it is crucial that the trainee is passionately enthusiastic about discovering and developing his or her own deeper framework. The teacher can do the work only when there is a passionate commitment on the part of the trainee. Whether or not the trainee has this passion is up to the trainee, not the teacher. Knowing if the passion is there depends almost exclusively on the trainee's personal honesty, and on the teacher's ability to invite, elicit, honor, and rely on this personal honesty.

Throughout each training session, in each tiny step, the trainee's personal honesty is an essential ingredient. When it is turned on, when it is present, teaching and training can move along. When it is low or missing, teaching and training stop. It is that important. It is that crucial.

The teacher's job is to foster and treasure the trainee's solid and strong honesty. If it is not there immediately, the teacher can enable it. If it is there, the teacher blesses and uses it. The teacher must be able to continuously invite, elicit, honor, and rely on the trainee's own personal honesty.

The teacher is good at creating a discovery-oriented atmosphere

If you sit in with a number of discovery-oriented teachers and trainees, you will probably notice some common characteristics in the general atmosphere. This atmosphere helps foster discovery-oriented work. The following are some of the things you might notice.

The teacher fosters and celebrates differences with the firm certainty that each approach is clearly superior to all others

There is a clear distinction between the people listening to the tape and the therapist on the tape. This distinction holds whether the therapist on the tape is the teacher, some noted exemplar, or, as is most common, one of the trainees. The teacher can say how wonderful or how awful the therapist on the tape is, even if the teacher is the therapist on the tape. The trainee can applaud or criticize the therapist on the tape, even if that therapist is the trainee.

The teacher's way of thinking, approach, perspective is clearly superior, and the teacher says so: 'Obviously, my approach is superior. My approach is the right one. No other approach comes close . . . If you accept that, you are a good trainee. If not, you are in big trouble . . . Of course, everyone thinks the same way. And of course, everyone is wrong, except me!'

The teacher creates an atmosphere in which each trainee is entitled to have a persistent inner voice proclaiming: 'Obviously, my way of making sense of things, my theory, my approach, is the clearly superior one. That is taken for granted.' There is a kind of refreshing whimsicalness in the atmosphere when each trainee is entitled to think this way even though each trainee may have a different way of seeing things, a different outlook or perspective. 'We all know that our approach is superior, and we all have different approaches! And somehow that makes sense!'

When one trainee questions the presenting trainee, the questioner asks: 'Have you thought about the impact of an emotionally abusive childhood environment? . . . What are the neurophysiological symptoms she showed during the bouts with the internal voices? . . . Are there fluctuations in her degree of contact with reality?' Underneath such questions is often a little voice saying: 'You should have thought of this. My approach is superior to yours.' The good teacher creates the kind of atmosphere where either the questioner or the presenting trainee, some other trainee, or the teacher can say out loud: 'That's right! Her approach is better than your approach!! So give up your inferior approach and adopt her superior approach!'

The atmosphere celebrates each trainee's inner certainty that that trainee's approach is the superior one, and that each trainee firmly believes this, regardless of differences between approaches. The atmosphere also celebrates the trainee coming up with a popcorn popper of possible ideas. Think of all sorts of answers to questions. What is valued is coming up not only with bunches of answers, but also with answers that can be silly, outrageous, dumb, ungrounded, ridiculous, altogether outside what the trainee usually believes.

Instead of an atmosphere in which there is to be one right answer, the atmosphere invites loads of answers. Instead of an atmosphere in which answers are to be smart ones, justified ones, the atmosphere prizes answers that are creatively wild, that come from what is merely possible.

The teacher fosters an atmosphere that welcomes all sorts of differences, differences in ways of looking at things, differences from the more or less accepted, conservative answers. The teacher fosters an atmosphere that openly acknowledges that each trainee's way of thinking is superior to all others, especially when each trainee has a different way of thinking. All of this contributes to a discovery-oriented atmosphere.

Putting the teacher's own magnificent approach on the table is good when done in the spirit of discovering and developing the trainee's own personal framework

There are times when the teacher can and does put her own approach on the table. However, it is important that the spirit can come out like this:

> 'Now I am going to put my own approach on the table. Of course mine is the best possible approach. Of course I am the teacher and you are the student. Of course I am older, wiser, and a far better therapist than you. Of course you should adopt my approach if you come to your senses.'

'Here is my answer to that basic question. Can you get closer to your own framework by trying to find your own answer? Here is my position on that basic issue. Can you get closer to your own framework by trying to find your own position? Here is what I would do right here. Can you get closer to your own framework by discovering what you are inclined to do?'

The teacher may say out loud what the aim is: 'If I am good, then my own view will get you to get closer to your own personal framework. I will tell you what I believe. I hope my telling you can get you to explore further, to dig into your own notions and ideas, to find what your own deeper framework believes. Now do you believe all this? Do you believe I am really that interested in discovering and developing your own framework? Or do you know that I am just being slippery and clever in getting you to adopt my wonderful approach?'

The trainee, on the surface, takes it for granted that the initial sessions are to be used to obtain a psychodiagnostic assessment and evaluation, some idea of the 'presenting problem' and the client's case history. This may be one position or answer to the basic issue or question of what the purposes and aims of the initial sessions are. However, the teacher puts on the table a position that the initial sessions may be used to accomplish the same working goals as each other session, namely to enable the person to undergo radical qualitative change toward becoming the person that he or she can become, and to free him or her of the painful situation and painful feelings in the situation that was front and center for the person in this session. Here are two different positions or answers to the basic issue or question. What might be a third position or answer, one that might come from the trainee's own deeper framework?

Right here, in the session, it as if the trainee takes it for granted that there are inner deeper forces inside the person, and these forces are bad, dangerous, to be closely monitored, defended against. The teacher is able to put her own position on the table. She views what is deeper inside as mere potentialities for experiencing, the nature and content of which can be grotesque and monstrous or deliciously wonderful seeds of the whole new person that the person can become, depending on his or her own disintegrative or integrative relationship with the deeper potentialities for experiencing. Here is where the trainee has a chance to explore inside his own framework. Perhaps the trainee truly believes that what lies deep inside most people is bad, awful, or mere possibilities for experiencing, or perhaps something different, something that gets closer to the trainee's own deeper framework.

The teacher can also call upon her own approach to offer possibilities for what the trainee seems to be seeking to accomplish right here, and also for the ways and means that the trainee is calling on to achieve what he is trying to achieve. The teacher says: 'Right here, you seem to be using this method to try to accomplish this in-session aim, goal, change. In my approach, I find it useful to rely on this other method to help achieve that same kind of in-session aim, goal, change. Take your time and dig down inside. Can you come up with some other way that you might be better able to accomplish that aim, goal, change, some way that is maybe more exciting and better than the way you use and the way I might use?' Or the teacher says: 'Right here, you seem to be trying to accomplish this in-session aim, goal, change. In my approach, I would probably be trying to accomplish this other aim, goal, change. So here is a chance for you to think. If you can let your own deeper inclinations talk, what might be some third in-session aim, goal, change, one that seems even more appealing than the one you had and the one I might have?'

The trainee seems to be using a common traditional way of listening to clients and making sense of what the client seems to be saying and doing. To enable the trainee to explore other ways of listening, perhaps even to discover his own deeper framework for listening to clients, the teacher may well demonstrate her own experiential way of listening by showing how to listen right here, and what the experiential way of listening can offer. The important spirit is given in words like these: 'You used one way of listening. I gave you an example of another way of listening. Are you interested in exploring your own inner deeper framework to find what might be your own, personal framework for how to listen and what you can get in listening in this other way? Maybe there is a third way of listening that fits your own deeper framework. What do you think?'

The teacher can put her own therapeutic approach on the table in such a way, in the proper spirit, so that the trainee can use that to help in discovering and developing his own inner deeper framework.

The passionate fun is discovering and developing the trainee's own deeper framework

Of course it is important that the trainee does a fine job with the client. Of course it is important that the trainee keeps getting better and better as a psychotherapist who will join the ranks of professional psychotherapists. Of course these things are important to the teacher.

However, in building the right atmosphere, what is truly important is that the teacher has passionate fun in working with the trainee to help discover and develop his or her own deeper framework. This is what is so enjoyable, so exciting, so much fun. The teacher's passionate fun creates the right atmosphere. It is contagious, infectious.

The good teacher has a beloved sense of genuine enjoyment when the trainee searches for the deeper framework, when he keeps finding bits and pieces of the deeper framework, when he continuously develops the deeper framework, and when he uses it well in actual in-session work. This is the good teacher's passion. This is what is sheer fun.

The value lies in the trainee discovering and developing the deeper framework, rather than voicing the 'professionally correct' response

In what is ordinarily known as supervision, most trainees know that there are right answers, professionally correct answers. There are right ways to think and do psychotherapy, and there are wrong ways to think and do psychotherapy. If the supervisor is psychoanalytic or cognitive–behavioral or Jungian, there are answers that are the right ones, the ones that show that the trainee is thinking and doing psychotherapy in the right way. Before entering the supervisor's office, the trainee does well to keep in mind that this supervisor is a cognitive–behavioral therapist or a psychodynamic therapist.

However, things are quite different when it comes to the creation of the discovery-oriented atmosphere. What is valued is that the trainee is searching, exploring, discovering his or her own deeper framework. What is valued is that the trainee is developing the deeper framework. When the trainee talks, answers questions, thinks out loud, makes sensible guesses, the value lies in a felt sense that what he or she is saying gets us further into the deeper framework, contributes to the further carrying forward, the development, of the deeper framework. The value lies in capturing the idea, in clarifying what seems there, rather than the trainee searching for and voicing what is the 'professionally correct' answer, the right response, especially as the supervisor nods in confirmation or grades the answer as wrong.

Picture that the trainee is talking about or playing a tape of the sixth session, and the focus is on how the session begins. Suppose that both the supervisor and the teacher ask: 'Do you think there is a better way to start the session?' The supervisor may ask the question in a friendly way, but it is as if the supervisor is also saying: 'Be careful. There are some right ways to open sessions, so you'd better answer the question with a right answer.'

The discovery-oriented teacher may very well ask the same question, but it is as if the teacher is saying: 'This is one of those basic questions that most approaches provide answers to, and there are different answers. But you seem to be face to face with this question right here, so what kinds of answers seem to be coming to you? Think of answers that may or may not make sense, that may be common or uncommon, but one or more might come from ideas deep inside you. Are you able to come up with appealing answers, or not much at all?' The teacher may attach all this extra baggage to the relatively simple question.

These are presented as some of the qualities of a good discovery-oriented teacher. If a teacher has most of these qualities, the chances are that the trainee can discover and develop his or her own deeper framework. If the teacher lacks most of these qualities, it is unlikely that the trainee will be able to discover and develop the deeper framework.

However, discovering and developing one's own deeper framework also depend on the trainee. There are some special qualities of the trainee who can benefit from what a good discovery-oriented teacher has to offer. This is what the next chapter discusses.

Chapter 5

Some qualities of a good discovery-oriented trainee

It seems to me that almost every trainee has an inner deeper framework that can be discovered. It also seems, however, that there are some qualities that go with a good discovery-oriented trainee. If the trainee has these qualities, the chances are relatively good that the trainee's deeper framework can be discovered and developed. If these qualities are not there, the trainee and the teacher may as well find something else to do.

In most psychotherapy training programs, what proportion of trainees seem to have these qualities to a reasonable degree? I believe that about 10–20 percent of trainees have at least a tiny glow of these qualities. What proportion of these 10–20 percent of trainees are ready to act upon these qualities and engage in the discovery and development of their own deeper frameworks? My impression is that less than half are likely to do so. I believe this to be sad, and I hope that both proportions can increase as the discovery-oriented approach becomes better and more at home in psychotherapy training programs.

If these estimates come reasonably close to reality, then perhaps 5–10 percent of trainees are inclined toward delving into their own inner deeper frameworks. In a training program of, for example, 25 students, we may be talking about one to three students who have the necessary qualities just to qualify.

The trainee with the right qualities

A passion to discover the secrets of psychotherapy

Most trainees share a generally common mind-set of attaining the level and meeting the standards of what the field stamps as competent and proficient professional practitioners. Most trainees are there to learn what is to be learned, to get the credentials and become accredited, find a fitting niche or specialty, and join the ranks of their chosen profession in pursuing their careers.

Most discovery-oriented trainees share these qualities, although they also have a genuine passion to discover the secrets of psychotherapy. This passion is of course not limited to discovery-oriented trainees, but it does seem to be a characteristic quality.

These trainees seem to share a reverence for the mysteries of psychotherapy, for what the field is and can become. They share a wonder and a pride in the field. These trainees seem to have high respect for the gifted masters of psychotherapy, and to have their own inner glow of becoming the finest practitioners, of reaching the highest levels of craftsmanship. These trainees seem to share the almost child-like naïveté of exploring the further reaches of psychotherapy, of being able to be surprised and fascinated with what remains to be discovered, with what can be achieved.

Discovery-oriented trainees do not hold exclusive rights over this passion to discover the secrets of psychotherapy, but they do seem to share this quality in common.

A passion to discover his or her own inner deeper framework for psychotherapy

This passion is much more than a nice helpful characteristic. It is an essential requirement. It must be there in some force, and it must remain glowing over most of the training sessions. There must be an inner hunger, a burning passion to discover one's own inner deeper framework for psychotherapy.

When the passion is there in the trainee, the teacher can do her or his work, can assist, guide, and help the trainee discover the deeper framework. The trainee may take the lead, or the teacher may take the lead, but the continuous effort is fueled by the passion of the trainee. If there is little or no passion, the effort cannot even get started. The effort comes to a halt, shuts down, fails, either for now or perhaps forever.

The passion includes an eagerness to enter uncharted territory, murky waters, the unknown, the uncertain, the unorganized, the unfamiliar. It includes the eagerness to tolerate the ambiguous in the enthusiastic search for the deeper framework.

The passion includes a powerful readiness and willingness to depart from what is known, the security of one's chosen approach, and to love the hungry risk of seeing what the inner exploration offers, whatever it may be. The trainee may have a tentative or firm commitment to brief psychodynamic therapy, or solution-focused therapy, or eye movement desensitization and reprocessing therapy, or cognitive–behavioral therapy, or feminist therapy. Yet the passion includes a glowing readiness to embrace whatever the deeper exploration uncovers, even if that means letting go of the chosen approach, whatever it is. The risk is delicious.

Addition of his or her own ideas to the established approach

The idea is that the trainee has a readiness or willingness to add his or her own ideas to some established approach, to whatever approach the trainee has or the supervisor is providing. The idea can come from an invitation from the supervisor: 'Go ahead, feel free to add your own ideas to cognitive therapy.' Or the readiness can come from the trainee him- or herself: 'I am ready to add my own ideas to cognitive therapy.'

It can be important for the trainee to have a readiness to add his or her own ideas to Jung's analytic psychology or to behavior therapy. This readiness can show itself as a jaw-thrust-forward cockiness and arrogance: 'There are some problems in cognitive therapy, and I would like to explain my solutions.' Or the readiness can manifest itself with a pinch of humility: 'I think this tape illustrates some things I was curious about in cognitive therapy, and I would like to get your ideas about something I did that seemed to work. But I would like your help here, your idea of what happened here.'

What the trainee adds may be a slight twist here or there, a stylistic extension that is mild, or perhaps a moderate or even major modification in something taken for granted in the particular therapy. In any case, the trainee has that quality of a readiness to add his or her own ideas to the established approach.

The passion is rare; most trainees are unwilling or unable to discover their own deeper frameworks

Many trainees can accept that there may be therapeutic approaches with which they are not especially familiar, or conceptual ideas they do not know much about, or that research might be able to tell them more than they now know, or that the next 20–40 years might offer some ideas beyond what we now are familiar with. But this is about territory that is outside, not deeper inside.

For most trainees, there is almost no conception of a deeper pool of notions, ideas. There is no deeper framework of notions and ideas that are outside their easy awareness, their easy access. There is no deeper framework that begs discovery, exploration, sorting out, organization, development. The very notion or idea of a deeper framework can be so alien that it can seem quaint, extraordinary, out of place.

For most trainees, there can be room for improving their conceptual systems, their theories, their cognitive systems. They can add to or modify their way of thinking, their conceptual frameworks. But 'deeper frameworks'? What are you talking about? The idea of a 'deeper framework' makes little or no sense.

For most trainees, there is little or no passion to explore 'deeper frameworks' that make no sense, no matter what you call them. When there can be nothing referred to as a 'deeper framework', it can be hard to have a passion to discover one's 'deeper framework'.

This approach is certainly not for trainees who are opposed to discovering their deeper frameworks

This approach searches for trainees with the glow of passion to discover their own deeper framework. Whether the search is loud and brassy or quiet and gentle, it is simply looking for the trainee with a glow of passion, even a token tiny glow. The search is friendly and respectful to trainees without the valued glow. A mild or even moderate interest is not enough, but that is all right. A mild or moderate disinterest is clearly not what we are looking for, but that too is all right.

The discovery-oriented approach is certainly not for trainees who are mildly or actively opposed to the discovery-oriented approach. It is certainly not for trainees for whom it can be important to dislike this approach, to rebel against it, to fight the approach, to attack it, and to do so politely or impolitely, indirectly or directly, professionally or in-your-face unprofessionally.

Some trainees have a glow of passion for discovering their own deeper frameworks. Most do not. Here are some ways that some trainees can show that they are not especially eager to explore down into their own deeper frameworks:

1. Instead of a passion for discovering their deeper framework, the trainee opposes the teacher. The trainee criticizes and attacks the teacher as being dismissive of most trainees and supervisors, as being supercilious to what trainees and supervisors are trying to achieve, as looking down on the enterprise of supervision and being supervised. 'You are being

offensive and insulting and arrogant . . . You have no respect for trainees and supervisors . . . You are critical of the training of psychotherapists . . . I like your enthusiasm, but I don't like your way of selling your ideas about supervision . . . So trainees who go through regular supervision are inferior?'

2. Instead of a passion for discovering the deeper framework, the trainee looks for problems. The trainee is drawn toward finding all sorts of problems, and can be inventive and creative in finding them: 'What if I dump the approach I have, and my other supervisors object? . . . Suppose I find a deeper approach that I don't like. Then what? . . . What if I find a deeper approach that is no good, that is not as good as the approach you have? What do I do? . . . If you say that is my framework, how can I trust you? How do I know you are right? . . . But what if I find just a little bit? How can I do therapy with just a corner of an approach? Suppose I like the approach I have? Why should I switch? Can I integrate the deeper thing into my approach?'

3. Instead of a passion for discovering their deeper framework, the trainee is drawn toward other matters. Engaging with the discovery-oriented approach, the discovery-oriented trainee has that glow of excitement in her or his face and voice. At the same time, another trainee goes for other matters, some relevant, some not so, some practical, some not so, but all without any passion for discovering the deeper framework, The trainee says, 'What about evaluation? Do I still evaluate you? . . . Can I just attend whenever I want to? . . . Do these qualify as supervision hours? . . . How do I identify this in my résumé? . . . What is the normal number of training sessions in this way of doing supervision?' These kinds of matters can be quite relevant and practical, or not especially so, but they can be an unfortunate alternative to having a passion for discovering one's deeper framework.

4. Instead of a passion for discovering their own approach, the trainee is ruggedly persistent in getting and having a wrong idea of what the discovery-oriented approach is. Almost from the very beginning, and after a fair number of training sessions, it is as if the trainee arrived with a wrong picture of the discovery-oriented approach, and doggedly clung to this wrong picture as if he or she had not been present in the training sessions. This is the trainee who, after a number of training sessions, can nevertheless proclaim: 'So this supervision is to help me do integrative psychotherapy . . . Do I have to do the approach you say I have? . . . So you do therapy on me to help me resolve my issues with doing therapy . . . What you do is to replace supervision with your "discovery-oriented supervision" . . . In your supervision, I can do anything I want to do with clients . . .' Such trainees are not especially blessed with a glow of passion for discovering their own deeper framework for psychotherapy.

5. Instead of a passion for discovering his or her own framework, the trainee prefers direct confrontational attacks, for better or worse. The spirit of the discovery-oriented training session is inclined to foster openness, honesty, discussion of issues that may not be especially common in many kinds of supervision. This spirit can sometimes welcome direct confrontational attacks on the discovery-oriented teacher and the approach. Sometimes these direct confrontations can come from and foster an inner passion for discovering one's own deeper framework. Sometimes these direct confrontations are fueled by something other than the glow of such an inner passion. These direct confrontations can be friendly or unfriendly, in keeping with or effectively defeating a spirit of open honest discussion, depending on the feelings of trainee and teacher. Comments such as the following can emerge out of and convey either spirit: 'What research supports this kind of supervision? . . . Do other supervisors let you do this kind of supervision? . . . If other supervisors did supervision this way, I'd never learn how to do psychotherapy! . . . I don't think this kind of supervision is any good! . . . What does the ethical code have to say about this kind of supervision?'

What can the discovery-oriented teacher do with trainees who are honestly opposed to discovering their own deeper frameworks? One answer is that these trainees are simply not geared to discovering their own deeper frameworks, so it can be sensible to part company. It is not their cup of tea. Another answer is for the teacher to learn and to try to do something constructive about the serious problems in this approach or in the teacher's way of carrying out the discovery-oriented approach. In any case, the moral is that a small proportion of most trainees come with a glow of passion to discover their own deeper frameworks. Those who are directly or indirectly opposed to this approach are simply trainees for whom this approach is not especially appropriate, and that is the way things are.

The trainee can select an approach or integrate several approaches without having a passion to discover his or her deeper framework

A fair proportion of trainees can find themselves in a position of selecting from a number of available approaches, or of being inclined to integrate a number of approaches. Doing either of these can be important, call for some careful thought, take some time, benefit from some helpful guidance from someone such as an interested supervisor. However, resolution of both issues can be achieved without the trainee having a passion for discovering his or her own deeper framework.

Most training programs introduce trainees to a variety of theories of personality and psychotherapy, and to a variety of therapeutic approaches. Trainees generally learn something about the variety of theories and therapies, especially in courses designed to acquaint students with the field's theories and therapies. Most training programs feature several theories and therapies.

Trainees typically select from the available menu of various theories and therapeutic approaches. They may make this choice earlier or later in the program, and with varying degrees of confidence. In any case, most trainees do select a theory and its therapeutic approach. What is noteworthy is that this selection can be made without, and does not require, any passion for inner exploration and discovery of the trainee's own deeper framework.

It can be relatively common for trainees to want to combine, to integrate, a number of therapeutic approaches. Sometimes the trainee simply likes two or three different approaches, and is drawn toward pooling a psychodynamic and a cognitive approach, or combining an Adlerian and a solution-focused approach, or a narrative and a humanistic approach. Putting them together is pleasing.

A trainee may be drawn toward several approaches because each is helpful in making sense of something important to the trainee, e.g. one approach makes good sense of the effects of culture, and a different approach offers good explanations of psychosomatic phenomena. One can offer worthwhile explanations of childhood traumas, and another is helpful in making sense of all sorts of addictive behavior, from drug addiction to sexual addiction to an addiction to criminal behavior.

A trainee may be drawn toward expanding her or his repertory of useful skills by combining the interventions of gestalt techniques, behavioral techniques, and techniques of dealing with grief reactions, or by being able to use both hypnotic and psychodynamic methods. Trainees can find it important to integrate methods of treating both this and that kind of mental disorder.

Trainees can integrate approaches that are effective in dealing with different kinds of in-session events. Here is an approach that helps with a patient who has little or no motivation for therapy. Here is an approach that is useful for patients who seem to show a sudden outburst of suicidal ideation or who have unexpected reactions to a change in drugs.

Whether the trainee is selecting one from a number of available approaches, or seeking to combine or integrate some appealing or useful therapeutic approaches, this can usually be accomplished without having a glow of passion for digging down into and discovering the deeper framework. Indeed, selection of an approach or integrating several approaches does not necessarily require exploration into one's own deeper framework. They can be, and usually are, separate enterprises.

Nevertheless, the discovery-oriented trainee has this glow of passionate enthusiasm for discovering his or her inner deeper framework for psychotherapy. It is an essential quality. The teacher can help, but the trainee must have this passion. This passion may well be a rare and special quality. This passion may not be called upon when the trainee is learning an approach, selecting from a number or approaches, or incorporating several appealing approaches, but it is a virtually essential quality in the discovery-oriented trainee.

The trainee is not encased in a rigid, single-truth mind-set

Most trainees appreciate that there are many different theories of personality, theories of psychotherapy, and an almost embarrassingly large number of schools and approaches to psychotherapy.

Nevertheless, most trainees seem to share a rather rigid, single-truth mind-set that includes such truths as the following:

1. There is a cumulative body of psychotherapeutic knowledge.

2. There is a body of foundational truths about psychotherapy.

3. There are generally accepted principles for how to do psychotherapy.

4. There is a research-based groundwork underlying the science of psychotherapy so that psychotherapy is a science-based enterprise with research-based principles and methods, and empirically validated therapies.

5. Accordingly, there is a right way to think about and to do psychotherapy.

Trainees with this rigid, single-truth mind-set are here to learn what is right and proper within this mind-set. The very idea of probing inside, looking inward to discover a supposedly deeper framework for psychotherapy is not right and proper. It smacks of being wrong, dangerous, as even daring to question and to attack what the single-truth mind-set holds dear.

The discovery-oriented trainee is not encased in this rigid, single-truth mind-set. Essentially freedom from this mind-set allows room for some excitement at probing inside to discover one's own deeper framework for psychotherapy (Mahrer, 2004a).

The trainee does not impose his or her rigid, single-truth mind-set on to the discovery-oriented teacher

It would be nice if the trainee were able to set aside the trainee's single-truth, here-is-the-right-way-to-think-about-and-do-psychotherapy way of thinking when he or she is with the discovery-oriented teacher. Perhaps a few trainees, with this mind-set, can do this, but most cannot. It is as if the single-truth mind-set has little or no room for setting itself aside.

The trouble is that this mind-set is very powerful, so powerful that it leaves little or no room for the discovery-oriented teacher to do discovery-oriented teaching. Instead, it locks the trainee into seeking to know how to do proper therapy properly, and it forces the teacher into being a supervisor who is here to show the trainee how to do proper therapy properly.

The trainee who speaks out of this mind-set will typically provide a description of the client, tell what the problem is, set the goal or desirable outcome, have an idea of how proper treatment ought to proceed, and seek an answer for some question for which the trainee seeks supervision.

For example, the trainee will say that the client has a secret that he has never shared with anyone, and the trainee would like the client to share that secret with the trainee. Accordingly, the trainee would like the supervisor to suggest some ways that he or she can use to get the client to share the secret.

Or the trainee says: 'Her problem is her relationship with her boyfriend. That relationship is bad for her, is leaving her confused and depressed, and is going nowhere. The trouble is that she runs from this problem. How can I get her to concentrate on this problem? Nothing seems to work.'

Or the trainee says: 'This fellow needs ways of coping with and reducing stress from a marriage with an alcoholic wife and her child with an attention-deficit disorder. I want to provide ways for him to control his stress, cope with it, and reduce the stress. I have tried some ways, and they seem to work for a while, but the stress is still there.'

Or the trainee says: 'I do cognitive–behavioral therapy, and I want to learn the methods such as self-monitoring, covert desensitization, attacking core cognitions, and other cognitive–behavioral methods.'

The trainee with the single-truth mind-set will typically want supervisory help in doing a proper job of assessment and evaluation, in problem identification, goal-setting, and dealing with therapist–client issues, and in the actual in-session treatment process, all in the context of the trainee's and supervisor's therapeutic approach.

All of this is fine, worthwhile, and eminently sensible within the single-truth mind-set. However, all of this encases the teacher in the trainee's single-truth mind-set and effectively handcuffs the teacher, preventing the former from being the discovery-oriented teacher. The bottom line is that the trainee with a rigid, single-truth mind-set is not especially a suitable trainee for the discovery-oriented teacher.

The trainee can be a discovery-oriented trainee with a discovery-oriented teacher rather than imposing a supervisee-supervisor relationship

When trainees and their supervisors or teachers meet with one another, it is as if each of them says: 'There are certain roles that I like playing, that are important for me to carry out, and this means that you are to play the right kind of complementary role. Let's see how we do with one another.' The roles may be rather general or rather specific, but each party seems to have a few favorite roles for him- or herself and for the other person.

The discovery-oriented trainee is ready and able to fulfill the role offered by the discovery-oriented teacher, or the discovery-oriented trainee comes with a built-in readiness and ability to be in the role of the discovery-oriented trainee. This role says in effect: 'I am here to find my own way, with your help. I want to probe inside, to discover and develop what may be my own deeper framework for psychotherapy. You can be the teacher who knows how to do this and who is here to teach and guide me toward discovering and developing the framework that I believe is deeper inside me.'

This role is appealing and important for the trainee, and the trainee welcomes and accepts the teacher in the role of the discovery-oriented teacher.

If the trainee virtually insists on being in most meanings of the supervisee role, and insists on imposing most meanings of the supervisor role on to the other person, there can be serious problems for the discovery-oriented teacher. Indeed, the discovery-oriented teacher is essentially unable to be one.

Here are just some of the more specific kinds of supervisee roles that trainees can play, and thereby impose some sort of complementary role on the supervisor, for better or for worse:

'There is a right way to do this therapy. Show me that right way.'

'I need to be told that I am an acceptable supervisee. You are here to tell me that I am.'

'I am like a child. You are to be like a parent to me.'

'I know I have personal problems. You are here to help me with my personal problems.'

'I am here to fear and dislike you. You are here to be feared and disliked.'

'I need an authority to be my friend. You are here to be the authority who is my friend.'

'I am here to be judged and evaluated. You are here to judge and evaluate me.'

'I am in trouble in the program. You are to be my defender.'

'I am your disciple and follower. You are my master, my guru.'

'I like sparring and fighting. You are to be the one I spar and fight with.'

'It is important for me to be led. You are to be the one who leads me.'

'I need spanking, punishment. You are here to spank and punish me.'

'I need straightening out. You are here to straighten me out.'

'I need special caring and nurturing. You are here to care for and nurture me.'

'I want to be like you. You are to be my hero, my exemplar.'

'I want to be a true professional. Make me a true professional.'

'I love being the favorite and best trainee. Make me your favorite and best trainee.'

The trainee is a discovery-oriented trainee by accepting a discovery-oriented trainee role, and by allowing the discovery-oriented teacher to be a discovery-oriented teacher. The trainee is not a discovery-oriented trainee when it is important for him or her to be in the traditional role of supervisee, and when it is important for him or her to impose the role of supervisor on the discovery-oriented teacher.

The trainee is refreshingly honest, rather than playing the professionally correct role

Trying to dig into and open up the trainee's own deeper framework counts a great deal on asking questions such as the following: 'When he asked if you were a real doctor or a student, what would you wish you were able to do? What do you think caused him to feel so much better since the last session? How come people change in psychotherapy sessions? So, if she was psychotic in adolescence, does that mean she is still psychotic today?'

Of course the trainee can give voice to the position or answer that is professionally approved, the safe response, the professionally correct response. Playing this role is relatively inviting, easy, and safe. It also defeats the aim of discovering the trainee's deeper framework.

What should the trainee do? It is not especially helpful if the trainee gives voice to some reasonable or ridiculous alternative such as a position or answer that is professionally incorrect, unapproved, dangerous, or risky, or one that is outlandishly wild and bizarre.

Instead, the good discovery-oriented trainee is ready and able to give voice to what is genuinely honest, to what the trainee deeply and seriously seems to believe. The trainee is able to say: 'I'm not really sure, but this is what I think I really think about that . . . Well, here is what I know I should say, and it may even be the best answer, but I know I personally believe this other way . . . My honest answer, my own personal answer, goes like this, but I've never really talked about it much. Really? Truly? I don't really know. I know what the field says, but I have no idea if I can go along with that. My honest answer is kind of weird, but I know it's what I honestly think.'

Being refreshingly honest is a requirement because it is the guide to finding the trainee's deeper framework. The teacher is wholesomely dependent on the trainee's honesty. Without it, the search for the trainee's deeper framework comes to a conspicuous halt. Here are some examples of the crucial role of the trainee's refreshing honesty:

- The teacher and the trainee have tried to get at an underlying principle in the trainee's way of thinking, and the teacher puts it into these words: 'Is this close? Once a person is psychotic, the person is always psychotic, and the best the therapist can do is for the person to be able to live a decent life without being flagrantly psychotic.' The trainee says: 'I never tried to say it like that, but yes, I think I do believe that! Hmmm.'

- The teacher and the trainee come up with three or four quite different things the trainee might have done right here in the session. 'Of these, which one seems to appeal to you a lot, to be what you would love to do? The answer is up to you! Go ahead, be as honest as you can!'

- Discovery-oriented work counts on the trainee selecting some moment on the tape when the trainee felt delighted, pleased, excited, wonderful when she or he listened to it. Finding and selecting that moment can call upon the trainee's true honesty, provided that the trainee is ready and able to be refreshingly honest and open in finding that moment. It calls for a good measure of honesty for the trainee to say: 'It happened right here, and I am ashamed to say that the best part of the session is right here where this girl cracks up. I was just silly. I was like a stand-up comic, and she cracked up! It was my best part of the session. Probably not hers!'

- Discovery-oriented work depends on the trainee finding some place on the tape that the trainee was bothered by, where the trainee felt awful, was in big trouble, was worried or concerned. The bad feeling might have happened during the session or afterward, in listening to the tape. The refreshingly honest trainee can say: 'He's going on and on about the weather! "I have a seasonal affect disorder!" He blames his irritability on the damned weather. Right here I wanted to tell him to shut up already – and I had to stop myself cause I almost started telling him what I really thought!'

Not all trainees can benefit from this kind of work with a discovery-oriented teacher. It does seem to call for trainees with some relatively special qualities.

What seems to be helpful is for the trainee to try having a few of these kind of sessions with a discovery-oriented teacher. If it does not seem to work out, that is that. It ought to be fairly clear right away that this trainee does or does not have the qualities that seem to be called for. If the trainee has the right qualities, these sessions can be fun and productive, and can have a powerful effect on the psychotherapist that the trainee becomes.

If the trainee does not have the right qualities, there is no law that he or she has to be a discovery-oriented trainee, or that the discovery-oriented teacher is the only supervisor available. Nor is there any law that the absence of the right qualities is an eternal characteristic, woven into the very essence of the trainee. It may very well be that the trainee has the right qualities in a month or in 6 months, or perhaps never. Discovery-oriented teaching and learning are mainly for trainees who have the qualities that are good for this method of teaching and learning.

Chapter 6

Some practical-logistical guidelines in discovery-oriented training of psychotherapists

Picture a teacher in an office, with perhaps one to four trainees, rather than a teacher in a classroom with 15–30 or so students. The purpose of this chapter is to deal with some of the practical–logistical matters.

The emphasis is on careful, in-depth study of tapes

In the office, the trainees and the teacher study tapes of the session. Videotapes are impressive and good to watch, but audiotapes can be easier to get and much less obtrusive, and are usually good enough for discovery-oriented training.

Whether you use audiotapes or videotapes, tapes are worlds better, for discovery-oriented training, than the trainee's reporting of notes from the session. It seems safe to say that discovery-oriented training can occur if you use tapes, and comes dangerously close to not occurring if you rely on the trainee's notes.

Tapes have some useful advantages over notes, at least for discovery-oriented purposes. I rely on and trust tapes as a precious resource of what happened in the session. The trainee, other trainees, and the teacher can focus on what happened on the tape. Special parts of the tape can be replayed and studied more and more carefully. The bottom line is that tapes are essential for careful and in-depth study of the session for purposes of discovery-oriented training.

In the teacher's office, the emphasis is on the trainees' tapes; in the classroom, the emphasis is on master therapists

In the classroom, the emphasis is on tapes of master therapists who are exemplars of a broad variety of approaches. It seems better to study tapes of actual sessions with actual clients, rather than demonstration sessions, sessions with volunteers or actors who play the role of client, or pre-therapy or post-therapy interviews, assessments, and evaluations.

The 'master therapists' usually consist of well-known authorities of each of the major approaches. In addition, it can be helpful to have tapes of fine practitioners who are merely fine practitioners, whether or not they are well known.

In the teacher's office, the emphasis is on the trainees' tapes; however, these may be complemented in two ways. One is that the teacher may also have a turn presenting tapes of his or her own sessions. Second, it can be helpful to include study of tapes of a few master therapists who exemplify the kind of approach or some particular method that seems to be emerging from a trainee's own deeper framework.

> 'You seem to be uncovering an approach that highlights the re-experiencing of childhood traumas. Here is a tape of a fine practitioner who does this well.'

> 'You are discovering a leaning toward therapist openness and self-disclosure. In this tape, the therapist can illustrate how to do this sensitively and well.'

How can the trainee select the right parts of the tape to be studied?

Before coming to the teacher's office, the trainee listens to the tape and selects one or two parts of the tape for careful study. The part may be short, perhaps covering 3–10 seconds or so, or it may cover a longer period of a few minutes or so. In any case, at least three guidelines are helpful:

1. Pick out a part that you like. There is something pleasing about this part, something you like, something you are proud of, something perhaps wonderful and exciting, the kind of thing that you would be inclined to play over and over in your own office, or you might even want to have a buddy trainee listen to and appreciate. Notice how important it is to be refreshingly honest in selecting a part for this reason.

   This wonderful part may include something you did, something that worked wonderfully. Or it may be that some delightful and prized change occurred here, whether or not you seemed to have much to do with the impressive change. It may be that you accomplished the wonderful change that you wanted to accomplish, or it may be that you were honestly surprised by the good change that somehow happened right here. It may be that you tried out something, you did what you wanted to do, and 'it worked', or it may be that something wonderful happened here and you have no idea what you did or if you had much of anything to do with whatever helped to bring it about.

I want to emphasize how crucial it is for the trainee's genuine honesty to be a main feature in selecting this part of the tape. It is so easy to select this part of the tape because 'the field' would agree, or because the trainee's colleagues would nod in agreement, or because most of the teachers or supervisors would be pleased that the trainee selected this part. In some contrast, perhaps, the trainee has done a good job if, for example, the teacher and the other trainees are impressed that he or she is being refreshingly honest, open, genuine, and real in selecting out that part to study.

2. Pick out a part that you do not like. Pick out a part where, either in the actual session itself or in listening to the tape, you were dismayed, felt bad, were bothered, wished you could have started over, were troubled, did the wrong thing, were embarrassed, failed miserably, were a rotten therapist, felt awful, got into real trouble.

Pick out a part that truly bothers you, rather than a part that is not devastating but shows you are human after all, a part where your bad feeling is mild or so very understandable, a part that does little or no real damage to your stellar reputation in the eyes of your colleagues or the teacher.

Picking out this part tests the guideline of your supreme honesty, your willingness to be exposed. The reaction of your colleagues and the teacher will be: 'Well, you are certainly a top scorer on the "honesty scale". I think I am envious of your being so honest. Wait till it is my turn. I am going to be more honest than you are.'

The part you pick out may refer mainly to the other person, rather than to you. Usually it refers to something you did or did not do. In any case, the feeling in you is strong and it is bad.

3. Pick out a part that is powerfully inexplicable. Occasionally, something happens in a session that is almost incredible and yet inexplicable. It is absolutely surprising, perplexing, unaccountable. It bowls you over. It is eerie, uncanny. It may be good or bad or neither, but mainly powerful and inexplicable.

Of course what happened may be well known to the teacher. It may have its own little body of literature. Or perhaps not. In either case, having happened to you first hand, it is powerfully inexplicable, to you at least.

All of a sudden, as if out of nowhere, the client looks at you, and you are convinced that the client knows everything about you, everything, completely. This lasted only 5–10 seconds, and the feeling in you was neither good nor bad, just powerfully eerie, bizarre, strange. For only a brief moment, you knew for sure that your mother was present, standing behind you, listening, so close that you can sense her breath. Then it was gone.

You suddenly are about 10 feet above where you and the client are sitting and talking. You are literally above the two people, observing them, and having thoughts about what they are doing with one another. It seems so natural, until you are once again inside the body and mind of the psychotherapist you are being right now in the session. Very weird.

Each training session begins with a tape ready to play the selected part. It is essential that the trainee be excruciatingly honest in selecting out one of these three kinds of excerpts, especially the first two, and occasionally the third.

How can a trainee be judged as 'good' or 'not so good' on his or her skills?

Picture that the trainee and the discovery-oriented teacher have a list of some explicit 'trainee skills' that the trainee is here to gain, and that they judge the trainee on each of these skills. From the very beginning of the training, the trainee knows what these skills are, and the trainee is eager to learn each of these training skills. Here are some of them:

- The trainee is able to select out the parts of the tape for careful study in the training sessions. Furthermore, the trainee can select out parts that are exciting and pleasurable, parts that are uncomfortable and bothersome, and parts that are perplexing and inexplicable.
- The trainee is gaining skills of discovering the deeper framework. There are a number of these skills. Each is somewhat distinctive.

For example, suppose the trainee and the teacher agree that right here something went wrong, and the teacher is ready to work with the trainee in studying what might have occurred earlier to help explain and understand what went so wrong right here. There are simple skills in examining what occurred before the targeted moment when something went wrong. Some trainees learn these skills well, some not so well, and some apparently not at all.

Discovering one's deeper framework calls for the trainee to learn and to develop some skills, especially in working with the teacher so that both teacher and trainee are working together in discovering the trainee's deeper framework. The trainee knows that she will be judged as doing all right or not so well in learning and developing these skills.

- The trainee is able to put each discovered part of the deeper framework into writing, to integrate it into and with the other parts, and to keep a continuously modified log of the developing deeper framework. This is more in the form of somewhat loosely changing notes than a formally organized and articulated conceptual system, or a disorganized jumble of words and terms that only the trainee might understand.

- The trainee is able to come up with positions on basic issues, and answers to basic questions. The trainee's notes include the basic issues and questions, and the trainee's own discovered and articulated positions and answers.

- The trainee must be able to carry out the homework assigned by the teacher. As a general rule, each training session ends with the teacher giving the trainee a homework assignment. It may be that the trainee had to come up with an answer to this particular question, or to read this article about the notion or method that seems to be emerging from the trainee's own deeper framework.

- The trainee is able to put the developing deeper framework to actual use in the actual sessions. It is one skill to discover and develop the deeper framework. It is a different skill to be able to apply the developing deeper framework in the actual session.

- The trainee has the ability to assist other trainees in the discovery and development of their own deeper frameworks. Training may well include a small group of three to five trainees. The teacher is here to work with the trainee whose tape is being discussed. So, too, can the trainees whose tapes are not being discussed be there. They can do things to assist the 'presenting' trainee in discovering and developing her own deeper framework.

These are some of the main 'training skills' that a trainee knows about, probably would like to become good at, and can judge how well she is doing on each of these skills.

How can a trainee be judged? The trainee can be judged by seeing how well she or he is doing on each of the skills she or he has to develop. Once there is a useful list of these skills, she or he may be judged by looking at each of them and asking at least three questions:

1. Is the trainee getting better, showing progress, on this skill, especially compared with the last few training sessions or so?

2. How good is he or she on this skill? Is he or she quite good, not good at all, somewhere in between?

3. Has training paid adequate attention to this skill or has it been generally overlooked?

It is relatively easy to ask and answer these questions when there is a list of the actual skills the trainee is to learn.

Assessment of the trainee on training skills is the responsibility of both teacher and trainee

In almost every training session, both the teacher and the trainee will almost certainly talk about how good the trainee is becoming on the skills involved in the training session, about his or her progress on the relevant training skills, and about which training skills have been relatively overlooked. The first two refer mainly to the trainee, and the last one refers mainly to the teacher.

If the trainee seems to be making little or no progress on the training skills, and if he or she seems woefully inadequate on most of the training skills, that is a reflection mainly on him or her. If training has failed to pay adequate attention to the broader range of training skills, that is a reflection mainly on the teacher.

If training is not going well, that ought to be rather clear almost from the very beginning. It is important that assessment is the responsibility of both the teacher and trainee (Mahrer and Boulet, 1997) Therefore, if training is to stop, this usually becomes clear relatively early, on the parts of both the teacher and the trainee. Discussing whether to end this training is an almost easy and natural responsibility of both the teacher and trainee.

What does it mean if both the teacher and the trainee arrive at a decision to end this kind of training? It can be taken that this kind of training is not especially fitting or appropriate with this teacher and this trainee. It is as if the first batch of training sessions is a kind of trial of the goodness of fit between this trainee and the discovery-oriented training, between this teacher and this trainee. Their decision to end this kind of training can be taken as having little or nothing to do with the worth of the trainee, the adequacy of the trainee, the status of the trainee in the training program. In other words, formal assessment to end this kind of training has a great deal to do with 'goodness of fit' between this trainee and teacher and this kind of training, and virtually nothing to do with 'pass' or 'fail' of the trainee in the larger training program.

Some helpful guidelines for a group

Discovery-oriented training can occur with a teacher and one trainee. I have done that often. However, I am more familiar with training occurring with a small group. Here are some guidelines for working with a small group of trainees.

Length of each training session

I have spent almost a whole day working with a small group of trainees. We meet about once a month, and spend the whole day in teaching and training. There are some reasons for spending so much time at once. One is that the 'trainees' are usually practicing psychotherapists, and these meetings are like little celebrations or friendly get-togethers, usually on the weekends. Another reason is that some of the trainees live an hour or two away, and it makes more sense to spend most of the day in training rather than just an hour or so.

It is perhaps more common that the teacher and trainees are part of a training program, and often work in the same building. Under these conditions, we generally meet once or twice a week, and the meetings seem to be about 2 hours.

The point is that the length of the training sessions can well vary, and there can be different considerations that justify whether the session is relatively short or long.

Size of the group

If each training session is approximately a few hours, and if we meet once or twice a week, I like to provide an opportunity for each trainee to be the center of attention at least once a week. I start feeling guilty if a few weeks go by and a trainee has not been center stage. Accordingly, I am relatively comfortable with a small group of perhaps two to four trainees, occasionally a few more.

In addition to the 'active' trainees, it is somewhat common to have a few others in the group. There may be a trainee or two who are mainly visitors, or perhaps friends of particular trainees in the group. Every so often, the group is asked if it is all right to let another supervisor sit in for a few sessions. Supervisors from the trainees' training program seem to be rarely welcomed, but supervisors from outside training programs are generally welcomed, especially if they are genuinely interested in this kind of teaching and training.

Level of experience

I had thought that the trainees would do better if they were all at essentially the same level of experience, if they were all beginning or advanced trainees, or all practicing psychotherapists. I was wrong. Whether the group works well or not so well seems to have little to do with uniformity of experience, at least in my experience.

Professed approach or orientation

Picture some trainees as not having any real preferred approach or orientation, some who have a tentative preference for a given approach, and some who are dedicated proponents of some approach or orientation. Picture some trainees as being Jungian, behavior therapists, client-centered therapists, solution-focused therapists, psychodynamic, integrative–eclectic, humanistic, and so on.

Does the group do better if most of the trainees share a single approach or have approaches that are compatible? How about a refreshing sprinkling of altogether different approaches, including no professed approach at all? I find that the group does well as long as the trainees are well suited to doing discovery-oriented work, regardless of their approach or lack of approach, regardless of whether they do or do not share a common approach.

What makes a group a 'good' group?

I do not have a solid grasp of what makes a group a 'good' group. In general, I do not have an answer to this question. Each of the trainees can seem to have the qualities of a good discovery-oriented trainee, and the group may be a good one or a poor one. Yet some groups work out well and some do not. I wish I could answer this question, but I cannot, not well at least.

There have been times when a new trainee entered a group, and the group seemed to become much better or much worse. There have been times when a member of an ongoing group did not show up, and the group seemed to be much better or much worse. It would make sense to think of a trial period, but I have rarely embraced and used this sensible idea except when a new trainee had a conspicuously shattering effect on a group, and then the new trainee faced the obvious and did the honorable thing by exiting from the group. I cannot take credit for these occasions. It still seems sensible to have a trial period.

There does seem to be a kind of magical quality that characterizes a good group in which the trainees feel comfortable with each other. Perhaps one characteristic of a good group is that the trainees trust each other. Another apparent characteristic is that the trainee who is center stage feels able to be honest, to search for his or her own deeper framework, and is relieved of having to be a knowledgeable student or trainee or therapist, sure of him- or herself, confident, and knowing what is right and proper as a fine therapist or therapist in training. Another apparent characteristic is that the trainee at center stage feels that the group is helpful in his or her own deeper searching. I can recognize and appreciate such a good group, even though I wish I knew how to bring it about and enhance it. I do not.

What should beginning trainees do with their first client?

It is relatively common that a trainee begins being in a group, and asks: 'This will be my first client? . . . Um . . . So what do I do?' The trainee knows that just about every supervisor, of just about every other approach, can tell the beginning trainee what to do in the first session with the first client. What can the discovery-oriented teacher offer as suggestions? There can be a number of guidelines.

One guideline is that 'what to do with the first sessions of one's first client' is a fitting and appropriate matter to talk about in order to get down into one's own deeper framework, and it is also a fitting and appropriate matter to talk about before the first sessions with one's first client. Before sailing into these first sessions, the guideline suggests that it can be worthwhile to start with this practical matter and to use it to explore down into the trainee's deeper framework.

A second guideline is for the trainee to follow the leads that have been given in the training program for what to do in initial sessions. Do what the trainee has been taught to do in these sessions. Just make sure that the sessions are recorded so that they can be studied in the training sessions.

A third guideline was introduced by several members of several discovery-oriented training groups: 'Count on your experience with friends who wanted to talk with you about something bothersome. Be this way with your client.' Each new trainee has been in the role of listening to and being with someone who is bothered about something, who may be ready to talk about something. The training program has prepared the trainee for this initial session. There are things for the trainee to do in the initial session. The trainee's personal experience with friends can be counted upon to provide the overall role, and also to fill in the gaps of what he or she actually does in this initial session with the initial client.

Fourth, older and more experienced trainees have emphasized that the beginning trainee can feel a little bit relieved knowing that the first session will be recorded and studied. An important use of the first session with the client is to have actual material to learn from, e.g. one older and more experienced trainee told the new and inexperienced trainee that in her initial sessions she tried to do what she was taught to do in initial sessions, that she modestly acknowledged wanting to be an impressive smash in her initial sessions, but that she was reassuringly guided through the sessions by knowing that the sessions were recorded, and that she could use the session to keep getting better and better – at an astounding pace, of course, and toward becoming a master therapist, of course!

Fifth, if the training session focuses on the issue of what to do in the initial sessions, further study of that matter can easily include the trainee examining a number of initial sessions as carried out by a variety of therapists. Studying these other tapes seems to be of help in getting at the trainee's own deeper framework, and also in seeing up close what the trainee may do in these initial sessions.

Sixth, trainees are reassured, by both the teacher and more experienced trainees, that discovering more and more about their own deeper framework usually leads to substantial changes in whatever the trainees did in their initial sessions with their first clients. Accept that whatever the trainee does in the initial session will probably change later.

Finally, emphasize the conservative and the safe. The profession, the training program, and the clinic or agency almost certainly have professional and ethical standards for what to do and what not to do in these initial sessions. Follow these guidelines. Do not do anything that is designed to antagonize or upset supervisors, the clinic or agency, the training program, colleagues, referral sources, the client's family, ethical boards, or especially lawyers. Stay out of trouble.

Start by going directly to the part the trainee selects out to study, rather than 'talking about' the person

When the trainee is center stage, the first thing she should do is to play the tape of the part that she wants to study. The trainee may introduce the part by saying that: (1) it is a part that the trainee liked, was special, was pleased with, a part where something good happened; (2) it is a part that bothers her, she worries about, she did something blatantly wrong or bad or dumb or worrisome, a part where something bad happened; or (3) it is a part where something inexplicable happened, something unusual and hard to make sense of, something truly out of the ordinary. The trainee may not be sure why this part is pleasing or bothersome or inexplicable, but it seems to be, and that is enough to start here and study it.

The trainee may not be sure exactly where the part begins and ends, but as we listen she can say that this or that is what she means by the part being pleasing or bothersome or inexplicable.

In any case, she does not begin with the common introduction, the common giving of some background. She does not begin with the common 'talking about' the person.

Bypassing the usual 'talking about' the person

For many supervisors and trainees, this can be hard. It is almost a natural law of the universe that trainees must preface a presentation by giving a little background, telling something about the patient, giving some preliminary and prefatory information, first 'talking about' the person. Giving this material is a knee-jerk reaction, essentially involuntary. Even seasoned presenters are inclined to put their hands over their mouth before we listen to the selected part of the tape. Beginning trainees, almost without exception, absolutely must begin by telling a little about the client – by 'talking about' the person.

Here is an example. Even before putting the cassette into the tape recorder, the trainee says: 'This client is in denial. On the intake screening, she indicated depressive thoughts, but I have had two sessions with her, and she just recites what happened in the week. In this session she mentions some concern about her mother's asthma, but mainly she just tells me about the week. She's in her middle twenties, works as a waitress at a restaurant. Not married. She and her mother have been here for over a year. Her father died in an accident when she was about 10 years old. They came here from Argentina. She lives with her mother, takes care of her mother, and has few friends. Another waitress. The problem is that she won't talk about her depressive thoughts, and it's hard to know why she's here. She doesn't seem depressed in the sessions, but fits the profile of a depressive denial.'

Probably the wisest and most helpful way of receiving this preliminary 'talking about' is to be polite, listen, and then invite the trainee to go to the part of the tape that he selected to play. The teacher may say: 'I know it is seductively important to give background about the person, so go ahead. Then we can get to the part of the tape you selected.' Or the teacher says: 'I will be polite and listen interestedly. Then can we go to the tape?' Or the trainee can say: 'I have to say something pertinent about my client. So I will. Then we can go to the part of the tape I want to play.' Be polite, listen. Get the 'talking about' over with. Then go to the part of the tape.

Here are some reasons why it is important to bypass the 'talking about', to avoid asking questions, getting more information, inquiring into the many things that the preliminary 'talking about' invites the teacher and other trainees to talk about:

1. What the trainee says in the prefatory 'talking about' generally comes from and represents the trainee's surface way of thinking, the trainee's surface approach, perspective. Asking more about this material, or questioning any part of this material, is very probably an effective way of locking it in, reinforcing this superficial framework, handcuffing the trainee to the superficial framework.

   If the teacher asks about more material, or further clarification, it is easy to see the teacher adopting and colluding with the trainee's superficial framework in order to do so. This might well tend to occur if the teacher says: 'Is there any other evidence of her tendency toward denial? . . .

Do you have any hints about the nature of the depressive thoughts? . . . Are there any other indicators of depression? . . . What about the nature of the relationship? . . . Why did she and her mother leave Argentina? . . . What about the medical history?'

On the other hand, if the teacher tries to use this 'talking about' to begin discovery, it is easy for the trainee to adopt a stance of defending the framework, locking it in, entrenching it further. This may well happen if the teacher says: 'You sound like your aim is to try to get her to talk about her depressive thoughts. Is that right? . . . Do you believe in letting the client proceed at her own pace, and bringing up what is important when she is ready? . . . You accept the idea of a profile of depressive clients? What is the profile? . . . How do you go about arriving at the goals of therapy? . . .'

In a sense, the trainee's preliminary 'talking about' is a trap. Whether the teacher tries to get more information or tries to use the 'talking about' to try to get at the trainee's deeper framework, the net result is usually a locking in, an entrenchment, of the trainee's superficial framework. Let it go. Bypass the introductory 'talking about'.

2. Preliminary 'talking about' the client is a poor entry into the trainee's deeper framework. Indeed, it probably will not work. Getting into the trainee's deeper framework is much better accomplished when you start with a part of the tape that the trainee is pleased about and happy with, bothered about and unhappy with, or blatantly surprising and inexplicable. Let the preliminary 'talking about' finish and go to the part of the tape the trainee selected to study.

3. When the focus is on a selected part of the tape, the trainee's 'talking about' has a fair chance of being useful to lead down into the trainee's deeper framework. 'Talking about' can provide exceedingly useful material once the trainee is attending to a particular part of the tape as the central focus. Throughout the balance of this volume, most of the methods of discovering and developing the trainee's deeper framework can and do use 'talking about' the client material.

In general, it seems best for the teacher and the trainee to bypass, graciously decline, starting with the common tendency to 'talk about' the client.

We now turn to the actual methods of discovering and developing the trainee's own inner deeper framework for psychotherapy.

Part II

Introduction to the methods of discovering and developing the trainee's deeper framework for psychotherapy

The remainder of the volume tells about the methods that a teacher can use to help a trainee discover and develop his or her own deeper framework for psychotherapy. For each method, the aim is to describe what it is and how to use it, and to provide some examples of how the method can be used.

If there is a course on discovery-oriented training, or if there is a section on discovery-oriented training in a course on supervision, these are the methods.

These methods can be learned. The teacher can become increasingly proficient in each of these skills. If a teacher is going to be a discovery-oriented teacher, it is important that the teacher be reasonably proficient in these skills. Teachers are invited to improve these methods, to reorganize them in a better way, and to add other methods of discovery-oriented teaching.

The methods are organized into five families. In other words, the discovery-oriented approach includes five general methods. Each of the following five chapters focuses on a particular general method.

Chapter 7

Method 1: identify and use the part the trainee selected to study

Identifying and using the selected part means first determining where it seems to start and end. Sometimes this can be relatively easy. Sometimes this can be hard to do. It can take some judgment to decide where it seems to begin and to end. Second identifying the part you picked out means describing it, and this can be a little tricky. To use the description, the emphasis is on a simple description, telling what that part is, rather than an in-depth analysis of how and why this part is so pleasing or displeasing or inexplicable. The emphasis is on a short-hand description, rather than giving deeper reasons to account for and justify why you might have selected this part. The emphasis is on telling what this part is. Once we have a description of what this part is, we can go into a deeper and more intensive analysis of underlying reasons why this part is regarded as good and pleasing, or bad and bothersome, or inexplicable and intriguing.

The emphasis is on using words and phrases that are simple, free of the vocabulary of any given approach, free of what may be thought of as technical terminology. Avoid psychobabble, even if the words or phrases have meaning for you. Keep the description simple.

Once you have identified the part, there are at least four ways of using this part to discover more about your own inner deeper framework. The purpose of this chapter is to show you how to identify the part you picked out, and especially how to use these four ways to get at and further develop your deeper framework. These four methods are dealt with a bit later in the chapter.

Identify where it is, where it begins and ends

The trainee has selected a part to study. Listen to that part to try to get a clearer picture of where it seems to begin and where it seems to end. The trainee says: 'It is roughly here. It is in here somewhere.' Sometimes the trainee says: 'It begins right here, and it ends right here.' However, it is common that it takes some work to identify just where it starts and ends.

It is easier to get a simple description when we can identify precisely where it begins and ends, and we can listen to that part carefully to try to arrive at a simple description. However, sometimes the actual part may be somewhat hidden, camouflaged, even though we know it is in this section right here, starting here and ending there.

Arrive at a simple description of the part you picked out

Picture the trainee, the teacher, and the other trainees trying to describe the part that the trainee picked out as a pleasing part, a displeasing part, or an inexplicable part. It can take a little time and a little work to find the right words, until the description seems right to the trainee.

By a 'simple' description, I do not mean one that has only a few words. I mean a description using words and terms and phrases that are simple, relatively concrete, free of the jargon of any particular approach, free of technical esoteric words, vocabulary that is free of 'psychobabble'.

The simple description typically focuses on the person, on what is happening in the person, on how the person is being, on what the person is doing. It can also extend to include the trainee's own thoughts and feelings.

For the purpose of this first method, simple descriptions of parts that the trainee liked, found pleasant, and is happy about, are most useful. Here are some verbatim examples, in the words of either the trainee or the teacher:

> 'Up to here, he was just mad, arguing with me, pissed off, fighting, and here he is so different. He's actually happy, laughing, making jokes about himself. What a difference!'

> 'You like when you are upbeat, funny, with a good sense of humor, and the client laughs, giggles, appreciates your good humor.'

> 'You like when you are thinking something the client ought to do, something you believe would be good for the client to actually do, you blurt it out, straightaway, and he grins and says, "Yeah".'

> 'You like it when she says how different things are, how much better she feels, and the good feeling in you is that you're a good therapist. You did well in helping to change her for the better.'

'I knew what he was looking for, what he was trying to say, and I said it for him. I said the word for him, and he agreed. That was what he was looking for to say. I love being able to do that.'

For the purpose of this first method, parts that are bothersome, that trouble the trainee, where he or she is upset and worried, can be somewhat useful, but less so than parts that he or she truly liked. Here are some examples of this second kind:

'It's right here where he's quiet, and says, "Maybe", maybe he's going to kill himself. I was scared, really scared. I could feel my pressure go up, and I had no idea what to do.'

'It's here where she says, "I don't think I'm getting any better; do you think this therapy is working?" She's not mad or anything, and she is really asking. I felt awful. Didn't know what to say. I just felt frozen, sort of numb. I hated that.'

'Here he's complaining, as usual, and I am supposed to just shut up and listen. And here I did. It's not therapy. I'm just supposed to be quiet and agree with him. I don't know what I'm supposed to do with him.'

'She's talking about the guy she's living with, and I'm being nice, understanding, empathic. But I feel two-faced, like I'm lying, cause I think she ought to drop the guy, and I can't just say that, or maybe I could. I don't know. I'm scared she can tell how I disapprove of her living with him.'

For purposes of this first method, simple descriptions of parts that are inexplicable are not especially useful. These parts are somewhat strange, uncanny, compelling, but they are not especially helpful in this first method. Here are a few examples:

'Right here I had a sensation that there was blood coming out of my nose. I was sure. But when I touched, nothing. I was sure there was blood.'

'Right here, I have no idea what caused it, but I got so dizzy when I shut my eyes for a second. When I opened my eyes, no dizziness. When I shut them for a second, I thought 1 was going to pass out cause I got so dizzy. And here it was gone. I have no idea what caused it!'

'She's telling about her uncle showing her how to play cards, and that's when it happened. I really felt like I grew up with her, like she was the girl from next door. I knew what she was going to say cause I knew we played cards together as kids. This was weird!'

What follows are some ways of using the four simple descriptions to get closer to your own deeper framework for psychotherapy. These methods rely mostly on parts of the tape that you picked out because you liked them, they were pleasing and exciting to you. A few of the following methods include parts that you picked out because you were bothered, upset, worried. None relied on parts that you picked out because they were inexplicable, weird, strange. You will use these parts in later methods.

Figure out your own list of impressive in-session changes

Gradually build your own personal list of whatever seems to be impressive changes that occur in sessions. It is an actual list, a written-out list. It is your list.

The actual items on the list may be similar to or different from what you may have expected, or from what other trainees have as their list. The items may lean toward a content that you can think of as psychodynamic or behavioral, or perhaps your items do not particularly fit any special approach.

Some items on your list may be bigger and broader and more general, whereas others may seem more particular, smaller. Some may be similar to what is ordinarily thought of as 'outcome' and some may not – they may be more of what you consider instrumental changes that can help lead toward bigger and more subsequent goals.

Start with the first few items you found. Then keep adding items as you find them. With each new item, see where it fits into the list you already have. Give yourself a chance to keep revising the list. You will gradually add some items by putting them under larger items: sub-items, subcategories. You will gradually add more major items. Keep revising, modifying, and reorganizing your list as you add items from studying your own sessions, the sessions of other trainees, and the sessions of seasoned therapists whose tapes you study. You are slowly and gradually assembling your own personal list of impressive in-session changes.

Here is a start list, after a few training sessions:

1   The client laughs, giggles, seems to be in good spirits, and this is different from the way the client usually is.

2. The client says how much better things are.

3. The client seems accepting of and even pleased with the therapist's suggestion of what to do.

4. The client thinks about things in a much better way.

Here is what the list looked like after a number of further training sessions with a number of clients:

1. The client sees others in a better way:
   (a) The client can understand the personal perspectives of the client's parents and older siblings.
   (b) The client can appreciate the worldview of significant people in the client's current personal life.
   (c) The client has a more realistic understanding of how others affect him or her.

2. The client adopts the therapist's outlook, perspective, worldview:
   (a) The client uses the therapist's own words and phrases in describing the client's way of seeing things.
   (b) The client solicits, invites, asks for the therapist's own view about particular matters and issues.
   (c) The client agrees with the therapist's assessment of the client's current state.

Keep adding to, modifying and revising, reorganizing the list of impressive in-session changes. Allow the list to be flexible, open to changes that are slight or large. Grant the trainee the right to change the list as the trainee comes across more and more impressive in-session changes, i.e. grant the trainee the right to change the kinds of impressive in-session changes that seem impressive. Their descriptions may change. They may combine with other impressive changes. They may be assimilated into other kinds of impressive changes. The list will almost certainly change over time.

Figure out your own sequence of impressive in-session changes

Sometimes a trainee will say that there were several changes that seemed impressive in the session, and it is hard to decide which to select for study. Sometimes, in studying one impressive change, the trainee will then go to another one that occurred earlier or later in the session. Occasionally a trainee will study a session to look explicitly for which impressive change occurred first, and which one or ones seemed to follow.

The aim is to try to identify a sequence or program of impressive changes for the trainee. Or perhaps a trainee may have a few sequences of impressive changes. This kind of study may culminate in identifying that the trainee first seems to get this kind of impressive change, and then this second kind, and the sequence ends with this third kind of impressive change. The sequence usually occurs over a single session, but it may extend to a few sessions or more.

Ordinarily, analysis comes up with couplings or pairs of impressive changes, e.g. one is followed by two or two is preceded by one. In another session, the coupling may consist of two being followed by three. If we put these 'findings' together, the sequence starts with impressive change one, followed by two, and ending with three. Here is a sequence of impressive changes for this particular trainee.

By studying the sequences in a number of sessions, it is possible to appreciate which couplings seem to occur more frequently than others. It is also possible to gain some confidence in the overall sequences or programs that seem to be used by this particular trainee.

All of this starts by seeing which impressive changes seem to precede and follow others, e.g. the initial impressive change in the session was described as the client accepting, even enjoying, attempts by the therapist to tell the client what to do, how to live life differently to be happier and less stressed. This was followed by another impressive change in which the client seemed to feel good with the therapist, to understand the therapist as a real person, to like the therapist as a person. This was an observed sequence. The trainee had not known or thought about this sequence, but there it was, or apparently seemed to be.

With another trainee, this three-part sequence seemed to occur in a number of sessions:

1. The client tells in some detail, and with a vibrant interest and involvement, about some pleasing childhood incident.

2. The client's level of distress seems significantly reduced.

3. The client is motivated to carry out a post-session homework assignment.

Not only was the trainee somewhat surprised by this sequence, but also it seemed rather out of keeping with his or her professed psychotherapeutic approach.

After many years of studying tapes of many sessions conducted by many therapists, including some of my own sessions, I finally ended up with a sequence of four impressive major changes that occur over each session:

1. The client discovers a 'deeper potential for experiencing'.

2. The client welcomes and accepts the 'deeper potential for experiencing'.

3. The client undergoes a qualitative change of actually 'being' the 'deeper potential for experiencing' in the context of earlier life scenes and situations.

4. The client is a qualitatively new person in the context of imminent post-session new scenes and situations of a qualitatively new personal world.

Arriving at this four-step sequence in each session was essentially a gift, a framework for what became my own way of doing psychotherapy (Mahrer, 1996/2004, 2002, 2004c). If that sequence had been offered by some established school or approach, I would probably have become a proponent of that school or approach.

In general, this method allows you to arrive at or figure out your own sequence of impressive in-session changes, whatever it may be, and whatever school or approach is friendly to that particular sequence of impressive in-session changes.

Whether the part you picked out was good or bad, figure out what you did to help bring it about

The part you picked out may have been one that you especially liked, was impressive, pleasing, good. Or it may have struck you as one that bothered you, was displeasing, unpleasant, bad. In either case, it can be helpful to try to figure out what you may have done to help bring it about. If the part is one you liked, you can have a good chance of being able to bring about these impressive changes more easily, more frequently, and better. If the part is one you disliked, you can reduce the likelihood of bringing about this kind of unpleasant in-session event in sessions from now on.

Ordinarily, you are studying your own tape. However, the same search can be done on tapes of other trainees, on the teacher's tapes, and especially on tapes of master therapists, exemplars.

Start with where the good or bad part occurred, and go back enough to be able to discover what the therapist seemed to do to help bring about that change. Go back as much as you need to get a good enough answer. What may seem surprising, but seems to happen most of the time, is that you only have to go back a little bit, perhaps a minute or so, 10 or 20 or so interchanges. Although it is helpful to go back further, perhaps 3–5 minutes or more, you usually do not have to go far back to be able to discover what the therapist did to help bring about that selected part.

Of course you may want to start from the beginning of the session, especially if going back just a little bit does not seem to offer a good-enough answer. In any case, study whatever seemed to help account for the occurrence of the selected part, whether you go back a little bit or a great deal.

Discovery of the principle usually takes care of the problem of myriads of cumulative influences in the therapist–client interaction

Clinical lore typically includes at least two 'truths' that can be taken as making it difficult to arrive at a clear picture of what the therapist did to help bring about the selected part. One 'truth' is that whatever is occurring right now is the culmination of a long history of subtle influences and determinants that gradually accumulate from the very beginning of the therapist and client being together. Therefore, it is almost impossible to identify what the therapist did to bring about the selected part.

The other side of this problem is that the therapist is not in this alone. There is a subtle interaction, a back-and-forth dialogue between therapist and client. This makes it almost impossible to highlight or to emphasize what the therapist does. It must be the interaction between the two that helps bring about the selected part.

There are at least two ways that identifying the principle seems to take care of both sides of this problem.

The principle starts with 'When the person is . . .'

When you go back a way, to try to discover what the therapist does to help bring about the selected part, you will almost always be able to find that things begin with the person being in a particular state or condition, with the person doing this or that. The principle typically begins with the person, rather than the therapist. This is so common that it is almost a rule. Compared with the way the person has typically been in the session, the person does something, is some way, is in a given condition or state. That is the beginning of the principle.

As examples, the principle usually begins as follows:

> When the person is on the verge of tears . . . When the person is expressing fondness and affection toward the therapist . . . When the person is now silent, withdrawn, pulled in . . . When the person is living and being in a childhood scene of arguing with a parent . . . When the person is in a pleasant state of self-satisfaction and well-being . . . When the person is in a state of dramatic strong feeling, a sudden outburst of strong feeling . . . When the person's attention is wholly targeted on the other person.

Starting with the in-session change and going back to try to find what helped bring it about almost always brings you to a point where the person is being this or that way. It is usually clear that the person's being in this particular state or condition is quite necessary. Without the person being in the particular state or condition, it is usually unlikely that the change would have occurred, that whatever the therapist or therapist and person did would have succeeded in bringing about the change you are studying.

The principle ends with: 'the therapist or therapist and person help bring about the change by doing this or that in this or that way'

You may be dealing with an in-session change that is appealing and valuable or that is bothersome and unwelcome. In either case, once you determine the requisite condition or state of the person, try to identify what the therapist seemed to do, or what the therapist and person seemed to do, that helped to bring about the change. In addition, try to identify the way the therapist or person did whatever you identified, the manner or style of doing whatever it was. Try to keep your description simple. Use simple vocabulary rather than using abstract generalizations or technical words and terms.

You are looking for what they seemed to do that helped, that contributed to the in-session change. You need not aim at pinning down all the causes. You are looking for what seemed to help, for whatever stands out. You are looking for something that the therapist can learn to do or avoid doing in subsequent sessions. You are doing your best to arrive at a working principle, rather than a law or rule, a working principle that will probably be revised and modified as you study other instances of the in-session change.

By paying attention to what the person may have done to help and what the therapist and person did together, you are thereby taking care of the other side of the problem of their interaction. You are identifying the specific ways that they may have combined or worked together to help bring about the change.

Usually, the identified principle includes several ways, or perhaps several alternative ways, that the change was probably brought about. Often the principle consists of a few steps or stages so that the therapist or therapist and person first do this and then do that, and the consequence is the occurrence of the in-session change.

Some examples

The first examples are of in-session changes that the trainee considered good ones, pleasant and valued ones. These are followed by in-session changes that the trainee thought of as bad, unwelcome, unpleasant, bothersome.

In each example, the trainee was rather surprised, both to find a working principle, and by the nature and content of the actual principle. Arriving at the principle was a matter of careful work, and also some genuine fun.

Throughout the session, the client was in the usual state of being pulled in, a tight ball of clenched anger. In the impressive change, the client is now excited, happy, self-assured, self-confident, on top of things. In studying what happened before the change, the client seemed to be fixed on her young niece, and especially on the way the niece coped with the family, around the dinner table, pressuring the niece to dress differently. The trainee seemed to join the client in being drawn toward the way the niece was being in the incident. Then the client was chuckling as she said what the niece had said: 'You're trying to get me to be like you? Good luck! Want to bet you can't do it?' Trying to arrive at what seemed to work led to this principle: when the client is compelled by, preponderantly attending to, a key other person, a dramatic change can occur when both client and therapist carry this forward, and the client shifts over to giving direct voice to what the key other person is saying and doing, almost as if the client is 'being' the key other person.

In rather sharp contrast to the depressed mood of most sessions, the impressive change was the client's enjoying some truly pleasant changes in him and his relationships at work. As this occurred close to the beginning of the session, studying the very beginning revealed that the client came into the office chattering about the delightful police-woman he met after parking his car and walking to the office some minutes ago. The trainee seemed pleased as the trainee kept saying: 'That's great! . . . A policewoman! Sounds like fun!' When they were seated, the trainee opened with a pleasant 'So are there any other nice things happening?' and the client launched into the unusually happy changes in him and his relationships at work. The principle was framed as follows: when the client enters the office in a light mood, join and share in the light mood, and then 'officially' open the session by inviting the client to look for nice pleasant changes in his current world. This can help lead to the client's telling about and enjoying nice pleasant changes in himself and his relationships.

The impressive change was the client's arriving at an exciting and workable solution to a seriously problematic situation: 'That's it! That's the answer! I think I'm going to do it!' In studying what may have accounted for this nice change, two things seemed to stand out as distinctive. One was that the trainee and the client were like bud-dies or co-workers who were a real team in trying to solve some problem. They genuinely solved it as a working partnership. It was often hard to tell who was trainee and who was client. The other was that they seemed like detectives or scientists carefully inspecting detail after detail of the problem situation that was so central. The principle was framed as follows: when the client is almost fully focused on a central problematic situation, the consequence can be an excitingly workable solution when (1) therapist and client are a working team of partners, co-workers who (2) carefully and fully study and analyze the details in searching for a solution to the central problematic situation.

The trainee was so proud of this part where the client was clearly so trusting of her, felt so understood by and close to her. Everyone in the group was so impressed. The group was even more impressed, however, with what close study seemed to indicate the trainee had done just before this expression of closeness with her. The client was talking about the two kids who lived next door when he was a little boy, and how they liked playing catch with his dog, when the trainee, without skipping a beat or interrupting what the client was relating, casually mentioned the name of the dog, 'Max', and slid in the names of the two kids next door, 'Peter and Marie'. The group was almost astounded. 'How did you know those names?' The trainee did not know how; she just remembers the cast of relevant characters in her client's past and current personal worlds. The group and the trainee came up with this working principle: when the client mentions relevant people in the client's life, it helps to bring about a close and intimate relationship when the therapist knows and mentions the names of these relevant people. The trainee added, 'and pets too'.

The rather dramatic change was when the client, who had been almost mechanically and dispassionately reciting horror stories about her life, suddenly burst into tears and was shaking and trembling in fear. Although the trainee saw this as an important turning point, he had no idea what might have accounted for this abrupt change until we took a closer look at what seemed to lead up to this change. As the client was telling about how her live-in partner was stoned, and slowly running a knife across the client's stomach, the trainee was, for the first time, caught up in this incident, was seeing the incident unfold in up-close detail, and quietly uttered: 'Oh God, this is scary . . . this is scary . . .' That was almost immediately followed by the client's suddenly bursting into tears, with shaking and trembling. The principle was framed as follows: when the client is describing an incident, and the therapist is so caught up in the incident that the therapist is having strong feeling, actually having and giving voice to this feeling can lead to the client's deeper and fuller involvement in the incident of strong feeling.

These were in-session changes that the trainee thought of as good ones, nice and pleasant ones, valued gifts. We can also study what he may have done to help bring about changes that he thinks of as bad ones, troubling and bothersome ones.

Once the trainee has a relatively clear picture of what she did that she believes helped to bring about the bothersome change, she can then concentrate on solutions. She can, for example, simply not do whatever it was that she now sees she did. She is also free to pursue bolder solutions and alternatives that do not set the stage for the unwelcome change, or that may even head in a better direction which she prefers.

She played a part of the tape that illustrated what bothered her so much. 'He does this all the time. Presents a problem, and I'm supposed to solve it. "Here's the problem. What should I do?" I hate that! He won't even talk about it. He won't go into any of the problems. I'm a fix-it doctor for him! When I try to bring this up and get him to see what he does, he just looks blank and then goes ahead and lays the problem on me!'

When we go back earlier in the session, we find instance after instance where the trainee virtually says: 'Just entrust yourself to me. Place yourself in my hands. I am all wise. I am the healer. I know everything.' Then, when the client does what the trainee invites him to do, she is so upset. The more we delved into the message conveyed by the trainee, the clearer it became that this is not the message the trainee wants to convey, nor the therapist role that the trainee wants to play. The way out, the solution, was searching for better therapist roles that the trainee would find excitingly fitting for herself in working with clients.

Another trainee played a part of the tape where the client was silent, and remained silent for nearly 2 minutes. 'That is what happens each session. She starts out talking, and then gets silent. I get so upset during those silences, and here, like always, I feel I am in a power fight with her. Those are awful times. I get so bothered, with her and with myself too!'

When we went back earlier in the session, what emerged was almost hilarious. Both the trainee and the others in the group were laughing. From the beginning of the session, the trainee and the client seemed to create and then engage in their own personal game. The client begins by starting a sentence and then pauses, as if groping for the right word. It is here that the therapist seizes the bait, jumps in, states the word the client was groping for, and goes on to complete the sentence. This game occurred throughout the beginning of the session, and it almost appeared that the client was baiting the therapist, the therapist accepted the bait, and the client then shut down, virtually saying: 'OK, you want to do all the talking? Go ahead.'

The trainee's giggling reaction was: 'I should just shut up and let her finish her sentence once in a while!' When we studied this game carefully, what seemed so important for the trainee was showing the client that the therapist understood, followed the client carefully, was truly listening. As we explored other ways to accomplish this, the trainee settled on a few that not only did the job but also avoided the game culminating in the client's silent withdrawal. The problem was resolved.

This other trainee was very agitated, quite scared as she blurted out that she was terrified that the client was going to kill himself. The moment of peak terror was in the third session when the client said: 'Next time? I don't think there'll be a next time . . . I finally made a decision for myself . . . Frank showed me the way.' Frank was the client's partner. Frank had died of AIDS about a month earlier.

When we went back to what seemed to culminate in these words by the client, it seemed relatively clear that the trainee was frightened about the possibility of suicide throughout the session. The trainee mentioned that behind everything she said was a private, hidden terror of the client killing himself, and the actual words she said managed both to hide and to convey hints of her terror, although all of this was covert, indirect, spoken in code. Just before the client mentioned 'next time', the trainee had said, in a conspicuously non-reassuring manner, 'That is good. I mean that you can talk about it. Maybe it will feel better by next time, next week . . .'

The trainee continued telling how terrified she was, from the beginning of the session, that the client was thinking about suicide, and she was puzzled and confused that she danced around this continuing fear, that she avoided saying anything about her fear, and that she virtually steered the client toward being the one to come close to spelling out the possibility of suicide.

What might be a careful statement of the problem that caused the problem? The trainee's version was as follows: 'What do I do when I have a private, hidden, near terror that the client, without saying it directly, is right now ready to kill himself, has decided to kill himself, is bringing up the real likelihood of suicide?' This question was the central focus of the training session. In going over several ways of answering this question, in probing into the trainee's own inner thoughts and ideas about this question and answers rooted in her own discovered framework, she arrived at an answer that seemed fitting, she read further about the answer that came from herself, and, in the next session, she put this answer into play. What had she arrived at? In probing deeper, she found principles of flagging, suddenly occurring feelings of fear and panic, of awful things about to happen. She found and practiced saying something like this: 'Wait a minute! Something's happening in me. I am scared, and I think it started . . . when . . . when you said "I don't think there'll be a next time . . . I finally made a decision for myself . . ." That scared me. That really scared me . . .'

What happened in the next sessions with her client? This serious issue no longer occurred with the client, or with any of the trainee's clients. She identified the actual things she did to help create the problem, and was able to find a solution by discovering more about her own deeper framework for psychotherapy.

Discover how to use the impressive in-session change once it occurs

Once you see the impressive in-session change, you have an opportunity to look carefully at whether or not the therapist seemed to use that in-session change or did not especially seem to use it in some way. You can see if the therapist seemed to use it in some helpful way, in some way that seemed familiar or rather surprising to you. You can study what the therapist actually did, and figure out some way that you believe might have been somewhat better or even much better. In any case, you can study what the therapist actually did, or could have done or perhaps should have done, following the impressive change.

Typically, you are studying the trainee's tapes to answer these questions. However, it is helpful, to answer these questions, to study tapes of other trainees and the teacher's tapes. In addition, it seems especially useful to answer these questions, to study tapes of gifted therapists, seasoned and experienced master therapists.

Studying what happens, or might have happened, or could or should have happened, can yield principles for what the trainee can do once the impressive change happens.

And there is more. Studying what the therapist did, or could or should have done, both comes from and sheds more light on the trainee's own deeper framework. Accordingly, you can frame principles about the trainee's deeper framework for psychotherapy.

Some examples

Throughout the session, the patient seemed rather mechanical, almost numb, dead, unfeeling. The impressive change was when the patient was clearly alive, filled with delightful feeling, spontaneous, happy, vibrant. This lasted about 5–10 seconds. However, it seemed that the trainee did not use this impressive change at all. As we tried to explore what the trainee might have done, what was especially appealing, we explored more and more of her deeper framework and emerged with the following principle: the therapy session is like a laboratory for finding and trying out whole new ways that the person might be in the post-session real world. What was somewhat surprising was that the trainee thought of a session in this way, or at least that this was a part of her own implicit deeper framework.

We also arrived at a working principle for how the trainee might use some impressive changes: when there is an impressive in-session change, the therapist can use it to see how that impressive change can be extended out into the patient's post-session world. She was both excited and surprised by this new way of using the in-session impressive change.

How might she have used the in-session impressive change? As she explained: 'This fellow was actually alive, spontaneous, happy, and he showed it here! He's never like that in his real world. Well, he could be. I think he should be. At least I can point this out to him. Leave the decision up to him. That's what I can do next time.'

With another trainee, there was an apparently wholesale shift in whom and what the client was. Up until the change, the person seemed to be a scared and anxious victim of the wishes and wants of others, the object of others' whims, the helpless subject of powerful and scary forces in other people. Then, for about a minute, the change seemed almost like an astounding transformation into a qualitatively new and different person who was somewhat removed, sound, intact, on top of things, and chuckling at the ridiculousness of life, of life situations and situations.

When we studied what the trainee seemed to do once this unusual shift occurred, what was so surprising and useful was that she talked to the radically new person as if this person was actually this person, was present, had actually replaced the ordinary former person. The trainee simply shifted from talking to the former person to talking to the altogether new person, and the consequence was that the transformed new person remained present, intact, and talking with her. The trainee was bowled over with what she had done, had no recollection of having switched to accepting and talking with the whole new person.

When we tried to spell out the working principle the trainee seemed to have followed, we arrived at this formulation: when the client undergoes a significant change, the therapist has a choice of talking to the 'new person' or to the 'old person'; talking to the emerged 'new person' is better. The trainee was pleased with, and somewhat surprised by, this working principle.

However, what was perhaps much more fascinating was tracking the inner deeper implications of what this might mean for grasping the trainee's inner deeper framework. We started by arriving at this formulation: the therapist's way of seeing the client is a powerful determinant of the limited and restricted or expanded and essentially unlimited degree of potential change in the client. This formulation captured something of her inner deeper notions. Even more importantly, this principle seemed to have powerful implications both for what the therapist can actually do in the session, and especially for her power in opening up or limiting the degree of potential change in the client. Here was an exciting core principle in her inner deeper framework, one with much further implications that might be spelled out. The trainee had discovered an exciting core principle.

Another example is of a client who is quietly pleased at how different he is in some rather subtle ways. He tells about how he was joking and friendly with his dentist and the technician, how this seemed so new and pleasing. The trainee regarded this as a valued in-session few minutes, but, when we took a careful look at what she did when this was occurring and after, she was disappointed. 'Listen, right here . . . and here . . . I just muttered "good" and "that's nice", and dropped it. I remember thinking whether this had anything to do with his problem of feeling rejected in the family, of feeling scapegoated and left out, and deciding it didn't, so I decided to just let it go. I think I made a mistake. I think. When I listened to the session, this was the best part!'

When we probed into her deeper framework, the trainee gradually moved toward a rather amorphous notion: 'I was taught that psychotherapy dealt with problems, you know, pathology, morbid things . . . But I think I always kind of believed. Well, I don't know.' Probing even further led to this formulation: psychotherapy is the business of changes, changes in what is bad, bothersome, problems, and changes in what can be happy, more fun, more enjoyable. This inner deeper principle seemed familiar to what she may have always believed, and at the same time rather new and surprising to her.

When we moved toward trying to clarify a working principle that seemed fitting and exciting, we emerged with this: when the client seems pleased with even subtle little changes in himself or in relationships, even if these changes seem unrelated to his 'problem', the therapist can use this (1) to explore the deeper meaning of this pleasant change and (2) to carry forward, extend, and expand the pleasant changes.

Arrival at your way of doing psychotherapy

You started by picking out some places, on the tape, that you liked, were pleased by, or that you disliked, were bothered by. Then you arrived at simple descriptions of the parts you picked out. This allows you to come up with your own personal list of impressive in-session changes. It also allows you (1) to discover or to come up with your own sequences of impressive in-session changes, (2) to discover what you and the person did to help bring it about, whether the change was impressive or bothersome, and (3) to discover how to use the impressive change once it occurs.

In effect, you are finding a way of doing therapy that comes from you and that fits you. It may be that you are essentially doing social learning therapy or implosive therapy or Jungian analysis. Or it may be that you are perhaps doing your own creative version of some therapy or other. Whatever it is, you are gradually assembling a way of doing psychotherapy that is true to you, whether it is what you expected or somewhat of a surprise, whether it remains your way for a while or is replaced by some other way as you discover more and more of your deeper framework for psychotherapy.

Chapter 8

Method 2: how and why is this part so pleasing, displeasing, or inexplicable?

In going over the tape of the session, the trainee has identified parts that are (1) pleasing, satisfying, exciting, pleasurable, (2) displeasing, bothersome, troublesome, or (3) compellingly inexplicable. The question is: 'How and why is this part so pleasing to you, or so displeasing to you, or so compellingly inexplicable to you?'

Arriving at an answer that is genuinely useful depends on the trainee's genuine honesty. The question can be hard to answer honestly. It is a sensitive and touchy question, in large part because the answer can easily involve some sensitive and touchy issues for the trainee. It is easy to give professionally correct and professionally acceptable answers. It can be hard to arrive at an answer that sparkles with honesty.

Arriving at an answer that is genuinely useful depends on the teacher's precious ability to provide an atmosphere that welcomes honesty. Furthermore, it can take some work, both on the part of the trainee and on the part of the teacher, to arrive at an honest answer. It takes an ability, on both their parts, to probe into the trainee's inner deeper ways of thinking, and to arrive at an answer that is accompanied with the right feelings of 'this is it; this is the in-depth and honest answer'.

Once the teacher and the trainee arrive at an answer to how and why this part is so pleasing or displeasing or compellingly inexplicable, there are at least three ways to use the answer. One way is to identify the highly personal in-session feelings that can be so important for the trainee, and to go from there to the kind of 'therapist role' that can enable the trainee to have those important personal feelings. A second way is to go directly from the trainee's identified answer to trying to discover more about the trainee's underlying deeper framework.

A third way is to use the answer to get at the trainee's personal impulses and taboo wishes, what the trainee would have loved to have done but should not and would not have done, and use that (1) to discover more about the trainee's deeper framework, and (2) to help figure out how to use that 'impulse' in actual in-session work.

Starting with how and why this selected part is so pleasing, displeasing, or inexplicable, the present chapter discusses these three ways in turn.

Use the question and the trainee's answer to discover his or her precious personal feelings and his or her valued therapist role

The question is to help identify the actual, honest, personal feeling that made this part so pleasing or displeasing. The aim is not to get at the trainee's conceptual system, way of thinking, theorizing. Nor is the aim to give the trainee a chance to give some sort of professionally correct, right, or acceptable answer.

Accordingly, the question may be worded somewhat along the following lines: 'You picked out this part. You may have picked out this part because you had some kind of good feeling. You were pleased, satisfied, happy. You may even have felt just great. Or you picked out this part because you felt bad, rotten, bothered, upset. Why did you pick out this part? What kinds of really personal feelings did you have, or do you have, when you picked out this part or when you listen to this part? Try to be incredibly honest. Find the personal feeling that is as honest as you can be. Forget about "theoretical" answers. Forget about answers that are professionally proper, correct, right. Is this all right? Are you ready to try to find the very personal feeling that made this part a wonderful one or an awful one? Yes? All right, what do you honestly think is the feeling?'

Once you can find the precious personal feelings, you can make a good guess about the therapist 'role' that can be important and valued for the trainee. The precious personal feelings are the juice, the fuel, that make the therapist role so valuable. Looked at the other way, the role is important and valuable largely because it enables the trainee to have, undergo, and enjoy these precious personal feelings.

Start from the trainee's wonderful feelings

Do your best to set aside muted feeling descriptions that reek with professional correctness. These are not especially wrong or right. They are mainly useless to arrive at the valued therapist role. Here are some examples of professionally correct answers that are both virtually feelingless and not useful:

> 'I believe there is a loosening of rigid cognitive structures. That is a good sign.'
>
> 'In this part I was satisfied with the development of a good alliance.'
>
> 'I was pleased that she was showing a better outlook on herself, more self-acceptance.'
>
> 'I liked that he is starting to work at therapy. He's starting to bring up material that is relevant.'
>
> 'Right here, she is beginning to accept my interpretations. That felt good.'

Do your best to accept these professionally correct 'feelings', and to set them aside. Now look for the real feelings that are so delicious, so preciously personal, so unprofessional. Right here, in this part, what is your truly preciously wonderful feeling that made this part so wonderful? Here are some answers:

> 'She took what I said so seriously, like gospel! What I said was important like I speak the truth, and she takes what I say seriously!'
>
> 'He looked at me and he is so attractive! I felt aroused. It was safe sex, and he is gorgeous. If I met him in a bar, he'd never look at me, but here, now, I'm as intimate with him as I can be without touching him. I am aroused. That's it!'
>
> 'She's telling me a secret that she's told no one. She trusts me. I'm her closest confidante. I feel so special. She really confides in me, and I am trustworthy.'
>
> 'I've got a great sense of humor. I'm funny. That guy's laughing, and he was thinking of killing himself! I get him to laugh. Hell, I crack him up, and he loves it. Listen to him here!'
>
> 'I hate to admit it, but I felt, right there, I felt superior, like I'm in better shape, and like I'm the doctor. See, he's the vice-president of this huge bank, and he's older than me, and I see his picture in the newspaper, and here he is scared and crying cause he's afraid he's gay, and he is like a little boy. I'm the doctor. I'm superior to him. That's what I feel and it sure feels great.'

Once you find the precious personal feeling, try to identify the 'therapist role' that is so important for the trainee, the role that allows for whatever precious personal feelings that are so important for the trainee to have. Start from the precious personal feeling and try to figure out the 'therapist role' that can give the trainee such precious personal feelings.

Most trainees are reluctant to accept the importance of such therapist roles. One reason for this reluctance is that it is then only a short step to thinking of psychotherapy as mainly a way for therapists to fulfill their own personal therapist roles in order to enable them to have their own precious personal feelings. That is not the way they like to think of psychotherapy. The related other reason is that most trainees much prefer to think of their professional role as the doctor, the helper, the one who provides psychotherapeutic treatment. The very idea of 'therapist roles' and 'precious personal feelings' is seen as cheapening the hallowed enterprise of professional psychotherapy.

Work with the trainee in arriving at his or her own 'therapist role'. Allow for the possibility that there may be a few favored 'therapist roles' for him or her. Leave open the possibility that he or she may accept or decline the therapist role, may modify and refine it, may move toward replacing current ones with future ones that have better fit with the trainee in 6 months or a few years or so.

Here are examples of some therapist roles (Mahrer, 1996/2004, 2001, 2002):

> 'I am the expert. What I say is important, true, correct. Patients look up to me as the knowledgeable one. They respect what I say because I know. I can testify in court. I have expert knowledge.'

> 'I can be so intimate with my patients. I can be closer and more intimate than anyone in their life. I never really was able to be really close with men, and very few women. But I can be more than my patients' best friend. I can give them an intimacy and a closeness they never had before. They can tell me anything, their deep secrets, their deepest fears, the special memories that they told no one. They can confide in me cause I give them intimacy and closeness.'

> 'I rescue my patients from becoming seriously pathological, from falling apart, from becoming crazy, from the horrible pit of agonizing feelings, from killing themselves. I am the grand savior. I keep them sane, whole, alive. If they are almost dead, crazy, enveloped by agony and psychopathology, I can bring them back. I am the magical one who can save them, their final hope.'

> 'I provide pure caring, concern, nurturing, understanding, empathy. No one knows you the way I do. No one understand you like I do. I know

everything about you. You have never known anyone like me in your life. I know exactly what you feel and exactly how you feel it. I understand more about you that you can understand.'

'I am the professional scientist who knows the professional science. I am the expert in the latest and best methods. I keep abreast of the science of psychotherapy, and I know and use the latest and most scientific methods. I know the scientific diagnosis, and I apply the latest and most scientific methods for treating that diagnosed problem or condition.'

'I am the model of an optimal person, the exemplification of a person who is mature, well-adjusted, psychologically sound. I can be your hero, your model, your exemplar, the kind of person you can become.'

'I am the wise older person, the elder. I know the world and its truths. I am the experienced one. I can tell you parables about life. I am the font of wisdom and knowledge. I know the way people are. I know how the world works. I speak the truth.'

'I am the God who can transform you, who can achieve miraculous changes in you. I can make you whole. I can resurrect you, I can inspire you, give you magical faith and hope. I am the grand healer.'

'I am the one who can see what is truly good and fine in you. I see far beyond all your human weaknesses and faults and flaws. I can see your essential goodness, the special qualities inside you, the precious soul that you truly are, everything that is to be cherished and loved inside you.'

'I am the one you are so attracted to. I am so appealing, attractive, personable, stimulating, arousing, seductive, and I love that you look forward to spending time with me in our sessions. This is truly safe sex. Even though I am so lovely, handsome, good-looking, I am also smart, knowledgeable, a doctor, and this combination feels so good.'

'I am the one who is on your side. I am your ally, your defender. I can appreciate and understand your side of things. Because I am a doctor, I have the power to defend you, do things on your behalf, prevent them from hurting you.'

'I am your rock, your ground, your solid anchor to reality. I am your solid base. When things are chaotic, I am the one you can count on. When you lose touch with what is real, I am the voice of reality. When you are fragmented and crumbling, I am your solid rock you can depend on and cling to.'

The search is not for some therapist role that the trainee might want to play or approves of. Rather, the search is for the therapist role that comes from an appreciative search from the good feelings that the trainee had in this part of the session, the therapist role that seems to allow for and provide for these kinds of good feelings.

Once the therapist role is discovered and described, of course the trainee is entitled to like or dislike it, and to regard a therapist role as either a central and important determinant or a secondary and relatively unimportant factor in the trainee's psychotherapy. Discovering the trainee's therapist role can be valuable especially if he or she welcomes the role and sees the therapist role as a centrally important factor in his or her deeper framework.

Start from the trainee's bad feelings

The guideline is to start from the trainee's honest bad feelings, the feelings that are bothersome, painful, uncomfortable, hurtful. Given that the trainee has these bad feelings, it is possible to do a superficial quick-fix by seeing the flip side of the trainee's bad feelings, and thereby to arrive at a cosmetic therapist role, e.g. if the bad feelings are a mixture of hurt and pain, inadequacy and irritation that the patient is making noises about leaving therapy, discontinuing treatment, not coming back, the quick solution can be a therapist role of being 'easy' with termination noises, being able to rise above and handle premature terminations, being self-confident, and well integrated.

Arriving at such a role can be cheap, quick, and easy. The therapist role is a sensible superficial solution to the problem of the trainee's bad feelings. However, the guideline can also be used to go deeper into the trainee's inner framework, to probe and explore whatever therapist role may underlie the bad feelings, may be discovered by going deeper into the trainee's bad feelings, may have been blocked by the situation of the bad feelings, e.g. with the above trainee, deeper exploration down into the painful feelings discovered a somewhat surprising central therapist role of the sensitive receiver of whatever the patient is saying and feeling, the carefully and competently understanding one, the one who knows whatever is occurring right now in the patient, the one who can clarify and carry forward whatever is occurring in the patient, and who is able to shift with the patient to whatever feeling is next, whatever it may be.

'Right here she is so hurting, and she is pleading for me to offer an answer, and I don't have an answer. I'm as stuck as she is! . . . I don't know what to say. She is asking for an answer. She deserves an answer. I don't know what to do . . . I feel awful right here.' The trainee went beyond wishing she could be an answer machine, could be a brilliantly creative resource of problem solutions. Probing and exploration slowly led to the discovery of a therapist role that was found by following the thread that started with the bad feelings. The valued therapist role was that of being exceedingly open and honest about her immediate feelings, whatever they may be, being a kind of exemplar of knowing and showing her own immediate feelings, even of being mixed up and confused, or being helplessly unable to meet her own expectations.

'I don't like what he's doing. He wants me to be his buddy, his good friend, and . . . he keeps asking me personal things, like here. I don't want to be his buddy. I don't even think I especially like him. I know he likes me, but . . . I don't know, this seems wrong, or something . . .' When we started from here and dug down deeper, we emerged with a clearer picture of the trainee's much preferred and valued therapist role as the problem fixer. Find the problem. Here's a solution. Three to six sessions or fewer. Problem. Solution. I am the consultant who fixes things right away.

Start with the part on the tape that is so pleasing or displeasing. Use that part to identify the trainee's feelings that are pleasing and wonderful or displeasing and bad, bothersome. The payoff is being able to identify the trainee's own, preciously personal feelings, and to go further by probing and exploring to discover the trainee's own valued therapist role that comes from and fits the trainee, and also that can provide those precious personal feelings. That is the payoff, the gift.

What can you do to have more and more opportunities to fulfill your valued therapist role and to undergo your precious personal feelings?

You can have a genuine choice. Here is one choice: it is bad to use therapy to fulfill these kinds of valued therapist roles and to undergo your own precious personal feelings. It is immoral, a violation of ethical codes, demeaning to the noble profession of psychotherapy. It is to be kept to a minimum. Instead, your role is to be the professional, the one who provides help to the anguished, the suffering, the unwell, the one who applies your competence and skills to your patients' mental illnesses and personal problems.

If this is your genuine choice, stop right here. Using your valued therapist role and precious personal feelings would probably be the wrong way to go. It would be conflicting, unsuitable, unpleasant, perhaps even immoral and wrong.

Here is a trainee who is liked by his colleagues because he has a light and playful sense of humor. He is so open, so revealing, so unguarded, and he is so able to see the lighthearted, playful, absurd, silly side of things. This is also how he is with his clients. When he plays his tapes, fellow trainees grin, admire the way he is, and respect the changes in his clients. However, he is bothered: 'But that's called the relationship, and that's all I know how to do! I'd be the same way if we were at a bar! That's not therapy. That's David being David! I don't know how to do therapy!'

He could have accepted and cultivated this particular therapist role, but he did not. He graduated, moved far away, and when he returned for a visit, he proudly displayed brochures and newspaper clippings and photographs of his clinic. He became an expert with biofeedback, wears a white coat, is a scientist–practitioner, has three rooms of scientific equipment. David, the trainee, had indeed found a way to set aside his therapist role, to hide that therapist role. A public relations video shows that he is the true scientist, doing scientific interventions. Nowhere on the video was there a fellow who is so open, revealing, unguarded, and who can see and enjoy the playfully absurd side of things. 'David, how do you like doing this treatment?' 'Well, it's a living. Actually, it's kind of boring, but it's a living. The old days in school were more fun. But that's life. You grow up.' 'It's a living.' 'Yeah.'

An alternative choice is to hold a position along the following lines: if this particular therapist role is indeed important to you, if these personal feelings are indeed precious for you, it makes solid and abiding sense to take steps toward maximizing this valued therapist role and precious personal feelings for maximal benefit to both you and the person with whom you are working. The following are some ways of doing this.

Choose a therapeutic approach that enables you to fulfill your valued therapist role and to undergo your important personal feelings

There are many different therapeutic approaches, including the one the trainee probably has selected and followed. The guideline is for the trainee to look for, to read about, and to try out whatever therapeutic approach seems to have a high probability of enabling the trainee to fulfill the valued therapist role and to undergo the trainee's important personal feelings.

Some therapeutic approaches can do the job. Some cannot. Some can do the job better than others. It can be up to the teacher to suggest some suitable and fitting approaches. It can be up to the trainee to become familiar with the approach that holds some real promise of fulfilling the trainee's valued therapist role and enabling the trainee to undergo the important personal feelings.

Start with the description of the valued therapist role and the important personal feelings. Then use this description to point toward a fitting therapeutic approach. Whatever therapeutic approach the trainee follows is tossed into the pot as the teacher and trainee use the valued therapeutic role and important personal feelings as the main tracking guide for the right and proper therapeutic approach.

For one trainee, the valued therapist role and important personal feelings involved being doctor fix-it, here is a problem and here is a solution, taking care of the matter right away, providing an all-purpose service, able to draw from any and all methods, able to handle any problem. This was the role the trainee loved, and these were the important personal feelings. The trainee's current cognitive–behavioral approach was friendly but not custom fitted, adequate but too restrictive. This trainee found a genuine eclectic approach to provide high goodness of fit with the valued therapist role and important personal feelings.

She was a trainee who was knowledgeable about constructivist psychology, helped teach courses in that approach, and was dedicated to that approach until she herself gradually found that her valued therapist role and important personal feelings did not really fit. These emerged as her being removed, watchful, knowing the patient's deeper world, being the source of wisdom, being looked up to as God like, being the guide through the mysterious intrapsychic world. She found her calling as a classic psychoanalytic therapist.

This trainee was almost naturally and effortlessly able to be most clients' best friend. Clients seemed to blossom and feel so much better when they were bathed in the trainee's genuine interest and charming friendliness. The singularly valued therapist role and important personal feelings included being truly interested in almost everything about the patient, genuinely liking the patient, being an unusually good person who felt close and loving with the patient, being the one the patient eagerly confided in. He was their best buddy. Most patients truly liked him, felt much better because of his true friendship, and lived happier lives as a result of knowing and being with him. This valued therapist role and important personal feelings were respected and acknowledged as the critical centerpiece of his way of thinking about and doing psychotherapy, i.e. whatever therapeutic approach he called upon was to fit itself to, adapt to, enhance this trainee's uniquely helpful therapist role and important personal feelings.

What can you do to have more and more opportunities to fulfill your valued therapist role and undergo your important personal feelings? One way is to choose a therapeutic approach that fits, that does the job. There are some further ways.

Work with clients who provide high 'goodness of fit' with your valued therapist role and important personal feelings

If being with this client means that you can enjoy fulfilling your valued therapist role and undergoing your important personal feelings, this client is for you. If you have little or no likelihood of fulfilling your valued therapist role and undergoing your important personal feelings, this client is not especially for you. In this sense, 'goodness of fit' is an important criterion of which clients to work with and which not to work with.

In the initial sessions, and perhaps later on, you can see if there is a high enough goodness of fit, i.e. you can determine, evaluate, assess the degree to which you can fulfill your valued therapist role and undergo your important personal feelings. Arriving at an answer can be an important part of assessment and evaluation, and having a reasonably clear picture of your valued therapist role and important personal feelings can help you do a good job of evaluating whether or not to work with this client. These initial sessions offer you good opportunities for trying out how the two of you work together, i.e. whether you can fulfill your valued therapist role and undergo your important personal feelings. The two of you can then continue or discontinue being with one another.

Her valued therapist role is laced with a strong component of social activism. In her therapist role, the important personal feelings flower when her client joins the cause, is ready to take action, is empowered by the trainee's spelling out of the principles of the cause, becomes a part of the sisterhood, voices the dictums of the movement. This trainee does not have much of a chance to fulfill this valued therapist role and to undergo these important personal feelings with the client who is the sullen older man in trouble with the law. She has much higher goodness of fit with the lost young woman who was such an angry loner.

He valued the therapist role of the special one who has the magical quality of being able to reach the unreachable, to make the precious contact with the withdrawn soul. The important personal feelings included the ecstasy of that first opening, the possibility of the connection, the meeting of the two people reaching out to each other, the initial touch that meant so much. He was deprived of this valued therapist role and important personal feelings with the talkative young university student who was so proud of manipulating her professors. On the other hand, the trainee was right at home with the silent woman who came so close to slicing her wrist and dying, and who was so out of reach of the staff of the psychiatric ward.

She was meant to fulfill the role of the Rock of Gibraltar, the solid anchor to reality, the one who was always here, the essence of stability and groundedness. With this client she had plenty of moments of important personal feelings when the client breathed a sigh of relief at the therapist's common-sense suggestions, when the client whispered how much he counted on the therapist just being here, when the therapist saw the look of trust in the client's eyes. On the other hand, the trainee was unable to fulfill this valued therapist role and to undergo her important personal feelings with the handsome young client who radiated seductiveness and male charm.

Work in a setting that provides high 'goodness of fit' with your valued therapist role and important personal feelings

Most trainees have a solid idea or two about where they want to work when they graduate. Whether their choices are rather general or rather specific, they can often say that they want to work in a neuropsychological clinic, a couples treatment center, the prison system, a women's center, a psychiatric hospital, the school system, a crisis center, pain management clinic, group practice setting, independent practice setting for adults, sexual abuse center, a divorce mediation program, trauma treatment center, geriatric center, eating disorders clinic, children's treatment center.

Perhaps the main reason for choosing a setting is that the trainee simply likes working with those kinds of clients. There is something appealing about working with those clients in the job setting, and that is that.

The discovery-oriented approach invites the trainee to play a game. Quite independent of whatever setting the trainee may be headed toward, and whatever reasons justify the choice, the game is to see what happens when the trainee allows the valued therapist role and the important personal feelings to point toward a setting with high 'goodness of fit'. It is only a game, whether the game ends up confirming the trainee's own selection or perhaps points in a surprisingly new direction.

For Douglas, the valued therapist role was being the expert, having power and clout, having expert knowledge that affected the lives of his clients. The important personal feelings occurred when he gave his expert opinions to people in the legal system, either in the form of reports or in court testimony as an expert witness. He wanted to work in a forensic diagnostic and treatment center, and the 'game' confirmed the choice he had already made.

Not so with Patricia. She too was headed toward a job in a forensic diagnostic and treatment center, and this was in line with her chosen specialty. However, her valued therapist role and important personal feelings seemed to involve offering genuine concern, caring, being a friend to the friendless, and when she allowed these to sketch out fitting settings, she became quite excited about two job settings. One was an Asian Center on the west coast, catering to recent immigrants from Asian countries where her own family was from. Patricia knew that many of these people felt relatively lost and alone, adrift and without someone from the new country to have as a trusted friend. The other setting was a walk-in center in town, where so many of the people were loners, without family or friends, drifting. Of course the actual choice was Patricia's, but the game at least offered an alternative possibility or two, and an alternative way of making the actual choice of where to work.

Karen was completing her residency in preparation for accepting a position as chief psychiatrist in two hospital clinics, one dealing with infertility and the other with sexually abused women. Drawn as she was to these positions, something happened when she discovered a valued therapist role and important personal feelings of going deep down into the bedrock of the agony, cauterizing the core of the suffering, joining with the patient in penetrating the very heart of the suffering.

As this kind of valued therapist role and important personal feelings seemed to become increasingly certain and increasingly clear, Karen found herself considering adding a part-time position in the same hospital's psychiatric program, and specializing in patients who were in deep-seated agony, wholly in the grip of serious psychopathology. For Karen, such a setting was soulfully satisfying in enabling her to fulfill what seemed to be her valued therapist role and to undergo her important personal feelings.

You have used the trainee's answer to discover his or her own valued therapist role and important personal feelings, and you have then used these to enable him or her to find more and more opportunities to fulfill the valued therapist role and to undergo the important personal feelings. There is another way to use the trainee's answer.

Use the question and the trainee's answer to discover his or her deeper framework for psychotherapy

The trainee began by having selected and then playing a particular part of the session, and here is the original question with regard to that selected part: 'How and why is that part so pleasing to you, or so displeasing to you, or so compellingly inexplicable to you?'

Asking this question in the right way can allow the trainee to answer sincerely and honestly enough to allow the answer to be used to discover the trainee's inner deeper framework for psychotherapy. You truly want to know how and why this particular part is so pleasing, so precious, how and why the trainee feels so good about this part. You truly want to know how and why this part is so displeasing, bothersome, troublesome. You truly want to know how and why this part is so compellingly inexplicable, like a magnet drawing and pulling the trainee. Then you can use the answer to help discover the trainee's inner deeper framework.

The proper way of asking this question includes being quite clear about using the answer to discover the deeper framework. Asking the question properly means your question is essentially free of challenging the trainee, pushing him or her to come up with the 'right' answer, making him or her even slightly defensive. He or she should want to answer the question as genuinely and honestly as possible so that you both can use the answer in this way.

If the trainee is pleased with this part, use this to discover his or her deeper framework

Begin by trying to be reasonably clear about what was so pleasing, satisfying, about this particular part. Spell out the answer carefully and specifically.

Then try to frame a working principle, based on the answer. This is typically a working principle for how to do psychotherapy, and yet the working principle also dips down into uncovering something of the trainee's own deeper notions and ideas about psychotherapy.

Then try to see how the trainee's answer, including the working principle, can shed light on something of his or her deeper framework. Given the working principle, it is likely that there are hints, implications, indications for what kind of deeper personal framework would probably go with such a working principle.

All of this is a matter of discovery. It is also a matter of thinking, figuring out. And it is often a matter of delicate and gentle exploration, little by little, of trying out, checking with the trainee if the teacher and trainee are heading in the right direction.

She was quite pleased with this part. Why? How? The answer seemed to be there in these words: 'He's finally able to say what he really felt about his brother!' These words seemed to capture and to help specify what was so pleasant about this part.

Now the teacher and trainee could try to frame a working principle, and the version that seemed to put it well was as follows: 'It is important for the client to identify and to actually say out loud the client's serious, unexpressed, real feelings toward a significant other person.'

Now that the principle is put into words, make a little effort to uncover something more of the trainee's inner deeper framework. What does the working principle imply about his or her inner deeper notions? Some gentle probing led to the following:

· Clients have specific real feelings toward significant people in their lives.

· When these feelings are not expressed, shown, directly carried out, clients will probably have pain and unhappiness.

· When these feelings are clearly identified and adequately expressed, shown, voiced, directly carried out, clients will feel much better, with less pain and unhappiness.

The trainee was pleased, and a little surprised: 'I think I've always thought that way . . . but not about therapy! I do believe that's true.'

She was pleased and somewhat surprised by how central and 'right' these deeper notions seemed to be.

The client is talking about how grateful he is for the way his grandfather used to be sincerely interested in the client's sketches and drawings when he was an adolescent. Then the client has an idea. He is going to do something he has never done. He is going to go to his grandfather's apartment, bring two of his grandfather's favorite cigars, and tell him how grateful he is for what the grandfather did. 'I'm going to do it tonight! Yeah! He'll be so surprised! I've never done anything like that!' These words are the highlight of the trainee's session.

We framed the highlight as follows: it is wonderful when the client spontaneously comes up with a happy new behavior, and is eager to carry it out right away, in the client's post-session world.

What light may this shed on the trainee's own deeper framework? Some exploration uncovered these two hints:

1. New behaviors can come about when the person is pleasantly excited about carrying out new behaviors that are pleasantly exciting.

2. There is something more than the therapist trying to get the client to behave in new ways. There is a pocket of exciting readiness for actually doing pleasantly exciting new behaviors.

The trainee could not say if these ideas were or were not a part of his avowed way of thinking about human beings, clients, and psychotherapy. In any case, there was something 'right' about uncovering these deeper notions and ideas.

With another trainee, the pleasing part of the session is when the client is telling a story about having lunch with a friend, and suddenly he is upset and bothered. None of the other trainees found this part exciting, yet she did: 'He hated being dispatched, overlooked, dispensed with, right here! It was great!'

All right, how and why was this part so great? She had a ready answer: 'We found a "sensitive spot".' And how is finding a 'sensitive spot' so valuable? She paused and wrote a few notes. Then she explained slowly: 'A person's "sensitive spots" are like windows into their insides. If we can follow these leads we can find out what the person's insides are like. We won't know what the insides are till we explore, and this is fascinating.'

Then she laughed. 'I was going to say windows into the soul, but that's not what cognitive therapy talks about. I do cognitive therapy. I don't know if this is cognitive therapy, but I think I sure believe in this. Is this cognitive therapy?'

For this trainee, the highlight was when the client finally stopped droning on and on about his buddies on the fishing trip, and was able to talk about his own thoughts, especially about his being so over-weight. Talking about others is resistance. Talking about oneself is helpful to be able to do something about the problem. The trainee explained that there was a 'self', and the best way to achieve change was for the client to talk about one's 'self'. You can learn a great deal by studying how the client talks about his 'self'.

As the trainee was explaining why talking about one's self is more valuable than talking about buddies on a fishing trip, the trainee paused. He had come across a new idea: 'Wait a minute! You can get a good idea of the person, how the person thinks, and talking about one's self is not all there is . . . If the person talks about anything seri-ous, that can show his thoughts, how he thinks. Yes! It doesn't have to be about his self. No way!' In the trainee's own framework, the way the client thinks is crucial, but getting at the way the person thinks is not limited to studying the way the person talks about his self. Access to the way the person thinks can come from the client's talking about other topics, as long as they are serious ones.

At this point, the trainee was excited about two issues. One had to do with how big a change this deeper principle can now make for what the trainee tries to get the client to talk about. The other had to do with an issue relating to the trainee's own deeper framework: what determines the degree to which the client's own personal thoughts are revealed, manifested, and shown? Are there some topics that are more important than others, in opening up the person's thoughts? Is it more than just the topics the person talks about? The trainee was almost entranced with trying to find answers to these questions, and both the questions and the answers were important in digging down into and discovering more about the trainee's deeper framework for psy-chotherapy.

This trainee was so pleased with playing the part of the tape where her client simply said that she is ready to end the marriage. Truly, the client seemed almost peacefully radiant, sure of herself. 'I don't belong in this marriage. I'm ready to get on with my life.' The trainee was grinning from ear to ear. 'She was so depressed! Up till now. All she did was complain about her husband, and I was so worried about sui-cidal ideation. And she was withdrawn, so withdrawn. And bitter and angry. Such anger! But everything changed in this session, and here it is! It's like she became a new person somehow. She's so different!' What was so important here? Why was this change so valuable? The trainee carefully explained that she had always thought in terms of 'problems' and treating 'problems'. But here was something more than the problem being reduced. Yes, that was impressive, but what grabbed the trainee even more was that the client was right. Maybe she did not belong in this marriage. Maybe a person can back up, take a new course, and get on with a better life. The trainee was slowly working her way into her own deeper framework. She was tip-toeing her way into a new set of deeper ideas about life and living.

For this trainee, the most pleasing part of the tape was when he intentionally reformulated what the client was saying, and the client merely said 'Hmmm'. The trainee explained that he intentionally looked for the positive side of what the client was saying in a negative way. What might this reformulation tell us about the trainee's deeper framework? The answer is that the trainee seems to believe in the importance of having a range of options, of choices. One dimension of options is from negative to positive. It is better, the trainee believed, to be able to see things both negatively and positively, rather than only negatively, or even rather than only positively. And there are probably other dimensions too, but that was for later scrutiny. The trainee was probing deeper within his own inner framework.

If the trainee is bothered with this part, use it to discover his or her deeper framework

There are at least two ways that the bothersome, troubling parts can be used to help discover more about the deeper framework. One is to go directly from whatever seems to be so bothersome and troubling. Another is to identify what might be much more preferable, and use that to discover the deeper framework.

A group of trainees had individually listened to a tape of an exemplar doing an initial session. One trainee was almost incensed at the therapist reflecting back what the client was saying. Yes, the therapist was doing a fairly good job of reflection. No, the trainee did not believe that it would have been better for the exemplar to do a standard intake. So what was so bothersome? The trainee had trouble becoming clear about what was so bothersome until she was able to say that the therapist might have gently and sensitively told the client some things that the therapist might do in this session, such as trying to find out why the client was here, or explaining something about the practicalities of their working together, or letting the client talk about whatever the client wanted.

Good enough, but what can this tell us about the trainee's deeper notions about psychotherapy? We hit pay dirt when she arrived at notions that there are plenty of protective barriers between people, that clients and therapists especially can have layers of defenses protecting themselves, that there are moats and safeguards to be respected. In this first meeting, therapists should be exceedingly gentle and sensitive because clients are in a state of vulnerability, and their defenses are up, strong, and vigilant. This is why the therapist cannot just intrude like a pile-driver. It is better for the therapist to spell out options, possibilities for how this initial session can be handled.

None of the other trainees in the group had notions like this. They just listened to the trainee with the delicate and sensitive notions from her inner deeper framework.

When the next trainee played the selected part of the tape, he was so frustrated: 'This client just tells stories about everyone: her daughter, her sister, her friend, and here, she's worried about her husband taking so much responsibility at work. It's the third session! I have no idea what her problem is! Right here, right here, I was so furious I could feel myself starting to get a headache. I did everything I could not to yell at her!'

This trainee seemed to have explicit rules for how clients and therapists are to be. When we explored the trainee's rules for therapists, therapists are to be aware of negative feelings toward clients, but not to let clients know of these negative feelings. On the other hand, clients are to identify their problems, to tell what bothers them, and to talk about these problems in their sessions. The trainee had quite explicit rules for what clients are to do.

If the trainee has such explicit rules for how clients are to be, then how is the client to know what these rules are? Should therapists tell clients how they should be? Should clients gradually learn them over the course of a fair number of sessions? The trainee sputtered in almost sheer excitement: 'It's all right to talk with clients about what I want from them? I always wanted to do this in the first session, but I never was told anything about this. Hell yes, I'd love to. I've never done that. It makes good sense to me, especially when clients don't naturally do what I want them to do . . . I'm going to talk this over with her next time!' His deeper framework included an explicit role for clients to fulfill, and he added another working principle, namely that it was helpful to discuss this role with clients when it was appropriate and timely.

Another trainee had similar rules, but her rules were for therapists, not for clients. She was devastated during one part of the session. Her client was describing a recent talk with her aunt. The instant the trainee played is where the client is saying: 'And she was acting as if she understood me, but she didn't, like you do sometimes, and . . .' The trainee had stopped listening right here. She was frozen, in a state of panic, numb. The client had never been 'that way' before, and the trainee was genuinely devastated. She was very upset even as she played the excerpt. What was so awful about this excerpt was that she had fallen apart, she was indeed frozen, unable to cope, in a state of panic.

What does all this indicate about her deeper framework? It means that therapists do not react that way. Therapists are in better shape than that. Anyone who actually is so vulnerable, who can be so easily decompensated, crumbled, torn apart, frozen, in panic, does not deserve to be a therapist. She truly accepted this part of her own deeper framework. She believed these beliefs.

She was not at all interested in trying to figure out what she could have done with her momentarily falling apart, how she could handle this if it occurs again. Nor was she interested in finding alternatives to the deeper principles she had painfully discovered. She was instead impressed with how certain she was that her own deeper framework included this fixed idea about the stability and unflappability of the therapist. She really and truly believed in this newly discovered part of her own deeper framework.

Another trainee was similarly bothered by his sudden and disruptive feelings about his client. He had moments of being utterly disgusted with her. In this part of the tape, he was quiet, but he was seized with a pure loathing for her as she is telling about how she knows that her daughter's boyfriend is attracted to her. The trainee is still bothered as he says: 'She's fat, and she's self-centered, and she stinks! I don't think she takes showers! And all I know is that I'm disgusted with that woman. I don't like her!'

It would be easy to stop here, and to talk about how to use the trainee's disgust and loathing in 'therapeutic' ways. It would be easy to talk about the therapist's strong feelings toward a client or how and why the trainee might have been so affected by the client. It would be easy to see what the trainee's strong feelings might indicate about himself. On the other hand, we were heading toward seeing what we might learn about his own deeper framework, so the question was: 'How and why was this part so exceedingly bothersome?'

The trainee clarified what was so exceedingly bothersome: 'I stopped being a therapist! I just felt things about her . . . I wasn't being a therapist! I was just feeling . . . I hated her!' Once we have a clear idea of precisely what was so bothersome, we could try our best to see if this could shed any light on the trainee's deeper framework. 'That sounds like you have ideas of how a therapist should be. Yes?' This opened up a picture of part of the deeper framework as the trainee surprises himself by announcing: 'A therapist has to be in control of the relationship!'

We inspected this rule a little further, and the trainee arrives at this deeper set of ideas: 'It's all right to have feelings about the client, good or bad ones, but the therapist is always in charge, always knowing what feelings he's having, always in charge of using the feelings. The therapist has to be in control of the relationship.' He was somewhat surprised by the strength with which he believed what was a part of his deeper belief system, but there it was.

It is rather common to start from the trainee's bad feelings toward the client. However, in order to be able to discover the trainee's deeper framework, it is helpful to pin-point, to get a clear picture, of precisely what is so troubling about having such bad feelings toward the client, e.g. another trainee was chuckling as he played the part of the tape that was so bothersome to him. Yes he was having nasty feelings about his client, and, in this particular part, the client was reciting how his younger sister showed up in town and stayed with him. He felt nothing about using his younger sister, and he was cold and uncaring about his sister's being beaten up on the streets, and his being called by the nurse at the hospital. 'Right here, he's telling about the phone call . . . I hate this guy! I want everything bad to happen to him! I wished that he got beaten up on the streets!' The trainee was chortling as he mentioned how he knows he should not feel this way, and he recited the standard guidelines for both reducing and using his personal feelings about the client.

But his negative feeling was not what bothered the trainee most. He was mostly bothered that in the part he played from the tape, he thinks he heard a voice saying 'You bastard!' That voice is what bothered the trainee. The more we carefully explored what the trainee believed was so bothersome, so scary, the closer we came to something intriguing of the trainee's own deeper framework. The trainee raptly explains: every so often, under the right conditions, the client and the therapist come right up to a thought or idea, perhaps a 'voice'. This thought or voice has almost a 'presence', and it can be sensed by both the client and the therapist. It was probably this 'presence', this 'voice' that the trainee heard as 'You bastard.'

The trainee was excited about what he seemed to believe, strange and weird as it seemed to be. A voice or presence suddenly appearing under the right conditions? Either the therapist or client or both can sense its presence? 'This is weird stuff, but I think I have ideas like that, at least in this part of the session! It's weird. But I do believe there is something there!'

You can start from how and why this part of the session seems to be so special, so precious and valued, and you can use your answer to shed some light on the deeper framework. You can start with why this part seems to be so bothersome and troublesome, and follow your answer down into the deeper framework. You can also discover the deeper framework by starting with how and why this part seems so compellingly inexplicable, strange, unusual.

If this part is compellingly inexplicable, use this to discover the trainee's deeper framework

The trainee looked for and found a part of a session that was very pleasing or was very displeasing or was compellingly inexplicable. Each of these can be used to help discover the trainee's deeper framework.

Suppose that the trainee has flagged a part that is compellingly inexplicable, perhaps even bizarre and uncanny. Often it is something that the trainee is eager to tell a trusted colleague, but rarely to admit to many others. The strong inclination is to explain it away, or to tuck it under some category that makes it explicable, or to say something about its prevalence, or to share stories about other such compellingly inexplicable occurrences, or to understand a corner of it by turning to the nature of the therapist–client relationship or the client as some sort of cause. On the other hand, the compellingly inexplicable occurrence can be used to shed some light on the trainee's deeper framework.

The trainee played a small part of the taped session, and said: 'And right there I felt blood coming out of my nose! I felt it! But when I touched, there was nothing. It was weird! I felt blood coming from my nose. I know I did. It was wet. I knew there was blood. It just happened, right here!'

There was a slice of the trainee's being quite upset, bothered. He was nervous as he dismissed this as indicating that there was 'something wrong' with him, but he was bothered, and somewhat relieved and scared, that he was actually playing this part and talking about what had happened. In trying to probe down inside, we arrived at this principle, coming from the trainee's own uncovered deeper framework: some occurrences, 'symptoms', can be exceedingly weird, bizarre, uncanny, but not necessarily indicative of psychosis. This principle was one he truly accepted, and it was compelling because, as the trainee said: 'If someone had this symptom, I would think of psychosis, but not now. There is more to psychosis. I never thought about that!'

When this trainee played the selected part, she was fascinated with a pronounced dizziness when she closed her eyes momentarily, and how the dizziness quickly disappeared when she opened her eyes and looked directly at the client. A few seconds later she did it once again, and once again there was sharp and pronounced dizziness which immediately disappeared when, seconds later, she opened her eyes and looked at her client. 'I tried it twice, right here, and I was so dizzy I almost passed out! I kept my eyes closed for maybe a second, and I think I opened them cause I was scared! It was unbelievable, and never happened before, or since!'

When we listened to more, and tried to describe what happened in greater detail, she said: 'I closed my eyes for a second, and I had this sort of image of her lunging at me, like a mad woman, with fangs! I remember now, and it went away when I opened my eyes and looked at her. It was that image! I was terrified!'

As we tried to explore what all this might indicate about her own deeper framework, she came closer and closer to this principle: there are special times when the therapist–client eye-to-eye relationship can foreclose the therapist accessing and receiving deep-seated, immediate imagery. This principle was utterly new for the trainee, and she was so impressed with what she believed she had discovered about her own deeper framework.

'Well,' the trainee announced. 'This was strange. Just listen.' He played a part where the client is telling about being a loner as a little girl, and how special it was to sit on the front porch and play cards. She mentioned how she used to tap the cards to make them be the right cards. That was the part the trainee played. He had said nothing. But he explained: 'While she's talking, I was being a little kid, she was the girl next door, we were playing cards. It was real. But here's the weird part: it was déjà vu! I knew what she was going to say! I knew she was going to say that about the tapping! I really think that happened to me! This is really strange!'

What might this strange experience indicate about his own deeper framework? He was playing with ideas about how careful attentive listening can bring back early memories in the therapist, but then we moved over to another aspect. 'I had a strange relationship with her. Like I felt kind of removed, friendly, but not too involved. Then this happened . . . It was a funny kind of closeness, like we played together as kids.' The more we explored this, the more animated the trainee became, until he arrived at this principle: 'The relationship – it can be powerful, and work in mysterious ways!' That is about all he could say, but he was now convinced of the powerful and mysterious ways that the therapist–client relationship can work.

We start from the trainee having some sort of feeling with the selected part of the session as either delightful or bothersome or compellingly inexplicable. Then we do what we can to move from that feeling and that part of the tape to trying to discover the trainee's deeper framework. This can be fun, it can be useful, and it can have the nice payoff of discovering something about the trainee's deeper framework.

Once you have discovered the trainee's deeper framework, see if you can find even more of what is there in the deeper framework

The trainee began with a part of the tape that was quite pleasing, or quite displeasing, or quite hard to explain, inexplicable. This was used by the teacher and the trainee to try to get down into the trainee's deeper framework. Now that the teacher and trainee have discovered this inner world, they have a chance to go even further, to look around even more.

Once again, the emphasis is on what seems to come from the trainee's own inner framework, rather than from either the establishment voice of the trainee or the voice of whatever approach the trainee espouses on the surface. Making sure this is the discovery-oriented atmosphere is the job of the teacher.

In this work of going further inside the deeper framework, the teacher and the trainee can have the advantage of the specific part of the tape that the trainee picked out to study. This can be an advantage because it allows for a specific focus, an explicit phenomenon to study, rather than cutting loose and floating around in diffuse generalizations or the world of cloudy abstractions.

The trainee was so pleased that the client accepted and seemed to grasp the connection between the tension in his neck and how that tension effectively prevented him from carrying out the work in his new job. Starting from there, the trainee arrived at a deeper framework that seemed to include this idea: bodily aches and pains may go away if the person sees and grasps the connection between the bodily aches and pains and what they seem to help the person attain, achieve, ways that the bodily aches and pains seem to be useful.

The teacher probed a bit further into the trainee's deeper framework by inquiring if this principle would seem to apply, or did not seem to apply, to what might be called the client's 'bad feelings'. If the focus were the client feeling depressed or angry or frightened, would the principle about bodily aches and pains stretch to apply to such 'bad feelings'? The trainee paused, thought about this, and decided that the answer is no. What was left to figure out is how the principle might include bodily aches and pains but not 'bad feelings', and that was as far as the exploration went, for now at least.

Another trainee started with a part of the tape where the client attacked the trainee, seemed critical and tough on the trainee. What seemed to add to the pain in the trainee was that the client was ordinarily so passive, dependent, wimpy, lacking in assertiveness, toughness, hardness. With a little probing into the deeper framework, the trainee arrived at this deeper principle: when the therapist–client relationship heats up, what can show itself is a deeper part of the client that is the other side of what the client seems to be like on the surface.

Going even further into the trainee's deeper framework, it almost appeared that the deeper framework might include polarities, with one pole being on the surface and the other pole being deeper inside the client. The trainee was the one who gradually arrived at this idea, one quite new for her. Perhaps, she wondered, there were indeed grand polarities in clients. Here was one, with the surface pole being one of passivity, dependence, weakness, and the other pole, the inner deeper pole, being one of toughness, hardness, assertiveness. Maybe there are more polarities. What an interesting new idea! Yet this seemed to come from and reveal more about the trainee's own inner framework. That was enough for now.

This trainee started with a high point in the session when the client seemed so much better as the trainee assumed the role of a parental figure who was solid, stable, reliable, trustworthy, always there. Using that to uncover the trainee's deeper framework bypassed the idea of the usual components of a good working relationship. Instead, the trainee discovered a meaningful principle that the relationship can be helpful when the therapist fulfills whatever role is especially important for the client at the time. Can we go further into the trainee's deeper framework? With increasing probing and increasing excitement at digging deeper, the trainee arrived at this principle: personality is laid down in the kinds of roles the parents played in the patient's infancy and early childhood; the job of the therapist is to fulfill the parental role that was missing or distorted in the patient's infancy and early childhood. The trainee was almost astonished at the nature of that belief, at the central importance she seemed to attach to this basic principle, and how alien this basic principle was to the approach she had been following until now.

For this trainee, the selected part of the tape was when the client finally arrived at the decision that had been such an issue. He was able to decide to leave his mother's home and to live with his friend. What was so impressive to the trainee was that it worked for the therapist to leave the client be, to not push or direct the client, to take whatever time it took and to go at whatever pace the client seemed to follow. The deeper principle was framed as follows: most clients have a built-in, healthy capacity to arrive at healthy decisions; by refraining from being directive in any way, and trusting in this capacity, the client can arrive at a healthy decision. This deeper principle was in accord with the trainee's chosen approach which featured a non-directive, low-pressure, respectful trust in the client's own intrinsic growth capacities. Can we go further?

We could because the trainee was drawn toward ways of mobilizing this built-in capacity for healthy and wise decision-making. Indeed, the trainee was passionate about finding how this capacity might be mobilized. As she probed deeper and deeper, she became increasingly enthusiastic and focused on finding an answer: 'If there is a capacity like that, why wait so many sessions, hoping it can come out?' Then she arrived at an answer that was filled with sheer excitement: 'Why not give it a chance to talk? Sure! I can ask if he's ready to let this capacity say what it has to say! Sort of like the two-chair technique? No, better. Only I can just see if he's ready. I know! I can describe this capacity and see if he agrees, then I can see if he can role-play this capacity, like giving it a chance to talk. It's not him. It's this capacity, and he can be its voice, like play acting. He doesn't have to do what it says, just listen. Let it talk! Yes! It makes sense to me! It's like a whole other person inside, and it's inside most clients. I think it'll work! Is there a therapy like that? Is this some crazy idea? Where can I read theory like this?'

Start by using the selected part of the tape to help enter into the trainee's deeper framework. Once you are in the deeper framework, you can look around. You can explore more. You can go even deeper. Sometimes you go only a little way. Sometimes you can see whole new vistas of the trainee's deeper framework. This can be fun, exciting, and so useful.

If this part is so pleasing or displeasing, what wild and crazy thing would you have loved to have done if there were no constraints at all?

You started with a part you loved or one that you hated, one that you felt marvelous about or one about which you felt miserable. Then the teacher asks: 'If this part is so pleasing or displeasing, what wild and crazy thing would you have loved to have done if there were no constraints at all?'

The right kind of answer is fueled by the trainee's deeper framework, and can shed light on it. But it has to be the right kind of answer, and there can be ways to tell if the answer is the right kind of answer:

- The answer exudes a sense of the weird, the wild, the wholly unconstrained, the truly bizarre. It is absolutely not something the trainee has done or would do, probably even in extreme circumstances. It is not included in a list of approved and recommended practices to be carried out by professional psychotherapists. It is something that would be considered offensive, unprofessional, unethical, maybe even illegal. If most supervisors even knew of the trainee having such an impulse, he or she would probably be thrown out of the program. Doing this wild thing would probably mean being sued, losing one's license, being thrown out of the profession. All of this defines what is meant by weird, wild, crazy, and beyond constraints.

- The answer is the right kind of answer when it is accompanied with a sense of devilish danger, sheer wickedness, violating professional taboos, wonderful excitement and titillation, sheer devilish fun. There is usually a nervous laughter, a sharp rising of the vocal quality, giggling, yelps and whelps, loudness and volume, a sudden blurting out of the impulsive answer.

Use the answer to help discover the trainee's deeper framework

There can be different ways of using the trainee's impulsive inclination to do this or that particularly wild and crazy thing. Professional ethics have a great deal to say about what the trainee ought to do with such impulsive inclinations. So does clinical lore. In addition, we can use the trainee's answer to see if we can help discover something about his or her deeper framework for psychotherapy.

The trainee was acutely bothered when the client asked, almost pleadingly, without anger or demand: 'I need some constructive suggestions.' What bothered the trainee so much was that this was the thirty-fourth session, the client tried her best to be a good client, but the problem was still there, and the client was right, she needed some constructive suggestions. What bothered the trainee so much was that he still had no idea of what the 'real' problem was.

What would he have loved to say? He would have loved to confess, with strong feeling: 'Bonnie, I don't know what's wrong! I know I should know, but I don't have the least idea what's wrong! ! I am so sorry! I wish I knew! Oh God, I feel miserable!'

Before we even turned to matters such as what the trainee might have done, we now had a chance to see what might be revealed about his deeper framework, and here is what we discovered: inside each client is a core problem, something that accounts for, explains, causes the client's troubles, symptoms, complaints, unhappinesses. It may be some psychodynamic, some trauma that happened, some core way of thinking, but, whatever it is, it accounts for and explains the client's problems because it is the true inner core, the 'real' problem. Once we find it, we can do something about the client's problems. But we have to know what that core 'real' problem is. This was a discovery in large part because the trainee had not known that he had such a clear and deep picture of this single, deep, core, 'real' problem in clients.

Another trainee was laughing as she played the selected part of the tape: 'Listen to her talk. Nonstop. And right here, listen. I am trying to say something, so she rushes. She out-talks me. She talks faster, and louder. And I just have to listen. I can only say something when she pauses, and then she interrupts me! I can't even get her to listen to me trying to get her to see what she does!'

What would the trainee just love to do under these conditions? 'You know what? I'd love to put my hand over her mouth and scream at her: "SHUT UP! I WANT TO TALK!! YOU DRIVE ME CRAZY!!" But I can't!' When all the laughing subsided, we tried to see what this might lead us to in the trainee's own deeper framework. The first new idea the trainee found was that she had an inner belief that the client brought out this reaction in her: 'I never feel this way! Not even with my husband or my sisters or my mom and dad. No one. And only with her. No other client. It seems so sensible. Sure. Somehow she makes me react that way, or feel like it.' But she went even deeper, and seemed to find this exciting related part of her deeper framework: 'I somehow have this idea that maybe there is something in her that has the same reaction: "Shut up! You never let anyone talk. You never listen. You drive everyone crazy!" I never thought about that before.'

We tried to put all of this into words that were somewhat more careful, and into a principle that was a little more general, and we emerged with this: there are conditions under which the therapist's pronounced reactions to what the client is, says, or does is also the reaction of some part of the client to what the client is, says, or does. Still, the trainee went further. She was puzzling about how this newly discovered principle might make a difference in what she does in actual in-session work: 'This would make a difference, I mean in what I do . . . How could I use this? I mean not just with her . . . with any client when it happens, when I have a reaction like that. I never thought about this . . .'

When the trainee played the part he selected, it was in the beginning of the session, and the client was telling about his week, especially about the wedding that he attended with his friend. The client seemed in somewhat good spirits, and seemed to have enjoyed the wedding, except that all the women seemed older, and he was on the lookout for perhaps meeting a younger woman. What would the trainee have loved to have done? He explains: 'I haven't the slightest idea what his problem is! This is the fourth session already, and we just talk! That's all! So here it starts again. You know what I wanted to do? I wanted to scream at him: "Either give me some problem to work with or GET THE HELL OUT OF HERE! Just leave me alone! WHAT'S BOTHERING YOU?" But you know what, HE WOULDN'T DO IT! . .

"GET OUT OF HERE!!" That's what I could hear myself screaming at him. And it happened again right here!'

In searching for what this may indicate about the trainee's deeper framework, he messed around with ideas about clients denying and avoiding problems. He played with ideas about how a proper relationship might have succeeded in getting at problems. He even wondered about serious psychopathological conditions, and how applying such labels to the client might well betray his own frustrations with the client.

And then he arrived at something he had kept off to the side, an idea that emerged from the shadows. 'Maybe some clients just want to talk . . . They have no special problems, well not in the usual sense, you know.' He wondered if perhaps he got so upset and wanted to scream at the client because he somehow dimly sensed that there was no special problem, and he did not want to face this deeper idea. But here it was. 'Wow! That's something. Do you think that's true? I mean about some clients? That's a whole new idea for me.' Yes it is.

'What wild and crazy thing would you have loved to have done if there were no constraints at all?' The answer can be a doorway down into the trainee's deeper framework. And there is another way the answer can be used.

Use the answer to figure out ways that the trainee could use that 'impulse' in actual in-session work

Here are a number of ways that the trainee's inclination to do that wild and crazy thing can be used in actual in-session work. The teacher may walk through these ways with the trainee, and it is up to the trainee to see if any of these are especially fitting and appealing.

- If the trainee has that sudden inclination to do such a wild and crazy thing, perhaps the client does too. Perhaps the trainee is undergoing what is also occurring in the client, or perhaps there may be a similar inclination deeper inside the client.

  Suppose that the trainee is on the verge of bursting into tears or of wanting to kill the bastard who stole the client's child. There can be ways that the trainee can use her own inclination to see if perhaps the client also has a similar kind of wild and crazy impulse, or perhaps not.

- Perhaps the client has similar hesitancies and fears about actually carrying out wild and crazy things. Perhaps the trainee is resonating with the client's own worries and bad feelings about constraints, about inner and outer pressures, rules, taboos. Could this be?

- The trainee may want to open up, disclose, reveal the sudden wild and crazy thing that is occurring in him. He is not going to do it, not going to carry it out, but he can describe what it is and how he feels about having such an impulsive inclination.

- 'If you affect me this way, perhaps you have a similar effect on some others too.' Suppose that the trainee has a wild and crazy impulse to rip off the client's clothes and have wild and crazy sex with him, or to smack him in the face because he is so mean and aggressive to the trainee. Perhaps the trainee is not the only person in the client's world who has such wild and crazy reactions to the client. Could this be? Could it be that the client evokes and provokes similar wild and crazy reactions in some others? How does the client manage to do this?

- Perhaps it would be nice if the client could actually find someone in her own personal world who can actually carry out this wild and crazy inclination in the trainee to take the client home and take care of her, or who can hold, stroke, cuddle, comfort the frail and hurting client, or who can actually accompany the client when she confronts her mean and nasty uncle who is in charge of her mother's estate. The trainee cannot carry out such wild and crazy things, but maybe this role can be fulfilled by someone currently in the client's world.

- The trainee may use his wild and crazy impulse in a friendly and playful way to enhance the relationship between them, to model a way of using such a wild and crazy impulse, or to shed some playful light on the client's ability to bring forth such wild and crazy impulses in others. This is the trainee who is able to say: 'Wait a minute! The rules say that you're not allowed to affect the doctor like this. You have to obey the rules, right? Say yes!' 'I just had this wild and crazy impulse to give you all my money! Now that is a wild and crazy impulse, and I am supposed to deal with it in a mature way. I just wish I knew how to do it!' 'Bingo! You scored a 10 on the hostility scale! That was good. Oh you are a pro at being hostile. You got me good! Have you always been so good at this?'

Depending on the trainee's discovered deeper framework and own personal reactions to each of the possibilities, he or she can find ways of using these wild and crazy impulses in actual in-session work.

You started from the part of the tape that was selected because it was so pleasing and exciting, or so displeasing and bothersome, or so compellingly inexplicable. Then you were able to use this selected part of the tape (1) to identify the trainee's preciously personal in-session feelings and also the trainee's valued therapist role, and then find ways that the trainee can, if this is welcomed and desired, build the trainee's therapy around these preciously personal feelings and valued therapist role. You were also able (2) to use these selected parts of the tape to discover the trainee's deeper framework, and then (3) go even further into even deeper parts of the trainee's own framework.

What you have found, in this teaching–training session, not only probes into the trainee's own deeper framework and way of thinking about psychotherapy, but also has direct applications for how the trainee can carry out actual in-session work both in general and in future sessions with this particular client.

And there are further ways to use these selected parts of the tape. You can use them by starting with what the therapist may be seen as trying to accomplish right there in the selected part of the tape.

Chapter 9

Method 3: what is the therapist trying to accomplish right here?

One way of using the selected part of the tape highlights that part as pleasing or displeasing or compellingly inexplicable. Another way is to start from quite a different angle, quite a different perspective. Study that part of the tape to identify what the therapist seems to be after, headed toward, trying to accomplish.

What can be so exciting is that the therapist is almost always after something, heading in some direction, trying to accomplish this or that. This can be so exciting because what the therapist is seeking to accomplish, there in the tape, comes from the deeper framework and can shed clear light on the content of the deeper framework. In other words, whatever the therapist seems to be after can be used as a clue to the deeper framework. This is the basis for studying whatever the therapist seems to be after.

The therapist is usually the trainee. However, this method is also useful and appropriate when the therapist is not the trainee, but rather another trainee or the teacher or some other therapist whose tape is being studied.

Get the answer from studying the tape, rather than asking the trainee to give some acceptable answer

The question is: 'What is the therapist trying to accomplish right here, in this part of the tape?' The best answer can come from studying the tape. Indeed, when the therapist is not the trainee or the teacher, the answer is almost certainly going to come from studying the tape. However, even when the therapist is the trainee, it is far better to get the answer when both teacher and trainee can study the tape to make some sensible guesses about what the latter seems to be trying to accomplish, rather than if the former manages to put him or her on the spot by asking, with a hint of accusation: 'What were you trying to accomplish right here?'

When the trainee is put on the spot, the conditions can be ripe for him or her to give the right answer, the answer that would please a supervisor, the professionally correct kind of answer. You also lose the opportunity to see just what the therapist seemed to be after in this particular part of the tape.

It seems better for the trainee to study the tape to see what the therapist seemed to be trying to accomplish. Of course the trainee has notions and ideas. He or she may well remember the intended aim or goal in that part of the session. In any case, the better kinds of answers seem to come from studying the tape, with the trainee as the main researcher, trying to figure out what the therapist seems to be trying to accomplish right here at this point on the tape.

Getting the answer can sometimes be touchy

Trainees will typically have answers to what they seem to be trying to accomplish. Even when the focus is on what is happening right here in the tape, they typically have answers. This is why a great deal seems to depend on the teacher's ability to see what the therapist is apparently trying to accomplish, and on the teacher's ability to allow the trainee to agree or disagree. After all, it is the trainee who has to do the learning. When the teacher offers an impression of what the therapist seems to be trying to accomplish right here, the trainee ought to be given plenty of room to be quite free to agree or disagree.

The teacher should be able to make a good guess about what the therapist seems to be trying to accomplish right here. The teacher should also be reasonably skilled in working with the trainee as a co-researcher ('Hmm. This is a tough one. You have any guesses?'), in acknowledging the touchiness of looking for what the therapist was seeking to accomplish ('This can be touchy. I wonder if we are going to agree or not'), in relying more on the teacher's impression ('You're probably so involved in this . . . I think I trust what I come up with more than I trust what you come up with, but I can be wrong, well every so often, maybe').

It can be touchy to study the tape and see what the therapist is accomplishing right here, e.g. the answer may be somewhat unpleasant to the trainee. The answer may well clash with what he or she believes the goals or aims ought to be, especially with regard to his or her chosen approach. Nevertheless, look for the answer even if it seems somewhat touchy, sensitive, surprising, or even embarrassing or bothersome to the trainee.

The enterprise has failed when the teacher falls into the role of the accuser, the prosecuting attorney, and the trainee adopts the role of the challenged, the accused, the one to have to come up with the right evidence to be acquitted. In these roles, the teacher accuses the trainee of having no basis for trying to accomplish what he or she is obviously trying to accomplish. The trainee says in effect: 'No, that's not true! I am totally justified in pursuing this goal.' He or she defiantly proclaims that the client wanted that goal, that the goal came from the client, and the evidence is somewhere in earlier, untaped sessions. Or the evidence consists of something from earlier sessions that absolutely justified his or her adoption of that goal. In any case, the teacher and the trainee have failed miserably, and have managed to turn the session into what it ought not to be.

It can be touchy to search for an answer to what the therapist was trying to accomplish right here, especially if the therapist is the trainee. The payoff is wonderful. Be careful of the dangers.

Try to identify what the therapist seems to be after right here and now

Start from the part of the tape that the trainee selected. You may of course study what happened before and after that part of the tape.

Try to identify what the therapist seems to be after. Look for the more or less immediate aim or goal of the therapist, as shown right here on the tape. Try to let the tape talk to you directly. Keep the search simple.

- Do not look for especially esoteric aims and goals. Do not be clever or creative or scholarly.

- Do not impose aims and goals that are personally or professionally acceptable. The task is to see what the tape has to show, rather than imposing what you want the tape to show.

- Emphasize the more immediate aims and goals, rather than trying to see way down the road to eventual long-term outcomes.

- Look for more or less simple, concrete, conspicuous aims and goals, rather than rising to highly abstract and generalized levels of description.

Here are a few examples of what the therapist seemed to be trying to accomplish right here. From studying the selected part of the tape, it seemed rather conspicuous that she was aiming toward assembling reasons, evidence, for the client to give up her excessive drinking. Right here, the therapist was making a case that the client's drinking would probably have negative consequences on the client's little daughter. Although the therapist was being somewhat gentle, indirect, it seemed relatively clear what she seemed to be after.

In a second example, the client and his wife work together in co-leading small groups dealing with departmental stress. From examining the selected part of the tape, it seemed relatively clear that the therapist was repeatedly trying to get the client to talk about his pride in the business becoming more and more profitable, whereas the client was apparently content to wander around from topic to topic. The trainee was not at all surprised by having an agenda for the session, but she kept cocking her head and grinning because she was clearly after something pleasurable, i.e. pumping up the client's satisfaction, and that was out of the ordinary for her because she thought her work was almost exclusively problem focused. What she was clearly after struck her as rather unusual.

In a third example, the therapist was trying to get the client to talk with more feeling, and the therapist was being so gentle, so persistent, in patiently using subtle little hints and touching the edges of the client's consistently neutral and low voice quality. In the selected part of the tape, the therapist had essentially given in to the client and was joining the client in saying fewer and fewer words, with more and more silences, and with the conversation becoming increasingly drained of feeling, on both their parts. Yet it was rather clear that the therapist was persistent in wanting more feeling in what the client was saying.

Identify the working principle underlying what the therapist seems to be trying to accomplish

Once the trainee and teacher can have a relatively clear idea of what the therapist seems to be trying to accomplish, it is possible to frame the underlying working principle. This calls for both the trainee and the teacher, and perhaps other trainees in the group, to work together to frame the underlying working principle. Here are some helpful guidelines:

- The working principle may be one that the trainee accepts and already seems to have adopted, and that is a familiar working principle. Or the

working principle may be alien, unfamiliar, one that the trainee is
somewhat skeptical about.

- The working principle should be framed so as to be relatively clear and
identifiable, concrete and specific, rather than essentially loose, diffuse,
and vague. Simple clarification is useful.

- The working principle should be a working principle, rather than some
sort of defensive justification, some sort of rationale in case questions are
raised about why the trainee did whatever he or she did.

- The working principle is illuminating. It is action friendly. It helps the
trainee in actual practice. It spells out what to do, the conditions under
which to do it, and what it seeks to accomplish.

One trainee was apparently trying to get the client to talk with more
feeling. In an attempt to frame a working principle, this is what
emerged: when the client's voice quality is significantly and impressive-
ly low, dead, mechanical, shallow, drained of virtually any feeling, it is
desirable for the therapist to try to raise the client's voice quality to a
minimally acceptable level of emotion or feeling. This principle applies
to virtually all clients, regardless of problem or mental disorder.

The trainee already tended to believe such a working principle. It
was working friendly rather than alien or hard to accept. What was
relatively surprising for the trainee was that this working principle
seemed to be one of the requisite conditions for him to do therapy.
Without a client having this minimal level of emotion or feeling, he
was lost, unable to do proper and acceptable therapeutic work. Seeing
and knowing the importance of this working principle were relatively
new for the trainee.

The second example was both more touchy and sensitive, and also
more surprisingly good-humored. The trainee started by proclaiming
that his aim, in this selected part, was to promote insight and understanding, and he was interested in what methods might be helpful.
However, with a little more careful listening to the selected part, it
became conspicuously clearer that the client was opting for one problem and solution, whereas the therapist was trying to get the client to
accept a different version of the problem and solution. The client
seemed to define the problem as being afraid of being rejected by the
wonderful woman, whereas the therapist was even more clearly trying
to get him to accept that the problem was being attracted to an
unavailable older woman, and the solution was to give up pursuit of
this woman.

When it came to trying to frame the working principle, the trainee, amidst a lot of friendly laughter, said: 'Here it is: the client is to accept the therapist's version of the client's problem because the therapist knows better! Besides, I think he mentioned it earlier. I think.' With further attempts to frame the working principle, the trainee came up with this version as acceptable and right: when there is a significant difference between what the client and the therapist see as the client's problem and solution, the therapist's is ordinarily the one that prevails. In other words, the client should ordinarily accept the therapist's version of the problem.

The trainee kidded himself about the importance of accepting the client's version of the problem, following this party line, and gaining his own 'insight and understanding' that this sounded good but was not what he actually did in practice. Here was an example of an emerged working principle that had bite, was rather unexpected by the trainee, and had direct and far-reaching implications for actual practice for this trainee, provided he accepted and adopted the working principle that was discovered.

Another trainee had started with a selected part of the tape in which the client was described as 'having problems staying on topic'. It was clear that the therapist was trying to get the client to talk about his feelings of anxiety and guilt at negotiating with a hooker who turned out to be a policewoman. The therapist kept bringing up the fallout in the client's family and friends and work, whereas the client was apparently more concerned with how clever the policewoman was at entrapping him.

Staying with what the therapist was trying to accomplish right here, the trainee arrived at this formulation of her working principle: the therapist knows the topics that are important for the client to talk about; if the client obviously avoids the important topic, the therapist is to get the client to talk about the important topic, or at least to help the client be aware of avoiding the important topic.

Having formulated the working principle rather carefully, the trainee was pleased with the clearer definition of a principle that she believed she was following in general, with all of her clients. She kept nodding as she came closer and closer to spelling out the working principle.

Finding the working principle was quite a different matter with another trainee. She was fairly certain that something valuable was happening here in the part she had selected to study, but she was not at all sure what it was. She had felt excited and on some sort of track in the selected part of the tape, but both then and now, listening over and over again to the tape, she was not at all clear what she was after, until she began opening up more and more of her thoughts in listening to the tape. Finally, the working principle seemed to take form and shape: when a client is starting to feel good, or heading toward feeling good, or even seems capable of feeling good, the therapist can help carry forward the client's sheer enjoyment and happiness in sheer living; psychotherapy can enhance pleasure and satisfaction in living.

Formulation of this working principle was so exciting for this trainee because it seemed to be a core principle, with deeper and broader implications for what her psychotherapy can be. The immediate aim was to formulate the working principle which seemed to her like a key to so much more of her own deeper framework for psychotherapy.

What can the teacher do when the teacher is threatened by what the trainee is trying to accomplish or by the working principle?

When I listen carefully to supervisors, and when I try to train teachers who are interested in becoming discovery-oriented teachers, it is quite common that a fair proportion of supervisors and teachers can be conspicuously threatened by what trainees are trying to accomplish or by the emerging working principle. My impression is that the supervisors and teachers then do at least two things that are not especially helpful to the trainee:

1. The supervisor or teacher is simply unable to see what the trainee is trying to accomplish, and is almost certainly unable to help him find and formulate his own working principle. It is as if the supervisor or teacher is saying: 'I don't like what I don't want to see and hear. What you are trying to accomplish is so threatening that I refuse to see and hear it, and I certainly cannot help you find and formulate the working principle.'

2. The supervisor or teacher attacks the trainee, criticizes her, educates and straightens her out. It is as if the supervisor or teacher is saying: 'What you are after is bad, wrong, not the way to do therapy. The way you seem to be thinking is bad. And you are also bad. I will show you what to accomplish, what to think in accomplishing it, and how to be good, professional, to think and act in the right way, my way.'

Of course, if the teacher is following the discovery-oriented method, none of this should occur, or should occur only rarely. But it happens.

Hopefully, the teacher can at least be aware of being so threatened by what the trainee is trying to accomplish and by the emerging working principle. Hopefully the teacher can graciously decline falling into the trainee-inspired or teacher-inspired trap of being threatened by what the trainee is trying to accomplish, or by the emerging working principle. But it is often a problem.

It is a problem for me. I come face to face with an explicit form of this threat for me. It happens when I am twisted into a knot of tension when I believe the trainee's working principle is something like this: 'I wear the black robes of the grand judge. I have a list of things I approve and disapprove of, and I want to get this client to stop the things I disapprove of, and to be the way I personally approve of. I want this client to be the way I want this client to be.' When I sense this working principle, I am marvelously threatened, and unable to be the discovery-oriented teacher. I fall apart.

Sometimes the trainee is quite explicit in fulfilling the role of the grand judge who imposes his or her own tough value system on to the client. Up front and explicitly, the trainee announces: 'This client refuses to acknowledge that she is hyper-sexual. I want her to see that she has this problem. How can I get her to accept this problem, and to have sex normally rather than whenever she feels like it, which is much too often?' Or the trainee puts her judgment right on the table: 'This client is not even bothered by his homosexuality. How can I get him to explore the causes of his homosexuality? He is much too resistant! I want him to be heterosexual.'

Sometimes the working principle is less up front, more implied or hidden, yet it seems clear to me that the trainee has an explicit list of what is acceptable and approved, and what is unacceptable and disapproved, and he or she is determined to get the client to conform to his or her personal value system. I see this trainee as using psychotherapy as a tool to impose his or her personal value system on to the client, and I am well and truly threatened.

What can the teacher do in these circumstances? Here are four ways I can try to cope with and use, for our mutual benefit, my being so threatened by what I believe the trainee is trying to accomplish, or by the working principle:

1. I can simply confess to being much too threatened, to be fair and clear about what threatens me. Perhaps we can decline working on this particular issue that the trainee is bringing up, and go on to other matters that are less threatening to me. Or perhaps these kinds of matters and

issues are so central to what the trainee wants, and so threatening to me, that it is best for us to part company.

2. I can say that I am unable to suggest some methods that the trainee requests because the whole idea is much too threatening to me, and because trying to find these methods both departs from and defeats the search for the trainee's deeper framework for psychotherapy.

3. I can try to clarify what I believe is the trainee's working principle, be honest about my own personal feelings of being threatened by such a principle, and acknowledge that I am unable to set aside these personal feelings. My doing this does not help the trainee get much closer to his or her own personal framework.

4. We can see if we can tip-toe our way to a pertinent underlying issue: how does the therapist arrive at the specific goals and directions of change in working with this client? If we are able to arrive at this underlying issue, perhaps we can take a step further and compare and contrast, with some mutual respect, our own personal positions on this issue or answers to this important underlying question. When both of us can arrive at this point, and the atmosphere is wholesomely non-threatening, it is both fun and instructive to appreciate our differing positions and answers.

Up to now, you have become somewhat clearer about what the trainee is aiming at accomplishing, and on the working principle that seems to be underlying what the trainee is trying to accomplish. You can go further. You can use your picture of what the trainee is trying to accomplish, and the underlying working principle, to peer down into the trainee's deeper framework for psychotherapy. You are fairly clear about what he or she is trying to accomplish. Use that as a point of entry into his or her deeper framework for psychotherapy.

How and why is it so important to accomplish what the therapist is trying to accomplish?

It is as if the teacher says: 'So now we are kind of clear about what you were trying to accomplish right here in the session. Let's see if we can make some guesses about how and why accomplishing that can be so important, helpful, valuable. There are probably some good answers. I am trying to look for answers that can tell us something about your own ideas, how you think. So what answers come to you – how and why is it so important to accomplish what you are trying to accomplish right here?'

The right atmosphere is where the teacher and the trainee(s) are detectives, inquirers, searchers for answers that might shed light on the trainee's deeper framework. You all are on the same side. It is just fine if any or all of you say: 'I don't know!' It is just fine if you come up with guesses that are kind of frivolous or silly or off the wall.

The right atmosphere allows the trainee to turn to his or her own personal system of values, of what he or she accepts as cherished and good. The right atmosphere (1) welcomes and accepts the trainee's personal value system, whether it is a religious value system, a political value system, a cultural value system, or his or her own personal value system and (2) accepts the trainee's value system as a welcomed and worthwhile answer to the question of how and why it is so important for him or her to accomplish what he or she is trying to accomplish.

Accordingly, the deeper framework may well be found to include the following values, and for these values to be the good-enough rationale for what the trainee is trying to accomplish:

- It is good for a person to live and be with people of his or her own kind, culture, ethnic background.

- It is good for a woman to be empowered, rather than depending on and living a life of inferiority to men.

- It is good, natural, and normal to be heterosexual.

- It is good for daughters and sons to take care of their aged parents.

- It is good to be faithful to one's spouse.

If the trainee's value system is meaningful, important, and cherished, the right atmosphere accepts that as a good-enough answer to how and why it is so important for him or her to accomplish what he or she is trying to accomplish.

The wrong atmosphere is where the teacher asks, in effect: 'Why are you trying to accomplish that? Are you out of your mind? What you are trying to accomplish is bad, wrong, dangerous, unprofessional. So defend yourself!' The wrong atmosphere is forcing the trainee against the wall, forcing him or her to grab an answer that can end the interrogation, and be acceptable, is safe and professionally approved.

There are at least two good ways of answering the question, two ways that the answer can be helpful. In one way, the question points directly to the trainee's deeper framework. How and why is accomplishing that so important? The answer comes from and tells about the trainee's deeper framework. Another way that the answer can be helpful is that the answer points toward a subsequent aim or goal. Achieving this is important because it helps to achieve that, and 'that' tells us about the trainee's deeper framework. Here are a few examples of both ways of using the trainee's answer to how and why it is so important to accomplish what the therapist is trying to accomplish.

The trainee had already said that the aim was to try to get the client to talk with a little more feeling. All he wanted was a little more feeling, not necessarily powerful outbursts or screeching voice quality. The client's voice quality was almost nil, unexpressive, dead, drained of any feeling or emotion. Furthermore, in discussing what the trainee was trying to accomplish, what emerged was his idea that a safe minimal level of feeling seemed to be a general requisite for getting psychotherapy started and moving it along.

How and why is this minimally acceptable level of feeling so valuable, important, helpful? It seemed to be almost a requisite because the trainee's deeper framework included ideas such as these: 'If the voice quality is dead, there is nothing to work with. The important data are what's happening right here and now. The client has to be involved . . . I think the important data are what's happening in the client right now.'

A little further probing, and the trainee was discovering more and more of the deeper framework: 'The important and useful data do not especially include whatever the client talks about in the state of dead voice quality. The important and useful data can include both whatever is occurring in the client when the voice level has at least a minimally acceptable level of feeling, and whatever the client refers to and talks about when the voice quality is acceptable.'

Even further, the trainee's deeper framework included two sets of data, with only a slight overlap. One set of data occurs when the client's voice quality is below the acceptable requisite, and one when the voice is at or above the minimal acceptable level. Both sets of data may be accurate, but only the latter set is useful, important, helpful. The trainee has opened up more about his own deeper framework for psychotherapy.

The second trainee had not been satisfied with just staying with the client naming the problem as being afraid of being rejected by the wonderful woman. Instead, the trainee had gone in what seemed to be a counter direction by trying to get the client to see that he was attracted to an unavailable older woman, and a better aim or goal would be to give up pursuit of that woman. The trainee was opting for what seemed to be the opposite of what the client wanted.

Now the question: 'Why was it so important that the trainee should try to get the client to accept the trainee's goal, rather than accepting the goal presented by the client?' The trainee was easily able to recite what he knows the field would probably say he 'ought' to do, namely to work from the client's presenting problem and stated goal of change. He also could easily recite that it is acceptable to find the problem underlying the client's presenting problem, and that doing something about the underlying problem is supposed to take care of the presenting problem, i.e. if the client is no longer afraid of being rejected by the wonderful woman, he can win the wonderful woman, and everyone lives happily thereafter. But none of this contained the trainee's right answer to the question of how and why it is so important not to honor the client's stated goal, and instead to try to get the client to accept a different goal.

The first wave of excitement came when the trainee said that he may not have found the right therapeutic goal, but that he had serious suspicions about just developing a program aimed at accomplishing what the client wanted. Carefully and sensitively following along this thread, we arrived at this set of ideas, all tapping the discovered deeper framework, and all accompanied wish sizzling excitement:

> Clients' presenting problems, symptoms, worries are indications of significant choice points, important decision points, ways that the client can take next steps, ways that the client might head off in a new and maybe better direction. If this is so, then merely accommodating to what the client wants is missing a chance to see what this might be. Actually, the 'presenting problem' or what the client seems to want from therapy is a trap, a ploy, a way of throwing both the client and the therapist off track, a way of masking, hiding, and avoiding what the 'better route' might be. Instead, the therapist is to avoid this trap by studying the presenting problem, by studying what the client wants, to try to find out the better way, the better decision, the better choice, the better avenue of change that is somehow hidden and yet contained within the presenting problem and the client's voiced wishes and wants from therapy.

The trainee could go no further at this time. Yet he had discovered an important part of his own deeper framework for psychotherapy. He knew he was on the right track of finding what he truly believed. All of this was new for him, and so seriously important and valuable.

The third trainee had selected the part of the tape to play because she was pleased with what she did, and yet she had some hesitation about what she was doing. She explained that the client had been both scared and depressed, angry and confused, all about her relationships with her daughter. They were fighting constantly, but over the last three or four sessions things were changing, and they were now getting along rather well. In this part of the session, the client was relaxed and happy, in rather good spirits, and the trainee was pleased with what she was doing with the client, with some hesitation. In studying what the trainee was doing, she arrived at this working principle: when a client is starting to feel good, therapy can enhance and carry forward the client's enjoyment and happiness. The trainee was trying to help the client feel even better, to put her good spirits to work making happy changes in her personal life.

Then the question was put to the trainee: 'How and why is it so important for therapy to enhance the client's enjoyment and happiness, or, in the trainee's words, to enhance "happy changes" in the client's personal world?'

The trainee had no ready answer, yet something in this part of the session seemed compelling to her. The more she probed into what was so hesitatingly exciting about this part of the session, the closer she came to a belief that psychotherapy usually ended without going on to the 'next phase'. The first phase was treating the problem. The next phase could be something more, something that built on the client no longer having the problem. 'She came because she had trouble with her daughter. That's over now. I think she could go on from there! Not just normal again, you know, the problem is treated. But then what? I think there is a second phase. You know, where she can do more than just get along with her daughter. She could feel better in lots of ways, now, with more than just her daughter.' She summed it up as follows: 'Therapy is to treat the negative. The next phase is enhancing the positive!'

She was surprised by what she seemed to have arrived at. She kept shaking her head and grinning sheepishly about having such ideas, and about what these ideas might mean for what psychotherapy might offer, for when to end therapy, for how to tell if therapy was successful, for what she had always conceived of as psychopathology and the structure of personality. She had dipped into her own deeper framework for psychotherapy

It is helpful to look for what the trainee seems to be trying to accomplish in this part of the tape. Once we can be reasonably clear, we can use what the trainee is trying to accomplish to see into the trainee's deeper framework. Then we are able to take a next step. Once we have a picture of what the trainee is trying to accomplish, we can then ask how and why it might be so important to accomplish what the trainee is trying to accomplish, and this further step allows us to see even more of the trainee's deeper framework. We have discovered more and more of the trainee's own deeper framework by paying attention to what he or she is trying to accomplish.

How can the trainee accomplish the newly discovered aims and goals?

It is common that trainees will ask supervisors how to accomplish what trainees want to accomplish: 'This client is not motivated for therapy, so how can I get her to be more motivated?' 'I'm not doing very well in getting this client to do her behavioral homework, so what can I do to get her to do the homework assignments?' 'I think it would be best if the husband came in for marital work, but he doesn't seem to want to, so what can I do?' For many supervisors, in many approaches, these kinds of questions are relatively common. The trainees know what they want to accomplish, and the supervisors usually know what methods the trainees can use to accomplish those aims and goals.

The situation is different in discovery-oriented training because it takes some work to be able to discover what the trainee is seeking to accomplish. Once we are sufficiently clear about what the trainee is seeking to accomplish, then the focus can shift to ways and means of accomplishing these discovered aims and goals.

The first trainee discovered that he wanted all of his clients to talk with a voice quality that exceeded a certain minimal level of feeling. He found that he was unable to work when the client's voice quality was almost dead, so neutral that it was essentially drained of all feeling, and came out mechanical, robot like. His minimum acceptable level was a moderate level of feeling quality. Clients do not have to scream or yell, to explode with feeling. His problem was when the feeling level was almost zero. This is what he discovered.

What might the trainee do to accomplish this minimally requisite level of feeling in his clients in general, or with this particular client right here in this session? The trainee was stuck. Both the teacher and other trainees in the group made some suggestions, each of which seemed sensible, none of which seemed to spark more than minimal feeling in the trainee: 'What about just telling the client to talk with more feeling?' 'How about modeling it for the client? You could talk with heightened voice quality. No?' 'If it's an issue, how about bringing it up for the client to talk about?' 'Have you pointed it out to the client – how the dead level might be a problem?' 'You must have some idea why the client talks that way, so could you help the client get at the reason?' These all seemed sensible. Nothing elicited much excitement from the trainee.

Then he grinned. He had thought of a way that seemed like a good one, at least on paper. 'You know what I could have done? I mean right here, cause I was so bothered by that dead voice? I could have played the tape for the client, and asked him if he was bothered by the way he sounded! And if he said yes, then I could tell him to talk with more feeling, at least in the sessions. If he said no or something, then I don't know. Sure, I could have him listen to the tape!'

There were some immediate reactions. The group was a wee bit stunned, but in a pleasant way. It seemed like a new idea, a simple and direct idea, a clever idea. The teacher was wondering what the trainee might read to learn more about such a way of accomplishing what he wanted to accomplish. And the trainee was eager to try it out, if he had the same reaction to the client's dead level of voice quality in the next session.

The second trainee discovered that she really did want clients to talk about the topics she thought of as important, especially when clients seemed to prefer talking about topics that she believed were not important. Once this general principle was found and put into words, the next issue was how she could get clients to talk about topics that she wanted them to talk about. She thought about this. The teacher thought about this. The other trainees thought about this.

Finding an acceptable answer was hindered by a phrase that kept coming up: 'It depends.' Riding with this disclaimer clause, the focus was on this particular instance in which the client was drawn toward the cleverness of the policewoman who entrapped him, whereas the trainee wanted him to talk about the feelings of guilt and anxiety the client ought to be feeling about being caught by the policewoman acting as the hooker.

There were a number of relatively standard suggested ways for the trainee to get the client to talk about what the trainee wanted him to talk about, e.g. the trainee might defer to the client for now, but bring up her favored topic later on. Or the trainee might have the client face the matter of avoiding the important topic, or at least what she believed was the important topic. Finally, the trainee found a way of accomplishing what she discovered she wanted to accomplish, a way that felt better than the alternatives. 'I could tell him that I have a problem right here, cause he obviously wants to talk about the clever policewoman, the hooker, and I want him to talk about how he feels about getting caught, the ridicule, how his wife and family would react, that stuff, which I really think bothers him, so how about our being fair. He can talk about the clever policewoman first, if he then will talk about what I think is the important topic. How's that?'

She had found a way of accomplishing the aim or goal that she had discovered was important for her. Compared with the other ways that were mentioned, this one made good sense to her, and it had the added feature of having high appeal value.

The third trainee had started with a part of the tape where she was so very pleased. Especially in the previous sessions, the client had been distraught, scared, doleful, depressed, angry, and confused about her fractious relations with her daughter. Here, in this part of the session, things seem so different with her daughter, and she is now relaxed, in good spirits, happy, and talking about both daughters, the novel she is working on, and a few other pleasant matters. The trainee had dug down and emerged with this principle: when a client is starting to feel good, or heading toward feeling good, the therapist can help carry forward the client's sheer enjoyment and happiness in sheer living. If this is the newly discovered aim and goal, the question is how the therapist can accomplish this aim and goal in the actual session.

Trying to figure out an answer came up with very little that seemed right and that touched off the right bodily felt signals in the trainee, until she came up with the following: 'I could ask her! Sure! Why not? I could tell her that things seem fine with her daughter, at least for now, and she's mentioning things that are pleasant, like laughing with the kids and working on her novel. So maybe she's ready . . . I could ask her if she is ready to do things, new things, that feel good, like with her daughters or with the novel, or anything. We could work on new behaviors that feel good . . . Is that allowed? It makes sense to me! Is this all right?' She is looking for and finding some methods to enable her to achieve the newly discovered aims and goals. She had not only learned a bit from her deeper framework, she was now dealing with in-session ways to achieve what the deeper framework told her she valued achieving.

What would the trainee just love to do or accomplish right here, even though it is outlandish, wild, impulsive, forbidden?

The teacher carefully explains what the trainee is to look for and why. Doing a good job with the explanation can be crucial because otherwise the trainee will almost certainly not be enabled to come up with an answer to this question: 'What would you love to do or accomplish right here, even though it is absolutely outlandish, wild, impulsive, and forbidden?' Here are some helpful guidelines:

- The trainee must not do it in the session. Whatever he comes up with is to be used to get at the deeper framework, and is absolutely not something he is expected to actually do in in-session work. Acknowledging the wish or impulse or fantasy is altogether different from actually carrying it out in the session.

- The right answer may have appeared, clearly and vividly, either at that moment in the session or right now as the trainee is studying the selected part of the tape. She knew or now knows what she would have loved to have done. Yes, it was a fleeting impulse. Yes, she freely admits that she had the inclination to do it. No, she would not have done it, but the impulse was delicious.

- If we set aside all the injunctions, all the 'shalt nots', all the sound and solid reasons for not doing it, and the virtual certainty that the impulse is wholly unacceptable to ethics, morals, professional standards, decency, if we wholly admit that doing it would plunge the trainee into big trouble, if we set aside all these reasons for not doing it - it would be absolutely fantastic to have gone ahead and done it!

- If we have to search for precisely what the impulse looks like, the tell-tale evidence is often found in the silly grin on the trainee's face or the spontaneous shriek, together with the bodily felt sudden puff of titillation, excitement, devilishness, joy, wickedness, mischievousness.

These guidelines help to pinpoint what the trainee would just love to do or to accomplish right here, and finding what this is helps to get a glimpse down into his deeper framework. Here are some examples:

In the excerpt that she selected, she described the client as lightly crying, being pitiful, fragile, vulnerable, helpless, and yet as being brave, doing her best to cope with obstacles. The trainee confessed to a momentary impulse of taking the client home with her. 'I have the weekend free. She was my last client for the day. I wanted to take her home with me and give her some chicken soup! Oh God! That's so

> awful . . . but you know, if she was a friend of mine, that's what I would
> do! I would! I had to fight from doing it! . . . And that's the first time I
> ever felt that with a client.'

The aim is not especially to make the trainee's impulse understandable, to explain it, to try to justify it, to make it all right. Nor is the aim to take the next step of finding acceptable ways of using her impulse to take the client home and take care of her. Useful and helpful and common as this may be, the aim is rather to try to use this impulse to shed some light on the trainee's own deeper framework. What might this impulse reveal about her deeper framework?

Both the teacher and the trainee went to a sensible answer that perhaps the impulse springs from the trainee's own wishes and wants, needs and inclinations. Or perhaps the impulse is a kind of testing of the limits of their relationship. Or perhaps the impulse reflects what the therapist and client somehow managed to be complicit in orchestrating together. All of these seemed sensible, but without ringing the right bells.

Then the trainee probed further, and what she arrived at was accompanied with the right bells and whistles, the right bodily felt sensations and feelings. 'She mentioned taking care of a bird when she was a little girl, a bird that was sickly or frail or something . . . and that her friend called her about her son hitting her and yelling at her and leaving . . . Maybe I was getting at something in her! Taking care of someone, being protective . . . Yeah. That fits!' She went on to frame the deeper principle: 'Maybe what . . . maybe my impulse tells something about her . . . about her own impulse. Maybe it's there in both of us . . . I think I believe that! I do!'

Now we were ready to see how to use this part of her deeper framework. It took very little encouragement for her to arrive at a way she just might use this deeper principle. 'Homework. Sure! Her friend? The one with the son? She mentioned it earlier in the session. I could have given her homework to go over to her friend's place and take care of her, give her chicken soup! For homework, go and take care of her friend. Comfort her. That would have worked!'

> This trainee clearly enjoyed playing the excerpt he had selected. He
> looked around the group as the other trainees and the teacher heard
> the client whining, complaining, in the hard-edged, grinding voice. It was
> pure whining. 'Right here, here's where I wanted to grab her and shake
> her and tell her to shut up! I was this far from telling her to just shut up!
> Give me a rest for a minute! That whining voice drives me crazy!'

As the teacher was trying to think how this could shed light on the trainee's deeper framework, such thoughts were quickly set aside as the trainee continued: 'I wanted to choke my client. God, I still do, just hearing that voice! And you know what? I know I got a problem. She drives me crazy with that whining. It's my problem. It would take a saint to just sit there and listen. And he'd be lying!'

This is where the teacher came a little closer to how the trainee could use all this to uncover something about his deeper framework. 'So let me see, in the session you get this impulse to do all that, to say all that, but you can't say or do anything. Right? If I were good, I could figure out what this can show about your own deeper way of thinking about therapy.' Without skipping a beat, the trainee says: 'I wish there was a law. In therapy you can be honest. I mean you could say what you can't say . . . I mean. You know what I mean?'

He was on a roll, and it seemed that all of this was coming from his deeper framework. He was laughing as he told us what he wished therapy was: 'I could say what I can't say, and so can she. Yes! . . . I can say: "I just got thought of something I can't say." And she can too. As soon as we get something we can't say, we say we got something. We raise a finger or something. Why not? We just raise a finger or we can say: "Right here I got something I'm embarrassed . . . I can't say." That would be so much fun!'

He had arrived at something new, something exciting. In therapy, both the therapist and the client have to have ground rules that tell them to signal when one has an inclination to say or do something that is taboo, not allowed. Then the person is free to say or not say what it is. The inclination can be with regard to one another, here in the session, or could refer to anything else. Psychotherapy can consist of clients and therapists saying things so that they can find an occasion when one or both have an impulse to say something that is forbidden, and then to tread lightly toward saying it or not.

On the other hand, this view of therapy seemed straight out of the trainee's own deeper pool of weird and bizarre, perhaps creative, deeper ideas. However, it was here that the trainee remembered doing just this with his childhood girlfriend who lived nearby for about a year. They somehow evolved the sign of sticking out their tongue when they had an impulse that was forbidden. This was their secret, and yet it was one that was so much fun for the two of them. He could barely remember if they said what the impulse was, but he remembered so many times when one would stick out the tongue, and they would laugh because each knew what the impulse probably was.

> A third trainee had an altogether different impulse. She wanted to just explode by saying, 'Just do it!' In the excerpt that she played, she was quiet, but inside she said she was so exasperated, so frustrated, that she wanted either to scream 'Just do it!', or she wanted to say, 'OK! That's it!', and grab the client, take the client to the client's sister's apartment, have her face the sister, and tell her sister that she is quitting.

The trainee explained that the client arrives at a point where she knows what to do, is so close to actually doing it, would love to do it, but never takes the next step of actually deciding to do it and going ahead and doing it. That is when she wants to scream out: 'Just do it!' This business with the client's sister is just another recurring example.

The trainee moved into accusing herself of having a problem. 'Maybe I have my own issues . . . Maybe I skirt around doing what I know I should do. That's possible. Maybe I just don't have enough patience or tolerance or something.' Although this may be a worthwhile avenue for trainees and supervisors to follow, it does not lead to discovery of the trainee's own deeper framework.

When she used her 'impulse' to lead down into her own deeper notions, she arrived at a picture of some massive force that acts against actually carrying out an important new act, especially when a client is on the cusp of actually doing it, actually resolving to carry it out and then going ahead and doing it. 'You know, I think I always believed something like that. Little changes, all right. But important ones? Something stops clients . . .' Then she became quite serious, and out came a statement that seemed bathed in truth: 'Therapy has to be able to do something about this . . . force or whatever it is. Something stops a person from making big important changes. I am going to solve this!'

She was deadly serious as she pursued this line of thought. She wanted to read what was written about this problem and how to solve it. She wanted to think about it more. She was seriously excited about finding a solution she could use at these critical points in her sessions.

This third method consists of (1) honest answers to the question of what the therapist seems to be trying to accomplish right here, in the part that the trainee selected to study, and then (2) using the trainee's answers as a tracking guide down into her or his own deeper framework for psychotherapy, and finally (3) applying what was discovered so that it can be used in actual in-session work.

Chapter 10

Method 4: what is the trainee's answer to the 'basic questions'?

An important and useful way of seeing and opening up and developing the trainee's deeper framework for psychotherapy is to help the trainee answer what may be called 'basic questions'. If the discovery-oriented approach is adopted in a training program, it is likely that the trainee will be introduced to 'foundational beliefs' and also 'basic questions' in didactic classroom work (Mahrer, 2004a). However, the study of actual tapes is much more likely to bring the trainee face to face with many 'basic questions' that would not probably be faced in the classroom, and even to provide a much more alive and challenging context for answering many of the 'basic questions' that came up in classroom work.

The teacher's job is (1) to know when the trainee is close to a 'basic question', (2) to know what the 'basic question' is, and (3) to help the trainee arrive at his or her own, custom-fitted answer.

The teacher knows what the 'basic questions' are

The discovery-oriented teacher knows what the 'basic questions' are. Few supervisors have much of an idea what the 'basic questions' are. Most discovery-oriented teachers have a respectful appreciation of the 'basic questions'. Only a few supervisors do. The discovery-oriented teacher knows what a powerful tool the 'basic questions' can be. Only a few supervisors do.

Here are some of the things the teacher knows about the 'basic questions':

- They are indeed in the form of questions, rather than simple statements, principles, assertions of truth. The statement may be: 'Clients seek treatment of their presenting complaints, symptoms, mental disorders, and psychological problems.' The basic question may be: 'What accounts for a person being with another person designated as a professional psychotherapist?'

- They can be found underlying most of what therapists do in sessions, whether the therapist is a trainee or a seasoned practitioner, whether the therapist does this or that kind of therapy.

- They are present whether or not the therapist knows they are present. Indeed, few therapists are aware of the presence of the basic questions, and even fewer know what these basic questions are, even though they have a large hand in determining what therapists think and how they go about in-session work.

- Virtually every therapist thinks and operates on the basis of his or her own answers to the 'basic questions', even though the therapists are typically unaware of their answers as answers to the basic questions.

- They are exceedingly powerful because the therapist's answers virtually determine what he or she thinks and does in actual in-session work. They are exceedingly powerful because adopting a better answer or shifting to a different answer can make a powerful difference in what the therapist thinks and does in actual in-session work.

- They tend to invite a number of different answers. Most 'non-basic' questions seem to have a more or less 'right' answer, e.g. 'Under ordinary circumstances, what is the chemical content of water?' 'What is the square root of 169?' 'What is the speed of light?'

  In contrast, what may be called the 'basic questions' seem to invite a number of answers, and a case can be made on behalf of each as fitting and appropriate, e.g. 'How can a person no longer suffer from this or that kind of painful feeling?' 'How does a person become the person that he or she is?' 'How can a person undergo deep-seated and substantial change in the person that he or she is?'

- They typically have a history of 'fashionably right answers'. If you go back in history, there have been 'fashionably right answers' to the particular basic question, and yet the basic question somehow managed to survive one fashionably right answer after another. Some of these basic questions seem to have originated mainly around the time of the beginning of professional psychotherapy in the early 1900s, e.g. 'What is the nature of a "good relationship" between therapist and patient?' Other basic questions seem to have a much longer history, going back hundreds of years before there was a professional field of psychotherapy, e.g. 'What seems to account for the onset of weird and bizarre behavior in this person?'

The discovery-oriented teacher has an appreciation for what may be called the 'basic questions' and a fairly good grasp of what these 'basic questions' are.

The teacher sees that the trainee is face to face with a 'basic question'

It is the teacher's job to see that, right here, the trainee is face to face with a 'basic question'. Trainees rarely know. Teachers should know. It is as if the teacher is saying: 'Right here you are face to face with a basic question. You don't know what the basic question is. I do.'

The teacher can see that what the trainee is thinking, saying, doing, is one answer to a basic question. The teacher can see that the trainee is holding to one answer to a basic question, and that he or she is almost certainly unaware that he or she is doing this, and what the underlying basic question is. For example, it is the initial session, and the trainee is asking the patient about her background history, specifically about whether she had brothers and sisters, and something about her mother and father when she was a child. The teacher is able to see that the trainee is taking a position of already having an answer to basic questions such as: (1) In intake sessions, what kinds of information are relevant? (2) What are the aims and purposes and goals of initial sessions with a patient?

The trainee understands the patient to have a deeper rage that does not show on the surface, and to have relatively inadequate defenses against the inner rage. It is the teacher's job to see that the trainee is face to face with a basic question, which can be formulated along these lines: 'If you believe in something "deep-seated", foundational, what determines if its nature and content are fixed or alterable, and to what extent they are fixed or alterable?' The teacher can see that the trainee already has an answer that the patient's 'inner rage' is essentially fixed and unalterable, and therefore is to be defended against and contained by means of adequate 'defenses'.

Often it is rather disconcerting for the trainee to be faced with some basic question. She is involved with this particular part of the session that she is playing, with what the client is doing and what is happening right here in the session. Suddenly, her attention is diverted to a question that seems out of the blue: 'This is interesting. So tell me, what do you think are the useful and effective ways for psychotherapists and patients to be with one another?' The trainee is entitled to pause, try to take stock, and to say: 'Um . . . huh? I don't quite follow.'

It is important that the teacher can see that the trainee is facing a basic question right here, and that he or she knows what the basic question is. It is helpful if the teacher is able to bridge the gap, i.e. to explain to the trainee that there is a basic question here, and maybe we can turn our attention to what that basic question is. This is a helpful skill.

Some examples of 'basic questions'

Some basic questions are more basic than others, and some relate more directly to in-session work than others, e.g. some basic questions relate more to 'conceptualization':

- What is the relationship between biological, neurological, physiological, chemical events and variables, on the one hand, and psychological variables, on the other?
- How can a conceptual system be constructed, originated, generated?

Some basic questions relate more to research:

- How can an hypothesis be shown to be wrong, false, refuted?
- On what basis is a piece of knowledge inserted into or withdrawn from the cumulative body of psychotherapeutic knowledge?

Here are some basic questions that relate to 'personality', touch the trainee's deeper framework, and can have some powerful implications for what he or she does in actual in-session work:

- Where does 'personality' come from in the first place?
- What are the components and parts of what is referred to as 'personality structure'?
- What accounts for substantial change in the way a person acts and behaves?
- How and why does a person have feelings that are good and pleasant or bad and unpleasant?
- What is the nature and content of what is presumed to be 'deep-seated', basic, foundational in human beings?
- Is there an entity or agency with the characteristics of 'free will'?
- How and why does a person construct, build, organize his or her own personal world?
- What accounts for change in 'personality'?
- Can there be dramatic changes in 'personality' that occur relatively suddenly?

Here are some basic questions that relate more directly to in-session psychotherapeutic work:

- What are the purposes, aims, and goals of an initial session?
- What identifies a change as a significant change?
- What are the determinants of the aims, goals of psychotherapy, the directions of change for the given patient?
- What kinds of information or data are useful in arriving at the aims and goals of psychotherapy for the given patient?
- Why do patients seek to have sessions with psychotherapists?
- Why do patients continue or discontinue having sessions with psychotherapists?
- What accounts for a psychotherapist maintaining and continuing or shifting to some substantially different way of thinking about and doing psychotherapy?
- Are the useful methods of change predominantly carried out by the therapist or by the patient?
- What are the useful and effective ways for psychotherapists and patients to be with one another?
- Are methods and techniques of psychotherapy owned and operated by given psychotherapies, or are they parts of a 'public marketplace' of methods and techniques?
- What kinds of past events are important and useful, and how are they important and useful?
- How can a person be free of bad feelings that (1) are relatively mild, (2) seem to be persistently present almost all the time and in almost every situation, and (3) seem to have been an intrinsic part of the person throughout his or her entire life?
- How can a person be free of situations that are painful, hurtful, accompanied by bad feelings?
- How can the post-session real world be used to help achieve personal change?
- How can a psychotherapist be aware of or reduce the effects of the psychotherapist's own personal value judgments in working with the particular person?
- How open and ready is the psychotherapist to undergo the degree and kind of change he or she is seeking to bring about in the client?
- How can psychotherapy enable the person to become what he or she is capable of becoming?

- How can psychotherapy achieve personal change that is deep-seated, fundamental, radical, foundational, transformational?
- How can deep-seated, radical, transformational change occur relatively quickly, in a single session, rather than gradually and cumulatively, over an extended program of sessions?
- How can readiness be increased for personal change that is deep-seated, radical, fundamental, foundational, transformational?
- How can a person become optimal, ideal, fully functioning?
- What is the conceptualization of what may be regarded as optimal, ideal, fully functioning?
- Are there specific, explicit ways of being and behaving common to people regarded as optimal, ideal, fully functioning, and, if so, what are they?
- How and why may dreams be used to understand a person?
- How and why may dreams be used to enable personal change?
- What does the therapist attend to as the person is being, talking, interacting?
- How does the therapist use his or her own immediate and ongoing thoughts, feelings, bodily sensations, images?
- How does the therapist arrive at a meaning from what the other person is saying and doing?
- How can a therapist know what the other person is thinking, seeing, feeling, undergoing?
- How can the therapist know what the other person may not know is going on inside him or her?

Guidelines for helping to get at the trainee's answer to the 'basic questions'

In effect, the teacher can say: 'You are facing a "basic question" right here. This is the basic question you are facing. What is your answer?' However, there are some guidelines that can make it easier for the trainee to arrive at an answer that seems to come from his or her own deeper framework. The following are some of these guidelines.

The search is for the trainee's own personal answer

The trainee must know that the search is for his or her own personal answer, rather than the 'right' answer for some particular approach, or the answer that the teacher of course knows is right. The right answer is the one that seems fitting and appropriate to the trainee, the answer that is accompanied by the right bells and whistles, the answer accompanied by a sense of being right for the trainee.

Let the trainee know that there may be several right and proper answers. One right answer is the trainee's own 'surface' answer, an answer that he or she genuinely accepts and believes in. What are the purposes, aims, and goals of the initial session of psychotherapy? The trainee can frame an answer that is personally suitable and fitting. And, yet, there can also be a more personal answer, a private answer, an answer that might well come from the trainee's own deeper framework, an answer that may seem somewhat uncommon, harder to defend, more devilish and risky. Give the trainee enough room to have several right answers.

Let the trainee know that the answer can be freely and easily altered, revised, revoked, replaced by another. He or she is not at all stuck with the answer. It is whatever answer he or she has now.

The teacher can provide examples of some different answers to the basic question

There are a number of ways in which it is helpful for the teacher to know and be able to cite some different answers to a basic question. One is to provide a context that there really can be and there are different answers to the basic question, that there need not be just one 'right' answer, that there are legitimately different approaches with identifiably different answers. A second is that the teacher may well offer the trainee an opportunity to select an appealing answer from a menu of answers, or for him or her to go beyond the different approaches to find his or her one fitting answer to the basic question.

Suppose that the trainee is face to face with this basic question: 'How and why may dreams be used to enable personal change?' A good teacher will at least have some idea of some different answers to this basic question, and will be able to make a stab at trying to identify some. A good teacher will be able to steer the trainee toward some resources that can provide some different answers to this basic question. A good teacher will be able to acknowledge that there are probably different answers, but he or she does not know enough to know of some legitimately different answers. On the other hand, most teachers may well know of their own answer to a basic question, and at least one or two different answers from one or two different approaches, e.g. here are some different answers to the following basic question: 'What are the purposes, aims, and goals of initial sessions?':

- The teacher's own answer is that the therapist must clarify the presenting problem and do a diagnostic evaluation. The good teacher should help the trainee by at least being able to identify some different ways of eliciting and clarifying the presenting problem, and several alternatives to what the teacher regards as a 'diagnostic evaluation'.

- The main goal of the initial session is to establish the groundwork for a proper therapist-client relationship, and this includes letting the client talk freely about whatever topics seem important to him or her.

- The main goal of the initial session is to define the roles of client and therapist, discuss the 'business' of psychotherapy, and explain the rationale of the therapist's approach.

- The main purpose of the initial session is to assess the appropriateness of this client for this therapy, and this therapy for this client. Check out the client's readiness for this therapy at this time.

- The main goal of the initial session is to accomplish as much as can be accomplished in a session. Rather than having unique and distinctive goals, compared with subsequent sessions, the goals of the initial sessions are to help accomplish what subsequent sessions aim at accomplishing.

The job of the teacher is to provide the trainee with some examples of some different answers to the basic question that he or she faces, or at least to let him or her know that there can be some rather different answers to the basic question.

The teacher can flag his or her own preferred answer

The trainee is here to discover his or her own deeper framework for psychotherapy, and the teacher must be of help. The trainee is not here to learn the teacher's way of doing psychotherapy.

Yet the trainee and the teacher, and the other trainees in the group, know that the teacher has a way of doing psychotherapy and that he or she probably has a preferred answer to the basic question. There are ways that the teacher can use his or her own preferred answer to help the trainee discover his or her own answer:

- The teacher can openly and honestly describe his or her own answer to the basic question about the components and parts to personality, about what accounts for substantial change in the way the person acts and behaves, about the kinds of information and data to obtain to arrive at the aims and goals of psychotherapy, about why patients seek sessions with psychotherapists, about what kinds of past events are useful and how they are useful. The teacher can say that here is my own answer to that question.

- The teacher can provide the precious atmosphere for different answers to the basic question. Of course his or her answer is the best of all possible answers. Of course any right-thinking trainee should adopt this answer. Of course the trainee can differ at the trainee's own peril. Of course there are altogether different answers in the field, and each constituency can provide evidence that its answer is best.

And of course the trainee's own answer will differ from the teacher's answer a little bit or a great deal. The atmosphere is good if it invites the trainee to come up with an answer that differs from the teacher's, even one that is widely afield from the teacher's, that is seriously alien to the teacher's, or goes as far as mirroring the teacher's own answer.

- Given the right atmosphere, and the teacher's own answer, what is the trainee's own answer to the basic question? This is the final payoff.

Some guidelines for how to use the trainee's answer to the 'basic questions'

The trainee has arrived at her own answer to the basic question, an answer that comes from her own deeper framework. There are ways the teacher can help the trainee use her answer to the basic question.

The teacher can show the trainee how to use the answer to make sense of and explain other topics

Once the teacher knows the trainee's answer, the teacher can help her broaden and expand the answer to make sense of and explain all sorts of other topics. If this is the answer to that basic question, perhaps the answer can be used with regard to other topics, other phenomena, perhaps even other related basic questions. The trainee found her answer, so maybe that answer is the answer to some other basic questions.

Where does it all come from in the first place? How does 'personality' get started? This trainee's deeper framework provided a distinctive answer: personality originates in the way a person handles important choices in life, important times of decision. It is at these choice points that the person becomes a person. Here is where it all comes from in the first place.

Now the teacher can help the trainee use her answer to shed light on some other questions, to answer other questions, to broaden the power of the answer by extending the answer to other topics, e.g. her answer may also apply to good parenting, to ways that parents can prepare a child to cope with later important choice points, personal life decisions. In addition, her answer can go a long way in understanding how personal change can occur, e.g. by going back to those incidents of important life decisions and enabling the person to make different and better decisions. Furthermore, her answer can help sort out the relative unimportance of so-called deeper and unconscious factors and variables, especially in comparison with the importance of early and determining life decisions. Even further, her answer helps to define what the person and the world bring to the person–world relationship, namely, the person brings past decisions and his or her decision-making apparatus, and the world contributes the conditions and circumstances for decision-making.

The teacher can help the trainee compare and contrast his answer with other answers

The trainee can now have a relatively clear idea of his own answer to the basic question, e.g. where personality comes from in the first place. Here are some ways that the teacher can help the trainee compare and contrast his answer with other answers:

- How does the trainee's answer fit in with his avowed surface approach? Suppose that he holds to a cognitive or to a person-centered approach. It may be that the trainee's answer does square well with the answer of the chosen approach. Or it may not. 'I don't really know what the person-centered answer is. I don't even know if it has an answer!' 'My answer is my approach's answer! I really do have a cognitive approach. It fits!'

- What are some common answers to that basic question? The trainee has discovered her own answer to the basic question of where personality comes from in the first place, how the person becomes the distinctive person that he or she has become. The teacher can help the trainee compare and contrast her answer with some other common answers to that basic question 'Here is a psychoanalytic answer to the basic question. Here is a social learning answer. Can you think of one or two standard other answers? There must be a few.' 'It looks like your answer has some fairly traditional alternatives, but they are different from yours, no?' 'It looks like yours is rather close to the cognitive answer, yes?'

The teacher can help show how the trainee's answer can have direct implications for what he does in the session

The teacher knows that the trainee's answer to the basic question can be thought of as abstract, conceptual, scholarly. There are conceptual works on the components and parts of 'personality structure', on what accounts for a person coming to have sessions with a psychotherapist, on the aims and goals of psychotherapy. The trainee can wax eloquent about 'archetypes' or core conceptual schemata, and stay in the rarified air of abstract conceptualization, far from the in-session trenches.

Whether the teacher and the trainee wallow in high-level conceptual discourse a little bit or a great deal, it is the teacher's job to see and to show how the trainee's answer can have direct implications for what he does in the session. The teacher must close the loop, to enable the trainee to use the answer to point back to the part of the tape that he started with, to show how his answer can make for significant differences in what he actually does in actual in-session work.

Some examples of how to find and how to use the trainee's answer to the 'basic questions'

The trainee began with a selected part, toward the end of the initial session, where she was telling the client how to answer the two sets of questions that he was to answer and bring in for the second session. The trainee was bothered by the way she waited so long to tell the client about the questionnaires, and wondered if she could have extended the appointment for another 15 minutes or so, or should have introduced the 'take-home' work earlier, or could have done a better job asking the client to answer the questionnaires.

The more she described what bothered her, the clearer it seemed to become that she was face to face with a basic question along these lines: 'What are the purposes and aims of the initial session? What do you want to accomplish in initial sessions?'

The trainee was able to recite what the program says should be accomplished in the initial sessions, and she knew that circumstances could alter the agenda. Nevertheless, when she was given a welcoming opportunity to address the basic question, and to delve into her own deeper notions and ideas, she found that she had deeper beliefs that emphasized the client's expectations about therapy, about what therapy would be like, about what he could get from therapy, and his highly personal hopes and dreams that might be achieved through therapy.

The trainee became excited at the importance she attributed to using the initial sessions to get this kind of information, and how this information was more valuable to her than the information yielded by the intake evaluation that the program said she should follow. She found herself explaining how special the initial sessions could be in opening up the client's own expectations, wishes and wants, hopes and dreams about therapy, about being with a therapist, about the kind of therapist he had in mind, about the kinds of changes that might be achieved. If the client's problems were touched upon, what was important was what might happen to these problems in therapy, what kinds of changes he wanted and hoped for, rather than the therapist's getting at the problem's severity or causes or history or diagnostic possibilities.

Once the trainee was able to explore her own deeper framework for answers to this basic question, she was able to move on to the practical and applied matter of how to use these answers in her practical and applied in-session work. She figured out ways to dedicate the initial session or sessions to enabling the client to provide these kinds of information. Her role was to elicit these kinds of information, to highlight and value them, to explore into and to carry forward the client's expectations and hopes for therapy, to have a menu of topics dealing with his expectations and hopes about therapy. For this trainee, here were the purposes and aims of the initial sessions of psychotherapy, and here were practical and useful ways of actually getting these kinds of information.

Another trainee had selected a part from the first 15 minutes or so of the session. It was the twenty-eighth session, and the trainee was bothered that his client was going on and on about her poor grades in some recent examinations at university. Why was the trainee bothered? He explained in depth that the client and her boyfriend had moved into an apartment paid for by the boyfriend's father, and the problem was that the father was so intrusive, i.e. the father shows up unannounced, when the client is home alone, and the father bothers her, makes her feel uncomfortable with his sexual innuendoes. This, the trainee believes, is the crux of the client's problems with being unable to sleep, being short-tempered, being reluctant to have inter-course, and feeling withdrawn and distant from her boyfriend.

In the session just before, the trainee wanted the client to be able to tell her boyfriend about the father's intrusiveness, and he had an agen-da for the present session, an agenda that included more focus on the client's feelings about the father, and her unwillingness to talk to her boyfriend about all of this. But, instead, the client is chattering about low grades in some university examinations. The problem, according to the trainee, was how to get her to talk about what he wanted her to talk about, instead of topics he deemed irrelevant.

It was here that the teacher invited the trainee to take a step to the side, and spend a few minutes dealing with a somewhat relevant 'basic question', namely: 'How can the therapist and client determine what issue, matter, topic is to be front and center for this particular session?'

On the surface, the trainee was drawn toward two apparently incompatible answers. One was that, in each session, the client is to be free to talk about whatever was on her mind, and the therapist is to accept and respect whatever she is here to talk about. The other answer is that once the therapist has a fairly good idea of what the problem is, he is to be the one who determines what the client should talk about. Unfortunately, it was these two answers that made for a problem in the twenty-eighth session.

The more the teacher offered some other answers to the basic ques-tion, and the more the trainee was able to dig into his own inner deeper framework, the closer he came to this answer to the basic ques-tion: 'It is the therapist's job to know what issues, matters, topics the client should focus upon. Once the therapist knows what these are, it is the therapist's job to make sure that the client talks about these par-ticular issues, matters, or topics.'

How could the trainee put these principles to work in the session? He figured out an answer that seemed right and fitting, and doable. At the start of each session, the therapist and the client can determine what matter to start with. The therapist can mention the topics that he believes are important, such as the client's feelings about not talking with her boyfriend about the father's 'visits', or her feelings about the father's visits, and she is invited to put on the table whatever is on her mind for this session. Then they decide together what topic to start with in this session.

The trainee was pleased with having an answer to the question that led to his playing this particular part of the session. He was pleased with discovering more about his own deeper framework for psychotherapy, and finding his own answer to a 'basic question'. And he was pleased about coming up with a solidly based way of using this answer in actual in-session work.

The next trainee was more than pleased with what she got from being able to face a basic question, and to think about her own answer to the basic question. She said, afterwards, that discovering this part of her own deeper framework apparently shaped the new way that she thought about and did psychotherapy from then on.

The session began with her playing a part of the session in which the client seemed to come out of his depression, for a few moments, and then went back inside the persistent depression. As was common in many of the sessions, the client was bitter and unhappy with his parents. He talked with a heavy and dead voice, with little feeling. There were extended pauses. The air was filled with uselessness, distancing, removal, withdrawal, depression, with the client and his brothers and sisters on one side, and his mother and father on the other.

But something interesting happened when the client mentioned that his much older sister had come for a brief holiday visit. She was an actress in New York. After a typical pause, the client's face lit up, and he actually giggled! His whole face brightened, and a whole different voice, one filled with bubbly animation, said: 'Gina doesn't take any crap from them. NO WAY.' And for the next 5 or 10 minutes, he was like a whole different person as he chatted on and on about Gina. He was giggling and laughing. He was happy. He was like a silly little boy who was having fun telling about Gina and how Gina was with their mom and dad.

Was it this dramatic change that so impressed the trainee? Was it the dramatic shift to this buoyant fellow that she wanted to show and tell? The trainee said no. 'This was a big change, and I think I was thrown off. I didn't expect such a change, and I was wondering what had happened. I didn't do anything to cause him to feel so different, and I just listened when he talked on and on. But here is what I wanted to play . . .' As she continued with the recording, the client is still being radiant, happy, silly, and then we hear the therapist saying, in a rather muted, neutral voice: 'How do you feel about the way Gina was with your parents?'

Within a few seconds, the client was back to being depressed, withdrawn, heavy. It was as if the therapist's question burst the bubble, and the client was back to being the unhappy way he had been. The trainee almost pleaded: 'What happened? This is what bothers me. What did I do?'

It was here that the teacher invited the trainee to shake hands with a basic question: 'Which part of the patient does the therapist talk to?' There can be choices. The trainee might have talked with the new and feisty patient, animated and happy: 'Gina can take charge of mom and dad! . . . You just watched Gina make fun of them? You didn't join in? . . . You sound like you want to applaud the way Gina is treating them like silly characters! . . . Gina's not afraid of them at all!' But, instead, the trainee talked to the depressed and distanced part: 'How do you [i.e. the depressed and distanced part] feel about the way Gina was with your parents?' And the depressed withdrawn part was once again present, and remained present when the session came to a close. It was as if the trainee refused to talk to the new and happy person, and instead chose to talk with the old and unhappy person. As a result, the new and happy person vanished and was replaced by the old and unhappy person. It was the trainee who seemed to be responsible for removing the new and happy person, and reinstalling the old and unhappy person.

The trainee seemed shocked by the idea that she may have choices of which part of the client to talk to. And yet, her opening concern with the powerful effect of her simple in-session question almost contained the seed of an idea that there are parts to the client, and that the therapist has choices of which part to select to talk to.

The more she thought about which part of the person the therapist talks to, and her own answer to the basic question, the bigger her answer became, and the more it seemed to have direct implications for what she does in actual in-session work. She came to four conclusions

1. The therapist almost always faces a choice of which part of the person to talk to.

2. There is usually a part that is being right here, immediate and present. There is usually a part that has reactions to the immediately ongoing and present part. There may well be one or more additional parts, if the therapist knows the person's 'insides' well enough.

3. Which part the therapist talks to can have exceedingly powerful implications.

4. Which part the therapist talks to can have a large hand in determining the kind of changes and the amount of changes that can occur in the person.

Simply by coming face to face with this basic question, and having a teacher who could enable the trainee to use the basic question to get at her deeper framework, the trainee was able to open up a whole new dimension of her own way of thinking about and doing psychotherapy.

There are at least three points that deserve to be highlighted in concluding this chapter:

1. This method of discovering the trainee's deeper framework is rather simple. It involves helping to put the trainee face to face with a basic question, and doing one's best to call upon his or her deeper framework in enabling him or her to provide an answer to the basic question. That is the method in a nutshell.

2. There is also a harder part. This method almost requires that the teacher and especially the trainee are able to get into a mind-set of 'basic questions', a mind-set in which most ways of thinking about psychotherapy, most theories and approaches, can be seen and appreciated as one of several ways of answering the basic questions.

3. When the deeper framework is discovered, it may be no special surprise, i.e. the deeper framework may fit rather well with the trainee's surface approach and way of thinking about psychotherapy. Often it may be somewhat different or even surprisingly different. In any case, the deeper framework is typically one of the more traditional approaches, but it may well be one of the more uncommon approaches, or perhaps have that special spark of originality. Regardless, the teacher and the trainee have come closer to discovering the trainee's own deeper framework for psychotherapy.

Chapter 11

Method 5: assign homework

With a few exceptions here and there, each training session ought to end with some kind of homework assignment. It is as if the training session produces a homework assignment, and the training session is not really over until the trainee has carried it out.

Assigning homework is more than a merely mechanical matter. It seems to take a certain amount of knowledge and skill for the teacher to know what kinds of homework to assign, and how to assign the homework effectively and well.

Both the teacher and the trainee have some responsibilities with regard to homework

It is mainly up to the teacher to find the homework assignment, to know what it can be, to identify it clearly and carefully. It is mainly up to the teacher to offer the homework assignment to the trainee, to assign the homework provided the trainee is ready and willing. In any case, homework assignment starts with the teacher. Usually, the homework assignment is hanging in the air, ready for the teacher to put into words, when the training session is coming to a close.

In the training session, it is up to the trainee to be ready and willing to accept a homework assignment. A trainee who profits from a training session tends to consider the homework assignment important, and is typically eager to find the fitting and appropriate homework assignment. Even more, the good trainee is eager to carry out the proper and fitting homework assignment after the session.

Later on, when the trainee is experienced, when he is moving well ahead in knowing and using his own deeper framework, he can do the work of the teacher, i.e. the trainee can accept the role of the one who ends the training session by finding and identifying the homework assignment and also by assigning it to himself.

The teaching session is over when the trainee does the homework

In one sense, the teaching session ends when it ends. But in another sense, the teaching session is over when the trainee leaves the teacher and carries out the homework assignment – carrying out the assignment is an important part.

Indeed, the trainee's carrying out of the homework can be seen as the highlight, the culmination of the session, the jewel. If the trainee carries out the homework reasonably well, she can gain the benefits of the discovery-oriented approach to training and supervision. She can find and clarify and carry forward her own deeper framework, and use that deeper framework to become the better and better therapist that she is capable of becoming.

If the trainee does not do the homework, in an important sense the teaching session was wasted, although each new training session offers the possibility of its own homework assignment. Sooner or later, she can begin to accept and carry out the homework assignments.

Add this to your notebook of your deeper framework

The trainee should have a notebook, a log, which may well be titled, 'My deeper framework for psychotherapy'. This notebook contains notes about what the trainee is discovering about his own deeper framework, what his deeper framework is, what the deeper framework has to say about conceptual issues and how to do psychotherapy.

If the trainee prefers, homework can consist of merely adding a few sentences or a paragraph or so to a running log of notes. The few sentences or paragraph are in no particular order. The log consists of disconnected notes. On the other hand, if the trainee is so inclined, the notebook may be rather organized so that there is a section on mind–body relationships, another on the initial sessions, a third on the origins of personality, and so on. In either case, the trainee has a notebook, and homework consists of adding something to that growing notebook of his own deeper framework for psychotherapy.

Some of the items that are added are likely to be well-accepted and well-known parts of other approaches, but they are nevertheless parts of the trainee's own deeper framework. Some may fit right in with what is already in the notebook, and some may be wholesale new departures. Some may be carefully worded, whereas others may be in the form of jumbled ideas. Some may be ideas that the trainee trusts and accepts, whereas others are going to have to be thought about for a while.

In any case, the homework assignment is to mark down the idea, the principle, or belief, which is part of the trainee's emerging deeper framework. It may be that most other trainees and most other therapists already know and accept this notion or idea. What matters is that the trainee has found something that seems to come from his own deeper framework, and here is a way of putting this notion or idea into actual words.

Some examples

Here are some verbatim examples of statements that the homework said the trainee is to add to the notebook or log of her deeper framework. Some of these statements are more about philosophical foundations or outlook, some are statements about what human beings are like, some about how psychotherapy works, and some refer to what she should do in actual in-session work.

Sometimes the statement is polished and finalized in the session, and the homework is mainly to add the statement to the trainee's notebook. Sometimes a general idea of the finalized statement is concocted in the session, and the homework includes polishing the statement to the trainee's satisfaction.

> 'When the client undergoes a significant change, the therapist has a choice of talking to the new person or to the old person; talking to the new person is better . . . The therapist's way of seeing a client is an important determinant of how far-ranging or limited the potential change can be in this client.'

> 'In just about every patient, there is a deep, hidden pocket of craziness, madness, psychosis. It may not show or affect the person, but it is there.'

> 'When the client comes up with a new behavior she can carry out in the post-session world, go along with the client. Give your approval. Encourage the client to carry it out.'

> 'If there is a bad quality or trait in you, such as being short-tempered or being cold and hard, you probably can't change that thing in you, but you can change your attitude toward it.'

'Bodily aches and pains can sometimes go away when the client has insight into the connection between the bodily aches and pains and the goals that can be achieved by having the bodily aches and pains, such as avoiding responsibility or avoiding doing things the person doesn't want to do.'

'An important job of the therapist is to fulfill the parental role that was missing in the client's infancy and childhood.'

'Important personality dimensions tend to occur in polarities, with one pole showing and the other pole deeper, hidden, buried, not showing.'

'This principle is just about a requirement before doing almost any intervention: when the client's voice quality is dead, contained, very low, without any feeling, the therapist should raise the voice quality to at least a moderate level of feeling and emotion. Otherwise, most interventions won't work.'

'If there is a big difference between what the client says is the problem or the solution, and what the therapist is fairly sure is the problem or the solution, the therapist's version is more important. I don't like putting this in words, but there are times when I do believe this principle.'

'Looking for causes in the client's past is not very useful. It is more important to get other information about a client's problem, information such as (1) how severe it is, how much it interferes with the client's life, or (2) the client's cognitions that account for the problem.'

Write about your creative new idea and its implications

In the training session, looking for the trainee's deeper framework can strike a goldmine. The goldmine can consist of the seed of a whole new conceptualization of psychotherapy, a big new idea about psychotherapy, a creative new idea with plenty of creative implications. When the teacher and the trainee come face to face with the creative new idea, both know that they are face to face with a creative new idea.

The teacher may actually say: 'This has the markings of a genuinely new idea. There can be something exciting here. I think you are on to something. Go for it. Obviously someone may have written about this, but this seems to be a seed of something creative, at least compared with what is commonly accepted in the field of psychotherapy.'

What the teacher does not think or say is this: 'You are so naive. What kind of training have you had? You think this is a creative new idea? Wrong! The whole field knows about this. To you it is a creative new idea. To almost everyone else, this is part of the accepted knowledge of the field of psychotherapy. Welcome to the field!' If this is what the teacher thinks or says, the teacher is not an especially good teacher.

The homework assignment is for the trainee to write anywhere from a few paragraphs to a few pages or more about the creative new idea and its implications for the field of psychotherapy. Treat the creative new idea as a creative new idea. Clarify the new idea. Spell it out further. Let it grow. Nurture and develop it further and further.

The teacher's job is to help the trainee be relatively clear on just what the creative new idea is. The trainee's job is to do the homework assignment.

Some examples

For a few moments, in the actual session, the trainee was not sure whether she was talking to the person who was psychotic or to the person who had thoughts and feelings about being psychotic. The trainee had come face to face with an idea of there being 'parts' to the patient, and what was so exciting was that she was starting to sense the vast power in which part she addresses, to whom she talks. Her homework assignment was to write about this, to explore some further possibilities. What are therapists missing when they essentially restrict themselves to talking to one main part of the patient? Are therapists squeezing their patients into being far less than the patients can be, restricting what patients can be, by confining the dialogue to just one part of them? Think about these issues. Write about these issues.

By probing in and near his deeper framework, the trainee arrived at the idea that this client really just wanted someone like him to talk to. There was no symptom, no presenting complaint, no psychological problem, no mental disorder. Not really. Well, the trainee could probably find one if he set his mind to it, but he was impressed that this person just wanted to talk with someone about all sorts of issues and matters, some personal and some just interesting to talk about. The homework assignment was to explore this idea, to see how far it goes, to write about the possibilities. Was this a rare exception? What might this mean about how the therapist and the client are with each other? Is the therapist showing the client how to talk this way with another person? Can the client find someone in his real world to talk with in this way? What does this mean for what psychotherapy is, does, is for?

The trainee found an interesting new idea as part of her deeper framework. The idea was that perhaps 'problems' were more than things to be treated, reduced, removed. They are all that, but perhaps they are more. Perhaps what look like 'problems' can also be seen as evidence of some important life choices, decision points, possible new directions. If the patient is gloomy and depressed, or agitated and worried, maybe the patient is dealing with, reacting to, some new possibility in life, a new direction, a choice that was not so present before. Think about all this. Write about this.

The trainee's deeper framework seemed to include an idea about a 'core' problem, something underneath and central to the more surface problems, worries, troubles. 'Doing something' about the more surface problem seemed to mean finding the deeper 'core' problem, and working on that. The trainee was excited about the idea of a 'core' problem, some underlying deeper problem, and the homework assignment was to write a page or so about this. Does the idea of a 'core' problem make solid sense? How can it be found? What is the relationship between the problem that the client talks about and the 'core' problem?

After about 20 sessions, the client and trainee agreed that the problem was now much less of a problem, and further sessions seemed unnecessary. It was time for goodbyes. However, the closer the trainee approached her deeper framework, the more something seemed unfinished, or perhaps an opportunity seemed lost. She was drawn to the idea that treating a problem, doing a good job in regard to the problem, was just not enough. Now that the big worry was generally gone, maybe therapy could do more. The trainee was not quite sure what this next step or phase might be, but she was almost convinced that there was a next step or phase. The homework assignment gave her a chance to think and write about these issues, these possibilities. Would she come up with something? What might be uncovered by some serious thinking about this matter?

Supervision is generally a matter of the trainee learning how to carry out some brand of psychotherapy, and learning how to act like a professional psychotherapist. Supervision generally is a matter of the trainee learning what the supervisor has to offer. In some contrast, this kind of homework assignment invites the trainee to think, perhaps to engage in some serious thinking, perhaps some creative thinking.

Figure out your answer to the basic question or the applied question

It is common for the trainee to be face to face with some relatively basic question or applied question of in-session operations. It is also common that he comes to some answer to these important questions. Helping him to arrive at an answer is what the teacher is there to do.

However, there are times when the basic question or the applied question seems to become tougher and tougher to answer. The trainee squares off against the question, may even gain heightened respect for the question, but he has not yet arrived at an answer that seems to be the right answer for him. He has not yet arrived at the deeper framework.

This is when the teacher can assign the homework. The question may be a basic one, dealing with conceptualization, basic issues, foundational matters. Or the question may deal with more practical in-session strategies and operations. In either case, the teacher should encourage the trainee to think about the question, to try to arrive at an answer, or even several answers. Here is an opportunity to involve the trainee's deeper framework in arriving at an answer.

Some examples

The trainee was bothered that the client just seemed to be dumping problems on her lap. It was as if the client were saying: 'Here is my problem, so tell me what to do about it.' This is not at all what the trainee preferred. When the teacher and trainee studied what happened earlier on the tape, and in the previous session too, it became embarrassingly clear that the trainee was playing the role of the great fixer. She had set the stage by saying words close to these: 'I fix problems. Tell me your problems. I will solve them for you. I am a trained professional problem-fixer. Just entrust yourself to me.' So the client did, and she was upset at the client doing what she invited him to do.

Here was the important question that the trainee was asked to think about and try to answer: 'When the therapist has a hand in helping to bring about the in-session problem, issue, matter that she complains about, is bothered by, what might she have done differently?' The case in point is this: 'What can the therapist do to avoid inviting the client to dump problems onto her lap, and for the client to expect that she will solve the problems as if the therapist were Dr Fix-it?'

A second example is of a trainee who alternated between being tit-illated by her handsome client and being bothered by being so taken by the handsome client. This was the second session, and the trainee told about the highlights with excitement and professional wincing. Her heart was racing as she walked to the waiting room. She tried so hard to be professional as they walked to her office. In excerpts she played from the session, she sounded all right, but she honestly confessed to trying hard not to stare at his handsome features. She confessed to going between wanting to tell a few of her colleagues about the handsome client and being bothered by her obvious attraction to good-looking clients.

In talking about this matter, she was not satisfied with her simply having some sort of a problem of emotional reactions to some clients, of being attracted to gorgeous male clients. She veered further afield, into matters of what she got out of being a psychotherapist, and how she felt when her colleagues talked about their clients in ways that seemed honest but not purely professional. The teacher asked her to write her answer to this question: 'What does the therapist get from being with a client? For the therapist, what are the important moments in the session, and why are these important?' The trainee was in the vicinity of some truly deeper issues in the field of psychotherapy, and the homework assignment allowed her to call upon her deeper framework in addressing these deeper issues.

For this trainee, the part of the tape that he selected was just another illustration of his quest to see what causes clients' problems. This particular client was bothered by a sense of being so alone, by herself, cut off and distanced from virtually everyone. In the course of studying the tape, the trainee was compelled by one thing the client said. It had stuck with him ever since the session. It was when the client offhandedly mentioned: 'My mother said I was like that since I was a baby.' That is all. The client then went on to something else, but he could not get that line out of his head.

Although the teacher recognized how important the issue was, it seemed that delving further into the matter was more a matter of it being prime material for a homework assignment, and the trainee eagerly agreed. Here was the question for the homework: 'Where does "personality" come from in the first place? What are the root causes of the basic foundation of "personality"?' The trainee had some understanding of psychology's stock answers to these questions. The homework assignment enabled him to delve into his own answers.

For this trainee, the problem came in the initial session, and consisted of a negative reaction to the client, not so much as a person, but rather as a client with whom to work. The trainee knew that she preferred other clients, that she just would rather not spend so much time in future sessions with this client. How come? It seemed clear to the trainee, the teacher, and other trainees in the group that this trainee was psychotherapy's answer to a Rock of Gibraltar. She was a person to be counted on, a solid and stable individual, a reassuringly dependable Rock of Gibraltar. It was also clear that this particular client would not especially fit the complementary role.

In considering a homework assignment, the teacher was going back and forth between two, and the trainee asked if she could write something about both, because both seemed so important for her to think about. Here were the two questions:

1. What could she do in initial sessions to see if she and the client might be a good fit or a poor fit in the balance of the sessions? Her present format for the initial sessions did not provide much of an answer. What would be a better way?

2. What kind of work settings might maximize her opportunities to be a therapist who provides stability, trustworthiness, solidness, dependability? A pain management clinic, private practice, school system, addiction center, psychiatric ward?

This next trainee had come face to face with a deeper issue, a basic question. The question was common enough, and may be phrased as follows: 'If you have some apparently lifelong quality or characteristic, such as having a pessimistic outlook or having a quick temper, are these qualities or characteristics fixed or are they changeable?' Although this was the basic question, the trainee was drawn toward two related questions from his study of the particular tape:

1. If these qualities and characteristics are fixed and stable, what can be done so that they do less harm? The trainee was thinking of the quick temper that flared and led to some big trouble for the client.

2. If these qualities and characteristics are changeable, what are the limits? Can a person be free of some of these bothersome and troubling qualities and characteristics? Can the quick temper go away?

The teacher had done most of the work in clarifying and putting into actual words the questions that the trainee would be thinking about. What seemed so special was that he was so eager to think about these questions, and hopefully to arrive at good answers.

In careful study of the tape, the next trainee was increasingly impressed with how she 'clicked' with the client, how she just happened to be the right kind of person for the client at this time. The trainee walked around the idea that what seemed to be of such help, what enabled the client to get over what he had to get over, was the kind of person that she was. In particular, she appreciated the client's wickedness and raucous impulsiveness. The client was like a little devil, and the trainee thought of this as a precious quality.

Now came the issue of framing the homework assignment. The teacher suggested that the trainee answer the basic question: 'What helps bring about change?' At first the trainee was somewhat taken aback, but then she realized that this was the very question she was circling around, and she was quite ready to delve into her own deeper thoughts about how the therapist fulfilling the right role could be an important factor in enabling the client to change.

This next trainee had come up against a fleeting moment in the session when what happened seemed so strange, so hard to understand, so mysterious. In the thirteenth session, he had a brief moment when he was absolutely certain that he and the client had played together as young children. He actually had a brief memory of their pushing a big plastic ball back and forth. What was so intriguing was that the trainee passed by easy and glib explanations, and seemed to be giving voice to explanations coming from his own deeper framework. The homework assignment was to try to explain this phenomenon by calling upon what seemed to be notions from his own deeper framework. A page or so would be sufficient. He brought in 10 pages of explanation.

In the course of studying the tape, the trainee arrived at this principle: 'There are conditions when the therapist's reactions to what the client is saying and doing, or how she is being, can also mirror or reflect her own deep-seated reactions.' In the session, the therapist was repulsed and disgusted with what the client was saying she had done, and, later in the session, the therapist was frankly surprised that the client, on her own, also mentioned that she was repulsed and disgusted. The trainee was not especially interested in why this might be, in looking for a way of making sense of why the therapist's reaction was also the client's reaction. On the other hand, the trainee was quite drawn to ways of using the principle. Here is the homework question that the teacher and the trainee arrived at: 'How can the therapist use his strong personal reaction to what the client is being like, saying, or doing?' This is the assignment the trainee much preferred.

The next trainee started the session puzzled, and was still puzzled when it came to defining what the homework should be. He began by playing a portion of the tape where the client seemed quite different from usual. She was laughing, making fun of her family, gesticulating with gusto, talking loudly, interrupting the therapist. When the therapist says that the time is over, the session is to stop, it is as if there was a moment where the animated, vibrant client receded back into the mousy little girl, pulled in and quiet, living inside a dead body that could barely move. Puzzled as the trainee was, he was even more puzzled in arriving at a homework assignment because he was facing a basic issue that was utterly new for him. 'I thought people want to feel good! Or at least not awful! Why did she switch?' He finally arrived at this wording of the question he wanted to address: 'Could it be more important for some people to feel miserable than happy?'

This was the opening of the ninth session. The trainee selected a part in which she and the client were jostling for what issue should be the focus of the session. Studying that part brought her to a principle of her deeper framework in which it was the therapist's responsibility to decide what issues the client should deal with in the session. She was surprised at what her own deeper framework seemed to believe, and she was ready and eager to address the issue: 'After the initial sessions, who has the larger hand in determining which issues should be the central focus of the session – the therapist or the client?'

To learn more about your deeper framework, study these readings

Once the trainee discovers something about his or her own deeper framework, a finger points toward some readings on that particular topic, that particular issue. The training session discovered something of the trainee's deeper framework. That sets the stage for learning more, for further study, which means that he she can be ready to study readings that go into depth on that issue or topic.

If the trainee knows something about those readings, has some familiarity, it is now time to study those readings again because his or her deeper framework casts a new and important light on these particular readings. If he or she has little or no familiarity with those readings, it can be even more important for him or her to study them. Usually, discovery of the deeper framework points toward the importance of readings that are unfamiliar to the trainee.

The teacher need not be an encyclopedia of what references the trainee can read. Sometimes the teacher can help by suggesting a particular book or author or journal. 'Start with this article by Sanderson in the last issue or so of the *American Psychologist* . . . There is this journal. Try glancing through its issues. Have you read anything by Assagioli? He writes about that matter . . . Here is a book of mine. Read this chapter to start with.' Often the teacher cannot be of much help in what the trainee can read, but can point him or her in a general direction.

There can be something precious in this reading, because the trainee may well have found a friend who is also interested in that particular topic. What is more, the friend has studied that topic, and has something to say that can tell the trainee more, can broaden and extend and clarify his or her newfound appreciation and understanding of the topic.

This homework assignment is over when the trainee reads the work, uses the work to know more about the deeper framework, carries the deeper framework further, and then actually writes a few paragraphs or more in his or her diary or log of his or her deeper framework. Some readings can be precious because the trainee has found a truly knowledgeable teacher on the subject of this part of the deeper framework. Study what that author has to say. Learn from that author. Then carry one's own deeper framework forward by writing in one's own diary or log or notebook.

Some examples

The trainee began with puzzlement. During the session with the client, she had a vivid private thought that the client was going to kill himself. What might she do with this private thought? How could she use this disturbing but vivid private thought? The trainee and the teacher found a way that seemed to come out of the trainee's own deeper framework, and that may well be useful, but the trainee wanted more. 'Has someone written about this – about when the therapist gets a thought like this, how to use it?' The teacher knew of nothing directly, but could suggest a reference that might help. As the trainee explained in the next session with the teacher, that reference pointed to a few sources that were right on the target, and she was so pleased that there were pieces written on the precise topic. She cited these references in the two pages she wrote about in-session situations when the therapist has vivid private thoughts that the client is going to do something serious like kill himself or murder someone.

In the course of examining the tape and in discovering a bit more of the trainee's deeper framework, she found that she loved playing the role of Dr Fix-it, the quick and effective problem-solver. It was, she believed, no accident that she was so drawn toward the solution-focused therapeutic approach, but she was puzzled that this approach did not seem to fit the range of problems that her clients seemed to present. What might she read? The teacher suggested that she start with readings on integrative–eclectic therapy and, some days later, the beaming trainee put on the table about a dozen articles by therapists who likewise embraced the Dr Fix-it role, all of whom took a broad and loose integrative approach that allowed them to select the most useful treatment for the client's problem. She had written a page or so about the advantage of this kind of integrative approach in allowing the all-purpose therapist to quickly and efficiently take care of almost any problem the client can present.

The trainee has discovered that his deeper framework included a principle that personality was made up of polarities, with one pole out on the visible, public surface, and the other pole buried deeper inside the client's hidden personality. The trainee saw this firsthand with this particular client where the manifest pole consisted of passivity, weakness, softness, and the inner deeper pole being that of coldness, hardness, ruthlessness. The teacher suggested that the trainee start by reading Perls and Jung. When the trainee brought in his log, in the next teaching/training session, he had devoured Jung's ideas on the grand polarities of personality.

This trainee was reluctant, at first, to consider that her deeper framework included an idea that she could have a deep connection with some special clients but not others. From the first sessions, with some clients, she almost seemed to know what they were thinking or feeling. The client had merely mentioned a little girl walking along the street, and the trainee somehow knew that the client saw herself in that little girl, and wanted to take her home. No one else, in the group listening to the tape, even came close to what the trainee somehow sensed. In describing the deeper framework, she said,: 'There are some clients where, from the beginning, I "resonate" with them. I know them. I know what's going on inside them, better than they do!'

She was so drawn toward reading about this. She discounted suggestions of reading about the therapist–client relationship. Finally, she accepted a suggestion to start with the literature on countertransference, and to search for reports of similar deep, hard-to-explain knowing of the client. She was eager to pursue her homework assignment, and perhaps to find ways she might be able to use her 'resonating' with some of her clients.

When this other trainee discovered a corner of her own deeper framework, she was wholesomely embarrassed and rather guilty. Her professed approach was cognitive, although she was not a fervid or an especially devout follower of cognitive therapy. She liked that approach and it made good sense. However, in probing deeper inside her own way of thinking, she uncovered a part of her own deeper framework that seemed to be as follows: 'Significant personality change comes from accepting the power of God!' She was embarrassed and guilty because her life had not been spent waving such a banner, she was surprised that such a belief was perhaps so central in her deeper framework, as a psychotherapist she spent little or no time thinking about the power of God, and she felt that such a belief had little or no place in scientific psychotherapy.

She was pointed toward a body of writings by respected contributors to 'scientific psychotherapy', and she was enthusiastic about finding answers to two questions especially:

1. Are there really other psychotherapists who believe in the importance of accepting God?

2. How can such a belief fit in with the tenets of scientific psychotherapy?

Reading can be so important and so helpful, especially if the reading carries forward the trainee's curiosity or excitement from something that happened in the session, something that touches or comes from his or her own deeper framework. What he or she reads may have to do with some in-session happening, or some conceptual matter, but what can make the reading so inviting is that he or she is with a person who is familiar with that in-session happening or that conceptual matter. The writer has been there, knows the topic well, and can talk with the trainee about what has intrigued him or her.

Reading can include much more than showing the trainee how to do the therapy that the supervisor supervises. Reading can help the trainee to carry forward, to further develop, his or her own deeper framework. The fruits of the right reading can include a paragraph or a page or so in his or her notebook.

Engage in skill-developing practice

The teaching session identified some skill. The homework is for the trainee to practice that skill, to do it over and over, to gain increasing proficiency and competency in the skill. It is practice time.

The teacher may practice the skill with the trainee so that he or she gets the idea of how to practice in a skill-developing way. The teacher may describe how the trainee can practice, but the homework is for him or her to engage in his or her own skill-developing practice.

There can be at least four ways to engage in skill-developing practice. Arranged roughly in terms of degree of increasing carefulness, they are as follows:

1. Write down the actual skill, describe it in some detail, then go ahead and practice it over and over again, e.g. picture that the skill is assigning homework for the client to carry out. Write down when you say it, the right circumstances. Write down carefully worded guidelines for what you say and how you say it.

   Then practice. Say aloud what you would say in the actual session in assigning homework. Say it over and over again, revising and modifying what you say until you are reasonably satisfied. Rehearse it until you are relatively skilled and comfortable in assigning homework.

2. Practice the skill with a partner. Suppose that the skill is the same one of assigning homework toward the end of the session. The trainee is with a partner, usually a fellow trainee. The partner plays the role of the client, and the trainee tries out assigning homework.

   Picture that the trainee and the partner discuss how that went, how it might be revised here and there, and the trainee then practices assigning the homework two or four times until he or she is reasonably satisfied and competent and comfortable in the skill.

3. Practice what the master does at the given point on the tape of the master's session. You have the tape of a master, an exemplar. It is not your tape. It is not your teacher's tape. It is the tape of a master

practitioner. Furthermore, you have isolated precisely where it is that the exemplar practitioner did what you would like to learn how to do.

You can play the tape up to that point where the master does the special thing that he does. You study what he does. You then replay the tape, stopping it at the right point, and then you try doing what the master does. Compare what you did with what he did. Try again. Keep doing this until you are close to doing it as well as he did, e.g. it is at this point that the master's client turns on him, attacks him, just as your client turned on and attacked you. Only this time you can learn from what the master did. Or, at this point, he did something you want to learn, namely how to be genuinely pleased with the changes shown by the client. Or, right here on the tape, he offered an 'interpretation' that genuinely impressed you.

In each case, you can practice what the master did under those immediate conditions. You can, compare your own level of proficiency with his, and you can keep practicing until your proficiency is in the same range as his.

4. Stop the tape at the point where you could have done something better, and practice doing what you could have done. It is the tape of your session, and you stop the tape where you could have done something better. You figure out what you should have done right here, and you try it out, e.g. at this point in the tape, your idea is that you could have used the sudden clutching up sensations in your abdomen. You didn't use these bodily felt sensations, but you could have. Or, at this point, you suddenly have two quite different and mutually inconsistent interpretations, and you could have mentioned both of them, but you didn't.

So you practice doing the newfound skill. But you practice by recording what the client says and then your attempt to do what you could have done at that point. You then listen to the recording, and record the second attempt to do it better. By studying each recording, and by trying it out over and over again, you are gradually refining the skill and gradually gaining increased proficiency in the developing skill.

These are four ways for trainees to do homework so as to increase their proficiency on given skills. They provide opportunities for skill-developing practice, opportunities for trainees to learn skills, and new skills, in order to attain a continually increasing level of proficiency, opportunities for seasoned practitioners to gain heightened proficiency in old and new skills.

The field of psychotherapy is not especially characterized by most of its trainees and practitioners engaging in skill-developing practice. It seems fair to say that, in the past year, precious few trainees or practitioners have accumulated 500 hours or 5 hours of dedicated, skill-developing practice, especially where they can provide convincing evidence of actual heightened levels of skill development. It also seems fair to say that the state of proficiency and competency of most practitioners seems to reflect the relative absence of hours and hours of actual skill-developing practice, and that trainees who engage in this kind of homework on a regular basis are likely to be functioning at a much higher level of proficiency and competency than the common level of most practitioners who have accumulated virtually no hours of skill-developing practice. Skill-developing practice helps, and its consequences can be impressive. Hopefully, the consequences might even impress the field of psychotherapy, including its teachers, trainers, and trainees.

When the trainee's deeper framework is sufficiently understood, homework can shift to studying and learning that psychotherapy

There will usually come a time when the trainee's deeper framework is lifted out, discovered, developed. The trainee and the teacher know the deeper framework rather well; the trainee has worked with it, tried it out in actual operation. The deeper framework is now understood sufficiently well.

Here is where the teacher and the trainee may well identify the deeper framework, recognize it, see what it is. It may be that the trainee's deeper framework is a little or quite similar to a given psychotherapeutic approach, one that is known. The trainee's deeper framework is that of solution-focused, Adlerian, primal, cognitive, psychodrama, fixed role, or Jungian therapy, eye movement desensitization and reprocessing, or behavior, person-centered, transpersonal, narrative, or psychodynamic therapy. Sometimes identification can pinpoint the therapy, sometimes only the general family. 'Your framework is of integrative therapy . . . Your framework is of this specific kind of integrative therapy.'

When this stage is reached, homework can consist of bringing this kind of teaching and training to a close, and shifting to the trainee's more or less direct study and learning of the approach that fits. Read about the approach. Study the approach. Learn that approach. Get supervision in the approach. It is your approach, or very close to your approach.

Sometimes, rarely, the trainee's deeper framework can gradually be discovered and slowly appreciated and understood. However, it does not seem to fit into any of the generally known approaches to psychotherapy. Under these special conditions, homework can consist of searching for the right family, even though the family may not be a solid fit. Or the homework consists of finding writings that speak to the trainee even though no particular therapeutic approach seems to be the one for him or her. But this is rare. It may be that the teacher is working with the special trainee who is truly creative. Keep working with that trainee, for some time at least.

I am still working on making experiential psychotherapy better and better, and I always have my eye out for the occasional trainee whose deeper framework is virtually that of experiential psychotherapy. By 'occasional' I mean that one in every 50 or so trainees. If I should come upon such a trainee, I am usually rather skeptical that I actually came across such a trainee. Then I am surprised because such trainees are exceedingly rare. Next I invite him or her to try a homework assignment of shifting over to studying and learning experiential psychotherapy.

Finally, I can say that this entire program of doing discovery-oriented teaching and training is a marvelously inefficient way of finding a trainee who can learn to do experiential psychotherapy!

Conclusions and invitations

1.(a) A case is presented that many trainees have inner deeper frameworks about psychotherapy, which can include notions and ideas about human nature and change, about how people get to be the way they are and what people can become, about how and why people can have pain and suffering, about how people can feel better, and how this can occur in what is called psychotherapy.

(b) The case suggests that these inner deeper frameworks are composed of notions and ideas that are rather loosely formed, undeveloped, shadowy, unclarified.

(c) The case suggests that the inner deeper frameworks may bear some goodness of fit with the trainee's chosen approach, outlook, psychotherapy, or the inner deeper frameworks may represent a substantial departure from the chosen approach to psychotherapy.

(d) Finally, the case suggests that most trainees can be essentially unfamiliar with and unaware of their own inner deeper frameworks for psychotherapy.

2. A review of the literature on supervision seems to indicate that helping trainees to discover, develop, and carry forward their own inner deeper frameworks is not an especially common component of supervision. Rather, it has received little or no mention in the literature on supervision.

3. A case is presented that there can be advantages for interested supervisors to be of some assistance in enabling interested trainees to probe down into, to search, explore, and discover, to develop and carry forward, their own inner deeper frameworks. One advantage can be for a higher goodness of fit between the trainee's inner deeper framework and his or her chosen approach to psychotherapy,

i.e. the chosen approach can be right and proper for him or her, not only at the working surface, but also with regard to his or her own inner deeper framework for psychotherapy. Among the other advantages, one may be especially speculative, untested, yet the possibility is raised that the trainee's general level of competency can be higher if there is a pronounced goodness of fit between the inner framework and the chosen approach.

4. There are methods of opening up and discovering, developing and carrying forward, the trainee's own inner deeper framework for psychotherapy. Five of these methods are proposed (in Chapters 7–11), and described well enough for interested supervisors and trainees to use.

   One practical and concrete invitation is for interested supervisors to make their own personal summary of the guidelines under each of the methods. Each of the five chapters describes a given method, and there are a number of working guidelines for each method. The invitation is for the supervisor to organize their own personal summaries of each of the guidelines for the five methods.

   The related second invitation is for the interested supervisor to learn these five methods and the guidelines underlying each. Learn them well enough to be able to put them to actual use in discovery-oriented training sessions with interested trainees.

5. For teachers, trainers, supervisors, and trainees who are sufficiently interested, who have a glow of enthusiasm, the invitation is to dedicate a component of training and supervision to enabling trainees to discover their own deeper frameworks for psychotherapy. Try using the methods presented in this book.

6. For the field of psychotherapy supervision, the invitation is to leave a little room for the discovery-oriented approach. This may well be a relatively new component, but it can probably coexist with the more traditional components of supervision.

7. For the field of psychotherapy, the invitation is for teaching and training to include a component of enabling trainees to explore, appreciate, and benefit from discovering their own inner deeper frameworks for psychotherapy. Of course there can be plenty to

teach students and trainees, plenty for them to learn. But if the field is to advance and improve, one little way can include students and trainees being able to explore their own deeper frameworks, to go beyond what they believe they know and are to know.

References

Alonzo, A. (1985). The Quiet Profession: Supervisors of psychotherapy. New York: Macmillan.

Andrews, J.D.W., Norcross, J.C., and Halgin, R.P. (1992). Training in psychotherapy integration. In: Norcross, J.C. and Goldfried, M.R. (eds), Handbook of Psychotherapy Integration. New York: Basic Books, pp. 563–592.

Blocher, D.H. (1983). Toward a cognitive developmental approach to counselor supervision. Counseling Psychologist 11: 27–34.

Burkhardt, B.R. (1980). Training and supervision of crisis workers. In: Hess, A.K. (ed.), Psychotherapy Supervision: Theory, research and practice. New York: Wiley, pp. 407–419.

Cooper, A. and Witenberg, E.G. (1984). Stimulation of curiosity in the supervisory process. In: Caligor, L., Bromberg, P.M. and Meltzer, J.D. (eds), Clinical Perspectives on the Supervision of Psychoanalysis and Psychotherapy. New York: Plenum, pp. 59–74.

Ekstein, R. and Wallerstein, R.S. (1972). The Teaching and Learning of Psychotherapy. New York: International Universities Press.

Gilbert, M.C. and Evans, K. (2000). Psychotherapy Supervision: An integrative relational approach to psychotherapy supervision. Buckingham: Open University Press.

Goodyear, R.K. and Bradley, F.O. (1983). Theories of counselor supervision: Points of convergence and divergence. The Counseling Psychologist 11: 59–67.

Greenberg, L. (1980). Supervision from the perspective of the supervisee. In: Hess, A.K. (ed.), Psychotherapy Supervision: Theory, Research and Practice. New York: Wiley, pp. 85–91.

Haley, J. (1996). Learning and Teaching Therapy. New York: Guilford Press.

Hart, G.M. (1982). The Process of Clinical Supervision. Baltimore, MA: University Park.

Haynes, R., Corey, G., and Moulton, G. (2003). Clinical Supervision in the Helping Professions: A practical guide. Pacific Grove, CA: Brooks/Cole.

Heppner, P.P. and Roehlke, H.J. (1984). Differences among supervisees at different levels of training: Implications for a developmental model of supervision. Journal of Counseling Psychology 31: 76–90.

Hess, A.K. (ed.) (1980a). Psychotherapy supervision: Theory, research and practice. New York: Wiley.

Hess, A.K. (1980b). Training models and the nature of psychotherapy supervision. In: Hess, A.K. (ed.), Psychotherapy Supervision: Theory, research and practice. New York: Wiley, pp. 15–25.

Hess, A.K. (1986). Growth in supervision: Stages of supervisee and supervisor development. The Clinical Supervisor 4: 51–67.

Hess, A.K. (1987). Psychotherapy supervision: Stages, Buber, and a theory of relationship. Professional Psychology: Research and Practice 18: 251–259.

Hill, C.E., Charles, D., and Reed, K.G. (1981). A longitudinal analysis of changes in counseling skills during counseling training in counseling psychology. Journal of Counseling Psychology 28: 428–436.

Hogan, R.A. (1964). Issues and approaches in supervision. Psychotherapy: Theory, Research and Practice 1: 139–141

Lewis, J.M. (1978). To Be a Therapist: The teaching and learning. New York: Brunner/Mazel.

Loganbill, C., Hardy, E., and Delworth, U. (1982). Supervision: A conceptual model. The Counseling Psychologist 10: 3–42.

Mahrer, A.R. (1985). Psychotherapeutic Change. An alternative approach to meaning and measurement. New York: Norton.

Mahrer, A.R. (1987). If there really were a specialty of psychotherapy: Standards for postdoctoral training in psychotherapy. The Humanistic Psychologist 15: 83–94.

Mahrer, A.R. (1988). Discovery-oriented psychotherapy research. Rationale, aims, and methods. American Psychologist 43: 694–702.

Mahrer, A.R. (1989). Experiencing: A humanistic theory of psychology and psychiatry. Ottawa: University of Ottawa Press.

Mahrer, A.R. (1995). A new departure in experiential supervision. Symposium address, American Psychological Association, New York.

Mahrer, A.R. (1996/2004). The complete guide to experiential psychotherapy. Boulder, CO: Bull.

Mahrer, A.R. (1998). A new departure in experiential supervision: Discovering the trainee's deeper personal approach to psychotherapy. The Clinical Supervisor 17: 125–133.

Mahrer, A.R. (2000). Philosophy of science and the foundations of psychotherapy. American Psychologist 55: 1117–1125.

Mahrer, A.R. (2001). An historical review of the field of psychotherapy – from the year 2199. Psychotherapy Bulletin 36: 9–14.

Mahrer, A.R. (2002). Becoming the Person You Can Become: The complete guide to self-transformation. Boulder, CO: Bull.

Mahrer, A.R. (2003). What are the foundational beliefs in the field of psychotherapy? Psychology: Journal of the Hellenic Psychological Society 10: 1–19.

Mahrer, A.R. (2004a). Theories of Truth, Models of Usefulness: Toward a revolution in the field of psychotherapy. London: Whurr.

Mahrer, A.R. (2004b). Why do Research in Psychotherapy?: Introduction to a revolution. London: Whurr.

Mahrer, A.R. (2004c). Experiential psychotherapy. In: Corsini, R.J. and Wedding, D. (eds), Current Psychotherapies, 7th edn. Belmont, CA: Wadsworth, pp. 439–474.

Mahrer, A.R. and Boulet, D.B. (1989). A postdoctoral plan for the education and training of counsellors. Canadian Journal of Counselling 23: 288–399.

Mahrer, A.R. and Boulet, D.B (1997). The experiential model of on-the-job teaching. In: Watkins, C.E. Jr (ed.), Handbook of Psychotherapy Supervision. New York: Wiley, pp. 166–183.

Mahrer, A.R. and Boulet, D.B. (1999). An unabashedly unrealistic wish list for the education and training of psychotherapists. Journal of Clinical Psychology 55: 393–398.

Nielson, J. (2002). Working in the grey zone: The challenge for supervision in the area between therapy and social control. In: Campbell, D. and Mason, B. (eds), Perspectives on Supervision. London: Karnac, pp. 141–156.

Patterson, C.H. (1997). Client-centered supervision. In: Watkins, C.E. Jr (ed.), Handbook of Psychotherapy Supervision. New York: Wiley, pp. 134–146.

Rogers, C.R. (1957). Training individuals to engage in the therapeutic process. In: Strother, C.R. (ed.), Psychology and Mental Health. Washington DC: American Psychological Association, pp. 76–92.

Shertzer, B. and Stone, S.C. (1968). Fundamentals of Counseling. Boston: Houghton-Mifflin.

Stoltenberg, C. (1981). Approaching supervision from a developmental perspective: The counselor complexity model. Journal of Counseling Psychology 28: 59–62.

Stoltenberg, C. and Delworth, U. (1987). Supervising Counselors and Therapists. San Francisco, CA: Jossey-Bass.

Truax, C.B., Carkhuff, R.R., and Douds, J. (1964). Toward an integration of the didactic and experiential approaches to training in counseling and psychotherapy. Journal of Counseling Psychology 11: 240–247.

Watkins, C.E. Jr (1990). The separation–individuation hypothesis in psychotherapy supervision. Psychotherapy 27: 202–209.

Watkins, C.E. Jr (1996). On demoralization and awe in psychotherapy supervision. The Clinical Supervisor 14: 139-148.

Worthington, E.L. (1984). Empirical investigation of supervision of counselors as they gain experience. Journal of Counseling Psychology 31: 63-75.

Yontef, G. (1997). Supervision from a Gestalt therapy perspective. In: Watkins, C.E. Jr (ed.), Handbook of Psychotherapy Supervision. New York: Wiley, pp. 147-163.

Index